AF553842

WOMEN'S EDUCATION

WOMEN'S EDUCATION

R.K. Arun
Principal, Islamia Teachers Training College,
Phoolwari Sharif, Patna

CENTRUM PRESS
NEW DELHI-110002 (INDIA)

CENTRUM PRESS
H.O.: 4360/4, Ansari Road, Daryaganj,
New Delhi-110 002 (India)
Ph.: 23278000, 23261597

B.O.: No. 1015, Ist Main Road, BSK IIIrd Stage
IIIrd Phase, IIIrd Block,
Bangalore - 560 085 (India)
Tel.: 080-41723429
Visit us at: www.centrumpress.com

Women's Education

First Edition, 2009

PRINTED IN INDIA

Printed at Balaji Offset, Delhi

Contents

Preface

There cannot be an educated people without educated women. If general education had to be limited to men or to women, that opportunity should be given to women, for then it would most surely be passed on to the next generation. The Education of Women as Women-General education for interesting and intelligent living and for citizenship in large part can be the same for men and women. We have heard frequent suggestions that women's education should run to pretty "accomplishments," such as drawing, painting or the like-skills which will enable well-to-do women to pass the' time harmlessly while their husbands do the really important work. This point of view should be obsolete. Women should share with men the life and thought and interests of the times. They are fitted to carry the same academic work as men, with no less thoroughness and quality. The distribution of general ability among women is approximately the same as among men. Yet, though men and women are equally competent in academic work, and though many subjects are equally interesting and appropriate, it does not follow that in all things men's and women's education should be identical. Indian universities for the most part are places of preparation for a man's world. Little thought has been given to the education of women as women. Women must, share the same programme as men or go without. There are ways in which many women's interests or appropriate fields of work diverge from those of men, and educational programmes should take that fact into account. In every country, no matter how far the "liberation" of women has gone, husbands and wives commonly play different parts. In general the man provides the income and the woman maintains the home. For many women who crave to achieve standards of excellence, the home provides an excellent setting. For a woman to give the home design, beauty, order and character, without being herself a slave to home- keeping and without imposing onerous prohibitions and restrictions on the freedom of movement of children, is a high art. It will not be acquired by chance, and for many women its acquisition will be impossible, except through education.

Women's access to education has been recognized as a fundamental right. The benefits of education are manifold. Educating women results in improved productivity, income, and economic development, as well as a better quality of life, notably a healthier and better nourished population. At the same time, it is clear that education empowers women, providing them with increased autonomy in every sphere of their lives.

The present book makes an overview of women's education. The book deliberates upon the appropriate measures that ought to be taken regarding women education so that an era of equality, dignity, esteem, self-respect and self-confidence dawns upon the Indian social order. The book is of tremendous value to students, teachers, educationists and general readers. An attempt has been made to cover up most of the topics included in M.Ed. syllabus of the Indian universities.

— *R. K. Arun*

UNIT-I

Introduction to Women's Studies

Concept and Need for Women's Studies—Scope of Women's Studies—Women's Studies as an Academic Discipline

Women'S Studies is an interdisciplinary university curriculum originating in the United States in the late 1960s. Almost simultaneously in 1969–1970, the first women's studies courses appeared in a handful of American universities, including Cornell University and San Diego State College (now University). By 1980 there were over 300 women's studies programmes and departments in United States universities. That number had more than doubled again by 2000, and included nine Ph.D. programmes (with at least one more in development). In addition, there were women's studies programmes and departments at universities around the world, including many sites in Canada, Europe, South Africa, the United Kingdom, and Australia, as well as Japan, Korea, Lebanon, Mexico, Ireland, Sudan, Turkey, and Uganda.

In the late 1960s, as the proportion of women enrolled in colleges and universities increased, feminists identifying with a new women's liberation movement criticized American higher education for failing to address women's concerns on at least three levels: the lack of equal professional opportunities for women scholars and graduates (the "glass ceiling"); the absence of curricular content reflecting women's lives and contributions in the liberal arts, sciences, and technical fields; and the skewed, diminished, and often insulting experiences of women undergraduates and graduate students in and outside the classroom.

Unsurprisingly, as Marilyn Boxer has pointed out, many of the pioneers in developing women's studies courses were political activists, using the free university and civil rights movements as models for developing feminist perspectives in various disciplines and expanding women's access to male-dominated classrooms, programmes, positions, and bodies of knowledge. Jean Fox O'Barr, for example, was five years beyond a political science dissertation that deflected questions about women when she began reading recent women's studies literature by Kate Millett, Robin Morgan, and others. As a result, O'Barr began questioning fundamental assumptions in her own discipline and eventually became a leader of the women's studies movement.

Women's studies scholars came from existing disciplines that, with the exception of home economics, were male-dominated. Women literary scholars and historians weighed in first, asking questions that repositioned women in their research and thus changed previous bodies of "knowledge." In literature, feminist scholars began to ask about the exclusion of women writers from the canon of "great" (and thus always studied) writers. In history, Marilyn Boxer cites Joan Kelly as recalling, "All I had done was to say, with Leonardo, suppose we look at the dark, dense immobile earth from the vantage point of the moon? ... Suppose we look at the Renaissance from the vantage point of women?" (Boxer, p. 129). Kelly articulated the core perspective of women's studies. The add-women-and-stir approach, pasting women into existing pictures of historical process or social dynamics, did not generate transformative insights. Nor did it help to recognize individual women who did things that men usually do. Instead, significant changes in scholarship stemmed from shifted "vantage points." This shift usually involved identifying systems of values and priorities practiced by women, systems that might either supplement or challenge prevailing value systems that are enforced socially or politically. An example from historical scholarship is Nancy Cott's seminal articulation in 1977 of a "woman's sphere" of interpersonal relations in colonial and early national New England. In women's studies, perhaps even more than in other areas of study, we can often identify "clusters" of significant works elaborating new insights. In this area of colonial and nineteenth-century European American women's culture, Cott's book had been preceded by Barbara Welter's work and enriched by complementary theses offered by Linda Kerber, Mary Beth Norton, Kathryn Kish Sklar, Carroll Smith Rosenberg, and others.

The floodgates of revisionist scholarship opened in the 1970s and 1980s, not just in history, but also in anthropology, sociology, literature, communication, and psychology. Simultaneously, women scholars began feminist activism within their disciplinary organizations, creating women's caucuses and women's networking mechanisms, agitating for greater representation of women scholars on conference panels and in governing offices and committees, and identifying ways of mentoring women graduate students. The National Women's Studies Association was founded in 1977. Several notable journals of women's studies were established, including *Feminist Studies* in 1972 and *Signs* in 1975. *Sage,* founded in 1982, has become a widely respected journal in black women's studies.

The proliferation of courses, programmes, and then departments of women's studies from 1970 through 2000 testifies to the development of an audience, a teaching faculty, and curriculum. Early women's studies advocates faced key questions about the content of the courses, the viability and structure of women's studies as a discipline, and the political mission of the enterprise. From the beginning, women's studies theorists have considered pedagogy an integral part of creating their discipline. Instructors have widely agreed that the dynamics of the classroom must somehow reflect and embody the theoretical struggles of the discipline. Would it be enough for a women's studies course to include content on women's lives, or must the course be taught from a feminist point of view? What was feminist pedagogy and what would a feminist classroom look like? Did traditional dynamics between instructor and students—grades, modes of address, even the arrangement of desks and chairs—echo prevailing power structures in a stultifying or an exemplary way? How would men experience a women's studies classroom, and how would a women's studies class experience men? Could men teach women's studies? Was there or should there be a difference between a women's studies course per se and courses in other home disciplines that reflected revised content on women?

The first courses constructed their content around women's experiences, which reflected the grassroots nature of liberationist politics as well as a democratic and particularist epistemology. Women's studies teachers found that the opening of the universities in the 1960s and 1970s brought in "nontraditional" students, often older women returning to school after raising children or after a divorce, to pursue education and credentials for new careers. This population has enriched women's studies classes by bringing perspectives and debates into the classroom that are relevant to postgraduate and non-college women. Most women's studies curricula are grounded by a specific introduction to women's studies course. Besides the introductory course, core curricula then may include courses on feminist theory and epistemology; political and legal issues; feminist perspectives on social structure and social power, race, class, sex and sexuality; and individual and family development issues.

Women's studies students generally take additional university courses allied with, or double-listed by, women's studies. These often include courses in sociology, history, anthropology, art and aesthetics, and literature. One of the thorniest sets of issues, and one that often lay beyond the control of the organizers of women's studies programmes, concerned the structure of the women's studies programme and the interaction between its administrative and curricular organization. Would it be more important to integrate women's content into a traditionally organized curriculum, or to create a beachhead of feminist scholarship and pedagogy? Would organization in a department isolate and "ghettoize" the women's studies endeavor? Would departmental status tempt faculty to abandon their mission to transform the entire university curriculum? Many early advocates of integration became converts to the departmental model because of the advantages of regular funding and tenure lines, which improved stability and seemed to bestow the stamp of legitimacy. Programmes still far outnumbered departments as of 2001, but the number of women's studies departments continues its proportional increase. In institutions where the programme model prevails, women's studies faculties usually have two homes, one in women's studies and one in another department.

Another set of issues that enriched and sometimes threatened to fragment the women's studies enterprise revolved around women's differences, particularly those of race, class, and sexuality. In 1969 Frances Beale updated the concept of "double jeopardy," the oppression of black women on the two counts of sex and race. African American women scholars, artists, and activists, as well as those of Asian, Native American, Hawaiian, Latina, and other racial and ethnic backgrounds, protested any assumption that women experienced a common set of life conditions, simply on the basis of sex. (The coining of the term "women of colour" presented some of the same pitfalls of unintentional homogenization.) Powerful writings and performances helped create a new mosaic of images and understandings of the multiplicity of women's lives as lived in the United States and in other parts of the world. Often painfully, women's studies absorbed the idea that privilege was not just a category that separated women from men, but also women from each other.

Though there were many lesbian and bisexual scholars involved in the creation of women's studies on campuses across the United States, the women's studies movement resembled the women's movement in general in its initial ambivalence toward full and integrated recognition of non-heterosexual women. Interestingly, the evolution of gay and lesbian studies courses and programmes in the last fifteen years has both reinforced the legitimacy of inclusion and, in some ways, diluted the impact of lesbian content in women's studies programmes.

The flip side of this dilemma, and one that echoes the uncomfortable position of black women in African American studies, is that lesbians often find themselves and their concerns under-represented in queer studies programmes that, of course, include gay men.

In the last decade of the twentieth century, women's studies scholarship grappled with the same theoretical dilemmas that troubled and enlivened other humanities and social science disciplines. Some scholars believed that postmodernist interpretations threatened to eviscerate feminism, while others saw postmodernist discourse as a meta language that would salvage the intellectual integrity of the women's studies project. As the ranks of women's studies professors increasingly include scholars exposed to women's studies as undergraduates, the professional as well as intellectual dynamics of the field will continue to evolve.

The Women's Movement—Pre-Independent, Post-Independent and Current Women's Movements

1880-1950

By the 1880's, women were seemingly on the road to achieving professional, legal, and educational equality with men. Elementary and secondary education was generally available to women. Higher education was also increasingly available to women.

States started to modify common law to give women more legal power. Wives were given control over their inheritance and earnings and even in some states, women were given a chance of winning at least joint custody of their children in the case of divorce. By 1900, 20% of the women in the U.S. were employed away from the home. In fact, a census taken in 1890 reported that women were represented in 360 occupations out of 369. Sadly, most employed women worked in textile and factory work with lower paid tasks and little chance for advancement.

On a more positive note, women's image also changes. Although there was an emphasis for women to marry, women were also encouraged to pursue higher education and even a career. Medicine also changed for women. The theory that a woman's reproductive system was the basis of her bodily functions started to be ignored. Menstruation and childbirth were looked upon as natural processes, not illnesses.

Public images like the "Gibson Girl" picture healthy and athletic women that were simply dressed, enjoying themselves playing tennis and golf, bicycling and even driving an automobile. Women, in turn, started to abandon trailing petticoats and ribbon gowns. Instead women slowly started to wear tailored suits or a dark suit with a simple blouse. Crinolines, bustles, and tight lacing of corsets were slowly abandoned, but most women wore some form of corset until the 1920's.

Beginning in 1900, women's attitude towards themselves started to change. Before, women's goals in life was to marry, have children, and obey their husbands. These women would often give up their careers and education to do so. In fact, in 1900, only 5% of married women in the U.S. had gainful employment outside of the home. By 1910, this number increased to 11%. This changed however. More and more women started to devote their lives to their careers. Studies showed that in major Eastern women's colleges, close to half of the alumnae were unmarried and supporting themselves in professional occupations. Women also had more information about sexuality and had more education and legal power. They now had more choices and voice in their relationships. One in twelve marriages in the U.S. ended in divorce by 1905. More and more women's organizations started to appear. Unlike the chatty, gossip groups before them, these clubs focused on women's concerns and rights. These groups brought public attention to issues varying from women suffrage to poor factory working conditions. Their impact was significant and useful, bring public support and demand for improved conditions.

Just as the women's suffrage movement started to come alive, an opposing movement, anti-suffrage, was born. The Anti-suffrage Society was formed in 1871. Typically, many psychologists and anti-suffragists associated feminism with mental illness. They came to the conclusion that most suffragists all bordered hysteria and their arguments could not be taken seriously. All women, they felt, were feeble minded, frail, physically weak, vulnerable, and intellectually inferior to men. By allowing the women to vote, it would expose and contaminate these women to the hysteric suffragist and it was their duty to protect women from such evil things. They also concluded that by allowing women to vote, the country's security would be jeopardized and ultimately lead to war. Also, because women were thought to be small brained, emotionally unstable, and irrational, voting would cause them added stress which they would not be able to handle. If women were to vote, they were thought by anti-suffragists to become more masculine. If men allowed women to vote, the men would become more effeminate. Quite bluntly, they felt the women's suffrage would turn the nation into a bunch of "transvestites".

Between 1890 and the First World War, the woman's movement was extremely active and vigorous. By 1914, the women's movement was focused on women suffrage. The women's movement suffered numerous set backs though. The National American Women Suffrage Association or NAWSA had abandoned the congressional campaign and concentrated on the states. By 1910, only four states had equal women suffrage. These failures were partly due to opposing organizations of anti-suffragists, who believe that politics was no place for women. It was not over yet!

With new leaders, including a woman called Alice Paul, the NAWSA brought all new tactics and ideas into their campaign. Paul was not used to and also not happy with her small role though. She started her own organization called the Congressional Union in Washington DC. Although NAWSA and the Congressional Union used similar tactics such as parades, rallies and protests, the NAWSA focused on the state legislatures and the Congressional Union concentrated on Congress. Later on, the Congressional Union broadened it focus to state level and even made itself into a political party, called the Woman's Party. Despite their differences, NASWA and the Congressional Union worked well together. When tension mounted and Congress repeatedly rejected the Women Suffrage Amendment, Alice Paul and the Woman's Party turned to extreme measures. In 1917, they organized round the clock picket lines in front of the White House. They were arrested and jailed and also received national press coverage when they were force-fed after refusing to eat. Eventually, Congress passed the amendment in 1919. The amendment was annexed and made official on August 18, 1920 when Tennessee approved, giving women the right to vote.

Unfortunately, the 1920's did not show such emphasis on women's issues. After the Women's Suffrage amendment was passed in 1920, women's organizations splintered and disagreed on valuable causes for the women's movement. Many veteran suffragists were worn out from the seemingly unending battle that took place just a decade before. They now felt that it was essential for them to return to the tasks they had pushed aside. Others felt women had reached liberation and equality, so there was nothing more for them to want.

This allowed anti-feminist undercurrents to rise up in society. The media was bombarded with the image of the happy housewife. Women were encouraged to take their place in the home again. In opposition to this image, the new generation of women took a whole new look. Rebellion against society's standards was prominent and a free morality was set in. Young women took an attitude of free and easy living, fun and freedom. These "flaming youths" or "flappers" as they were later called, wore short skirts, smoked cigarettes, danced wild, new dances, and in general, enjoyed themselves.

The Great Depression hit the U.S. hard in the 1930s. It also started a work war among women. With the failing economy, the first to be laid-off were the married working women, who were "taking jobs away from men", despite the fact that men now had reduced salaries that couldn't support their families. Legislature in 26 states even had proposed bills that would prohibit the employment of married women. Women organizations took on a determined resistance against these and only one bill was passed, which was in Louisiana. Later on, it was ruled unconstitutional in the courts. Despite all the hostility, the number of employed women stayed basically the same as the 1920s. Women workers were still cheaper and certain fields of work were considered virtually closed to men. Men found themselves unemployed and often lost track of time, wandering the streets in disarray. Women's lives were less disrupted by the depression than their husbands. Because of this, women became the center of stability in the family. Another result of the depression was a decline of divorces and an increase of marriages. Divorce was simply too expensive and marriage was seen as emotional support for young, single women in a time of uncertainty. Concerned about jobs and housing, people lost interest in the rebellious young style of the 20s and also the new moral standards.

Among all women, working or not, the return of tradition in their dress was evident. Although clothes remained loose and free flowing, skirts became longer and bosoms and small waistlines reappeared. This return was influence by new actresses and cinema queens, in which people in despair, felt they could some how live their lives through. The sweet virginal blond and the eluded temptress became a new twist of good-bad girl that dominated films. Women in the movies returned to their proper place, denied any real power. This came as a discouraging role model for women. Luckily, women's screen roles changed slowly over the next few years. Their intelligence and strength started to shine through.

World War II brought major changes to the women and American work force. Six million additional women went work for the first time in the Second World War. Initially, it was not easy to persuade women to go to work, but the media slathered the image of "Rosie the Riveter", the temporary women at work, everywhere. Women's guilt for working was a thing of the past. During the war years, four times as many women than men found employment in the federal bureaucracy. The government even paid lip service to the idea that men and women should receive equal pay and that childcare services should be established throughout the nation. Women were courted to join the work force, but they filled a majority of the factory, clerical, war related jobs. Once the war was over, some women happily left their jobs to return to their homes and marriages that were denied to them throughout the war. Other did not leave so happily. Cut-backs of women in the work force happened as soon as peace was declared. Business and factories simply did not need so many workers. Women were the majority of those laid-off.

By 1947, the number of working began to rise again. In 1951, 31% of all women worked. Conditions weren't as bright as they seemed though. Women received lower paid salaries in factory and industrial work. There was nothing they could do though. No state legislature protected them. Despite these discriminations, a majority of these women stayed working. Women's role in American society was changing constantly from the 1880s to the 1950s. Their experiences and memories, defeats and triumphs are everlasting though. Women manage to catch America's attention. Our founding mother's cries were finally heard. Some equality was finally met. Women were finally recognized as humans and the path for future generation's achievements and success was now laid out before them.

Educational Development of Women in Pre-independence Period

Although education in India started receiving some attention under British rule with the Charter Act of 1813 and obtained full recognition in the famous Macaulay's Minute of 1835, education of women in India still remained absent from the Indian society. It is only when the "Wood's Dispatch", containing Educational development programme was passed in 1854 by the East India Company that a special reference was made of education and employment of women and the Government assumed direct responsibility for making women literate. Some progress of women's education particularly at first stage of education that is primary level, was reported only in respect of a separate school for girls. Some women were also imparted training for appointment as teachers in girls' schools. But it is only from the year 1882, when systematised educational data began to be collected quinquennially, that the progress of women's education came to be assessed.

From 1882-1947, the progress of girls education was reported to be slow but steady, confined as it was to the affluent sections of the society or those families which were in the favour of foreign rulers. Nevertheless, starting from no education at the advent of British rule that is 0 per cent of the total enrolment of educational institutions under formal system, the enrolment of women increased to nearly 25 per cent of the total enrolment by the end of the British regime (1947) and this, is in no way a mean achievement. Due credit should be given to the foreign rulers at least for initiating the process of educational development of women as a part of the formal system of education in India. Table at a glance, the progress of education of girls and women in Pre-Independence period:

Table: Education of Girls and Women in Pre-Independent Period

Years

Percentage of literacy of women	*Primary Schools*	*Middle Schools*	*Secondary Schools*	*Univer-sities & Colleges*	*Other Institu-tions*	*Total*
			1981-82			
0.2	124491	*	2054	6	515	127066
			1901-02			
0.7	345397	34386	10309	264	2812	393168
			1921-22			
1.8	1198550	92466	36698	1529	11599	1340842
			1946-47			
6.0	3475165	321508	280772	23207	56090	4156742
	No. of girls enrolled per zoo boys in					
36	22	for middle and 14		12	for general coll- 12 for general	
			1946-47			
for secondary schools egiate education			education and 7			
for professional education						

Source: Quinquennial Report-Ministry of Education and Culture.

*Included in secondary schools.

Highlights of the progress of women's education in Pre-Independent period with an interval of two decades is briefly narrated below:

1881-1902

As indicated in the quinquennial reports of Education in India, the significant achievement between 1881-1902 in the field of Women's education was the entry of women in colleges. For the first time, two Indian women graduated in 1883 and enrolment in women's schools and colleges rose to 3.93 lakhs in 1902 from only 1.27 lakhs in 1882. Similarly, people began to recognise the importance of Secondary education for women and social taboos of stopping girl's education maximum up to primary level began cracking under the weight of social amelioration. The enrolment of girls in secondary schools during these two decades increased five times. Primary education enrolment, of course, expanded from 1.24 lakhs to 3.45 lakhs, during this period. While in 1882, only one girl out of 3 was studying in mixed school, the ratio went up, to one out of two in 1902. bidding a farewell to the malice of age-old prejudice against co-education, at least in the primary schools.

1902-1922

The two decades from 1902-22 witnessed a more active role of the Government in the field of women's education on the one hand and impact of Freedom Movement on women's education on the other. It is during this period that Lord Curzon supported the cause of Women's education and the similar policy was enunciated by a Government Resolution on Education Policy (1913). As is evident from the above table the growth of women's education was noticed at all stages of education, particularly at collegiate level and their passing out in examination with excellent results exploded the myth of inferiority of women. However, the landmark in the history women's education in India during this period was the establishment of an Indian Women's University in 1916 in Bombay, which is now known as Shrimati Nathibai Damodar Thackersey Women's University, catering to the needs of higher education of nearly 10 thousand girls and women every year. This University was established with the following objectives:

(a) To make provision for the higher education of women through modern Indian Languages (mother tongue) as the media of instruction;

(b) To regulate pre-university education; to start, aid, maintain and affiliate institutions for such education and to formulate courses of studies specially suited to the needs and requirements of women;

(c) To make provision for the training of teachers for primary and secondary schools;

(d) To institute and confer such degrees and diplomas, titles, certificates and marks of honour in respect of degrees and examinations as may be prescribed by the regulation; and

(e) Such other objects, not inconsistent with these as may be added from time to time by the senate.

While girls' enrolment in primary schools recorded an unprecedented increase from 3.45 lakhs in 1901-1902 to 11.99 lakhs in 1921-22, the increase in secondary education was from 10309 to 36698 during this period. The enrolment in colleges increased six times during these two decades. More girls came up for higher professional courses like medicine and teaching, where the enrolment of girls was of the order of 197 and 67 respectively in 1921-22. Technical and Vocational schools showed a record increase from 2812 to 11599 during this period, the vocation-wise break up of which is given below:-

Schools for	*No. of Girls under Instruction*
Teaching	3,903
Art	32
Medicine	334
Technical and Industrial Careers	2,744
Commercial careers	308
Agriculture	79
Other carters	4,199
Totat	11,599

1922-1947

During this period, women's education got a further fillip, as a result of the rise in the marriage age of women, and the awakening among women injected by Social Reformers and Mahatma Gandhi's Movement and also by the establishment of the All India Women's Conference (1926). The significant event of the period was the emphasis laid on women's education in the Report of the Hartog Committee which stated that education should not be the privilege of one sex only, but equally the right of both the sexes and that women's education would be expanded further for the advancement of education in India.

It is during this period that a visible progress of women's education was witnessed. The enrolment of girls in primary schools moved up from nearly 12 lakhs in 1922 to nearly 35 lakhs in 1946-47 and enrolment in secondary schools increased from about 37 thousands in 1921-22 to a record of 281 thousands. But the significant progress occured in higher education where the enrolment of girls increased from merely 1529. In 1921-22 to as high as 23,207, followed by improvement in the demand for women in the employment market. In spite of all this expansion, the enrolment of girls was only 2.4 percent of their population.

Women in Post-Independence India

In 1947, India won freedom from foreign rule. In 1949 a Constitution was drafted which gave equal rights and status to all Indian citizens. Independent India has seen various reforms and programmes for the uplift of women of all communities. Indian women have played an important role from the very beginning of Independence in different walks of life. Women have taken bold steps in all nation building activities, which started with education and has now blossomed into women's involvement in every activity of India. They have participated in all activities such as education, politics, media, art and culture, service sectors, science and technology, etc.

National Committees and Commissions for Women

There have been a number of important ad-hoc bodies that have reported on issues important to women over the years:

a. Committee of the Status of Women in India (1971-74)- produced a report in 1974 that raised the profile of women's issues in India, and led to a number of legislative changes, such as the Equal Remuneration Act 1976 and amendments to the Factories Act 1948.

b. National Commission on Self Employed Women and Women in the Informal Sector (1987-88)-produced a reported entitled "Shramshakti" which makes a number of important recommendations for legislative change.

c. National Commission on Rural Labour (1991)-produced a report which included consideration of rural issues as they affect women and recommended increased self employment, wage employment and diversification in order to redress inequality. It called for amended of patrilineal inheritance laws, training in technological skills, and increased legislative protection for home workers.

d. National Commission on Labour (1966-69) established important principles of labour policy in India which has included an emphasis on women.

National Commission for Women

It is often said that the status and position of women in society is the best way to understand a civilisation, its progress and its shortcomings. In case of India, women have come a long way from women sages and scholars in the Rig Vedic period to women in the armed forces, IT sector, politics ,industry and other significant areas while balancing their role as a daughter, wife and mother. This journey towards modernization has not been easy.

Women have had to fight the traditional Indian male-dominated society to emerge as stronger and independent entities. While all these are positive developments, cases of rape, harassment at workplace and dowry deaths are rampant. Illiteracy and ignorance about their rights are still prevalent among a majority of the women. It was in this background that the Committee on the Status of Women in India (CSWI) recommended nearly two decades ago, the setting up of a National Commission for Women to fulfill the surveillance functions to facilitate redressal of grievances and to accelerate the socio-economic development of women.

In January 1992, the National Commission for Women (NCW), was set up as a statutory body under the National Commission for Women Act, 1990 (Act No. 20 of 1990 of Govt.of India) to review the constitutional and legal safeguards for women; recommend remedial legislative measures, facilitate redressal of grievances and advise the Government on all policy matters affecting women.

As the problem of violence against women is multifaceted, the NCW has adopted a multi-pronged strategy to tackle the problem. The Commission has initiated generation of legal awareness among women, thus equipping them with the knowledge of their legal rights and with a capacity to use these rights. It assists women in redressal of their grievances through pre-litigation services. To facilitate speedy delivery of justice to women Parivarik Mahila Lok Adalats are organized in different parts of the country to review the existing provisions of the Constitution and other laws affecting women and recommending amendments thereto, any lacunae, inadequacies or shortcomings in such legislations. It organises promotional activities to mobilise women and get information about their status and recommend paradigm shift in the empowerment of women.The Complaints and Counselling Cell of the commission processes the complaints received oral, written or suo moto under Section 20 of the NCW Act. The complaints received relate to domestic violence, harassment, dowry, torture, desertion, bigamy, rape, refusal to register FIR, cruelty by husband, deprivation, gender discrimination and sexual harassment at work place.

NCW tackles the problems by ensuring that investigations by the police are expedited and monitored. Family disputes are resolved or compromised through counselling.

As per the 1997 Supreme Court Judgement on Sexual Harassment at Workplace, (Vishakha Vs. State of Rajasthan) every employer is required to provide for effective complaints procedures and remedies including awarding of compensation to women victims. In sexual harassment complaints, the concerned organisations are urged to expedite cases and the disposal is monitored. For serious crimes, the Commission constitutes an Inqu ...mittee which makes spot enquiries,examines various witnesses, collects evidence and submits the report with recommendations. The implementation of the report is monitored by the NCW.

The complaints received by the NCW show the trend of crimes against women and suggests systemic changes needed for reducing them. The complaints are analysed to understand the gaps in the routine functioning of government in tackling violence against women and to suggest correctional measures. The complaints are also used as case studies for sensitization programmes for the police, judiciary, prosecutors, forensic scientists, defence lawyers and other administrative functionaries.

From time to time the Commission conducts seminars, workshops and conferences and sponsors such events by providing financial assistance to research organisations and NGOs. The important areas so far covered include women in detention, violence against women; sexual harassment at work place; educational, health and employment aspects; women in agriculture and panchayati raj sector; custodial justice and mental health institutions.

The NCW holds public hearings on issues affecting large sections of women such as crime against women, women in unorganised labour sector, women in agriculture and women of minority groups. The deposition at these enquiries helps in appreciating the problems and initiating remedial action. As a measure of arousing public awareness and breaking bureaucratic apathy, public hearings under vigilant activists like Justice V.R. Krishna Iyer and Swami Agnivesh were held to understand problems and expedite solutions in the case of Kol women of Bundelhekhand; deserted women of hill districts in U.P., rape case of girl children of Tamil Nadu, unorganised women labour and minority communities of Tamil Nadu; creche workers' enquiry and tribal women of Dindigul, Tamil Nadu.

Special studies are conducted by the NCW on social mobilisation, maintenance and divorced women, panchayat raj in action, women labour under contract, gender bias in judicial decisions, family courts, gender-component in various

Commissions' reports on women, violence against women, women's access to health and education in slums to help in formulation of NCW's policies for recommendations. Special studies of NCW focus on development of health facilities among women belonging to the scheduled tribe communities; women of weaker sections-socio-economic development of scheduled caste women; mentally disabled women; credit needs of women-the Gramin Banks and the widows of Vrindavan.

The NCW also constitutes Expert Committees for dealing with such special issues as may be taken up by the Commission from time to time. Some important issues taken up by the NCW include sexual harassment at workplace, women in detention, anti-arrack movement, issues concerning prostitution and political and technological empowerment of women in agriculture.

Government Organisations for Women Department of Women and Child Development

General Grant-in-aid Scheme for Assistance to Voluntary Organizations in the field of Women and Child Development: The role of voluntary organizations and their participation in social welfare activities has been well recognized by Government both as an important resource as well as to emphasis that social problems and social issues require active participation of the community, Government and the voluntary organizations. The policy of the Government is to promote, stimulate and develop them and to provide opportunities to train their manpower so that the commitment of voluntary organization is mobilized for the well-being of the community. The scheme focuses on projects that aim to tackle problem areas which are relatively unserviced but where need is urgent; projects which fill in essential gaps in existing services and complement them so as to maximize the impact; projects which provide integrated services, all the components need not be financially supported by one source; projects which build the capacity of the individual to be self-reliant rather than dependent; projects located in backward, rural and tribal areas urban slums which are poorly serviced by existing services;

projects not covered by any of the existing schemes of the Department of Women and Child Development including the Central Social Welfare Board (CSWB); projects to mobilize public opinion and support to tackle pressing social problems.

Organizational Assistance to Voluntary Organizations: Assistance under his scheme is given to voluntary organizations working in the field of Women and Child Development. Department of Women and Child Development has adopted the policy of promoting, developing and assisting voluntary organizations to implement welfare schemes for women and children. Under most of the schemes grants are given only for projects. However, voluntary organizations also need some support to maintain their central office so that various activities can be carried out in a smooth manner, as the efficient running of the central office is a vital input for its activities. The Department of Women and Child Development have, therefore, a scheme for giving maintenance grants to voluntary organizations.

Vocational Training in Tribal Areas: This scheme was introduced realizing the need for skill upgradation to equip the tribal youths for employment/ self-employment. It also aims to improve the socio-economic condition of the tribal youth by enhancing their income. The scheme covers all states and union territories, the only restriction being that free vocational training facilities are extended only to the tribal people. Under the scheme 100% central assistance will be given to States/ UTs/ NGOs for setting up and running of vocational training centres.

Grant-In-Aid for Research, Publications and Monitoring: Under the scheme financial assistance is extended to undertake research/ evaluation/ monitoring studies, organize seminars/ conferences/ workshops, capacity building for monitoring activities, promotion of innovative activities etc. in the area of nutrition, women and child development The objectives of the programme are:

- To sponsor research/evaluation studies
- To sponsor research studies to individual scholar

- To sponsor seminars/ workshops/ conferences.
- To provide publication grant.
- To provide grants for monitoring activities/training of personnel/promotion of innovative activities.

Swawlamban or NORAD Scheme: The Norwegian Agency for International Development (NORAD) offers assistance for setting Lip of such projects on a sustained basis for poor and needy women both in urban slums and in rural areas. NORAD scheme aims to combine the necessary linkages in traditional as well as non-traditional activities to implement programmes in collaboration with industrial units. NORAD assistance is to be utilised in giving assistance to projects sponsored by public undertakings/ corporations/ women's development centres of universities/ autonomous organizations/ voluntary organizations for setting up of "Employment and Income Generating Training-cum-Employment cum-production Units for Women." In cases where the sponsoring organization is not in a position to assume direct responsibility and absorb trainees as its own employees, emphasis should be given on formation of a co-operative of women producers as a modality of employment. NORAD assistance can also be utilized for assistance in the formulation, appraisal and documentation of Projects/programmes. Emphasis of the project must be on income generating activities with the aim of achieving self-reliance on a Sustained basis.

Support to Training and Employment Programme for Women (STEP): The Programme of STEP aims to make a significant impact on women in the traditional sectors by upgrading skills and providing employment to such women on a project basis by mobilizing women in viable groups, improving skills, arranging for support services, providing access to credit, awareness generation, gender sensitization, nutrition education, sensitization of project functionaries. Thus, STEP advocates an integrated package of inputs aiming at the integrated development of poor women in traditional sectors. The ultimate endeavour of each project is to develop the group to thrive on a self sustaining basis in the market place with the minimal Governmental support and intervention after the project period is over. The programme of STEP advocates the objective of extending training for upgradation of skills & sustainable employment for women through a variety of action oriented projects which employ women in large numbers. The Scheme covers 8 traditional sectors of employment, viz. Agriculture, Small Animal Husbandry, Dairying, Fisheries, Handlooms, Handicrafts, Khadi and Village Industries and Sericulture. Two more sectors, namely, Social Forestry and Waste Land Development have been added later.

Swayamsiddha: The scheme was launched with the long-term objective of the all-round empowerment of women, especially socially and economically, by ensuring their direct access to, and control over, resources through a sustained process of mobilization and convergence of all the on going sectoral programmes. The vision is to develop empowered women who will demand their rights from family, community and government; have increased access to, and control over, material, social and political resources; have enhanced awareness and improved skills; be able to raise issues of common concern through mobilization and networking.

Swadhar: This scheme has been designed with a flexible and innovative approach to cater to the requirement of various types of women in distress in diverse situations under different conditions. The Swadhar Scheme aims to address the specific vulnerability of each of the groups of women in difficult circumstances through a home-based holistic and integrated approach. The objectives of the scheme are:

To provide primary need of shelter, food, clothing and care to the marginalized women / girls living in difficult circumstances who are without any social and economic support;

To provide emotional support and counseling to such women;

To rehabilitate them socially and economically through education, awareness, skill up gradation and personality development through behavioral training etc.;

To arrange for specific clinical, legal and other support

for women / girls in need of those intervention by linking and networking with other organizations in both Govt. & Non-Govt. sector on case to case basis;

To provide for help line or other facilities to such women in distress; and To provide such other services as will be required for the support and rehabilitation to such women in distress.

Scheme of Short Stay Homes for Women and Girls: The scheme focuses on women and girls belonging to the disadvantaged and under privileged groups. These homes are meant primarily for those women and girls who are either exposed to moral danger or are victims of family discord and the resulting strain of relationship or emotional disturbances. The effort has to be to help the women to rehabilitate themselves within a short period of time through institutional services where counseling and guidance, medical and psychiatric check-up and treatment, facilities of development of skills and relationships are provided. They need help and guidance to regain confidence in themselves to meet the situation and to acquire skills to become self-reliant and to develop relationships with people that could help in the re-establishment of their status in society. These homes should not be equated with destitute homes or orphanages.

Financial assistance is provided to institutions/organizations with experience in running Social Defence Programmes. Preference is given to voluntary organizations that already have sufficient infrastructure to run the homes. Assistance of the CSWB or the Ministry can be sought to set up a Training-cum-Production Centre for the benefit of not only the residents but also the poor residents of the locality. Vocational Training Programme, for which the State Social Welfare Advisory Board gives financial assistance can also be introduced in theInstitution.

Implementation of this scheme has been transferred to the Central Social Welfare Board (CSWB), which will sanction admissible grants to homes. However, the Department of Women and Child Development would deal with all the policy matters of the scheme. Child Development Programme Officers (CDPOs) have been designated as nodal officers for all schemes of Department of Women and Child Development.

Nutrition Education and Training through Community Food & Nutrition Extension Units (CFNEUs): CFNEUs organize live demonstrations supported by lecture-cum-discussions, film and slide shows and exhibitions on various aspects of food, nutrition and health in collaboration with the concerned Departments of the State Governments, Educational institutions and Voluntary organizations. The basic objectives of the schemes are:-

- To create nutrition awareness among the people particularly the women and adolescent girls;
- To impart skills and education for achieving adequate nutrition within their available means;
- To train housewives and adolescent girls in fruit & vegetable

preservation;

- To explain the importance of non-food factors like hygiene, sanitation, safe drinking water etc. for nutrition and health of the people;
- To equip the grassroots level workers of concerned sectors with basic messages on food, nutrition and health so as to enable than to communicate to the community during the Course of their duties.
- To enlighten the people about the existing health, nutrition and welfare services for promoting their optimal utilization.

Scheme on Community based Production of Nutritious Food: The scheme provides supplementary food of high quality to vulnerable groups particularly pre-school children, pregnant and lactating mothers attending ICDS or creches/ balwadies run by the NGOs. The type of food prepared at these units would invariably be the 'Ready to Eat' RTE type prepared by roasted, cereals and pulses or the freshly cooked food. A one-time UNICEF financial assistance of Rs. 5.0 lakhs maximum is given for this project and thereafter, the project should be self-sustainable. Therefore, a tie-up with the State Government/

organizations running the feeding programmes is necessary to make the project viable. The unit should be set in close proximity of ICDS project. The number of beneficiaries should be about 7500. The NGOs which are already engaged in nutrition and health activities and have experience of running the supplementary feeding programmes in creches/ balwadies/ ICDS and have firm linkages with the State Governments for supply of supplementary food to feeding programmes run by the Government are eligible for the assistance under this programme.

Early Childhood Education for 3-6 Age Group Children under the Programme of Universalization of Elementary Education: Financial assistance would be provided to the voluntary agencies to run early childhood (pre-schools) education centres as adjuncts of primary/middle school run either by Government, local body or private management, particularly for the disadvantaged sections in rural/ tribal/ backward areas, in nine educationally backward States namely, Andhra Pradesh, Assam, Bihar, Jammu & Kashmir, Madhya Pradesh, Orissa, Rajashthan, Uttar Pradesh and West Bengal. To avoid any duplication of efforts in an area, the Early Childhood Education (ECE) centres run with central assistance under this scheme should be in blocks and villages that do not have similar centres run by ICDS/ Social Welfare Sector or any other schemes of Government or non-Government body.

UNIT-II

Women and Her Family

Liberal Feminism

Liberal feminism asserts the equality of men and women through political and legal reform. It is an individualistic form of feminism and theory, which focuses on women's ability to show and maintain their equality through their own actions and choices. Liberal feminism looks at the personal interactions of men and women as the starting ground from which to transform society into a more gender-equitable place.

Liberal feminism tends to have a neutral vision towards different gender; it requires women to mold themselves to fit a citizenship that it perceived to have already been constructed in the welfare of men. Frequent criticisms of liberal feminism that suggest it overemphasizes equality, causing it to fail as a response to development of women's citizenship. According to liberal feminists, all women are capable of asserting their ability to achieve equality, therefore it is possible for change to happen without altering the structure of society. Issues important to liberal feminists include reproductive rights and abortion access, sexual harassment, voting, education, fair compensation for work, affordable childcare, affordable health care, and bringing to light the frequency of sexual and domestic violence against women. Susan Wendell, who is not a liberal feminist herself, proclaimed that contemporary liberal feminism is "committed to major economic re-organization and considerable redistribution of wealth, since one of the modern political goals most closely associated with liberal feminism is equality of opportunity which would undoubtedly require and lead to both."

Liberal feminists generally work for the eradication of institutional bias and the implementation of better laws. In the United States, liberal feminists have historically worked for the ratification of the Equal Rights Amendment or Constitutional Equity Amendment, in the hopes it will ensure that men and women are treated as equals under the democratic laws that also influence important spheres of women's lives, including reproduction, work and equal pay issues.

Feminist writers associated with this tradition are amongst others Mary Wollstonecraft, John Stuart Mill; second-wave feminists Betty Friedan and Gloria Steinem; and the Third Wave feminist Rebecca Walker.

Mary Wollstonecraft has been very influential in her writings as *A Vindication of the Rights of Woman* commented on society's view of the woman and encouraged women to use their voices in making decisions separate from decisions previously made for her. Woolstonecraft "denied that women are, by nature, more pleasure seeking and pleasure giving than men. She reasoned that if they were confined to the same cages that trap women, men would develop the same flawed characters. What Wollstonecraft most wanted for women was personhood."

John Stuart Mill believed that men are not intellectually above women and much of his research centered on the idea that women, in fact, are superior in knowledge than men. Mill frequently spoke of this imbalance and wondered if women were able to feel the same "genuine unselfishness" that men did in providing for their families. This unselfishness Mill advocated is the one "that motivates people to take into account the good of society as well as the good of the individual person or small family unit.

Rationality

In philosophy, rationality and reason are the key methods used to analyze the data gathered through systematically gathered observations. In economics, sociology, and political science, a decision or situation is often called rational if it is in some sense optimal, and individuals or organizations are often called rational if they tend to act somehow optimally in pursuit of their goals.

Thus one speaks, for example, of a rational allocation of resources, or of a rational corporate strategy. In this concept of "rationality", the individual's goals or motives are taken for granted and not made subject to criticism, ethical or otherwise. Thus rationality simply refers to the success of goal attainment, whatever those goals may be. Sometimes, in this context, rationality is equated with behavior that is self-interested to the point of being selfish. Sometimes rationality implies having complete knowledge about all the details of a given situation.

Debates arise in these three fields about whether or not people or organizations are "really" rational, as well as whether it make sense to model them as such in formal models. Some have argued that a kind of bounded rationality makes more sense for such models. Others think that any kind of rationality along the lines of rational choice theory is a useless concept for understanding human behavior; the term *homo economicus* (economic man: the imaginary logically consistent but amoral being assumed in economic models) was coined largely in honor of this view.

Rationality is a central principle in artificial intelligence, where a *rational agent* is specifically defined as an agent which always chooses the action which maximises its expected performance, given all of the knowledge it currently possesses.

Freedom

The movement for women's rights arose in the early 19th century as an off-shoot of abolitionism, the anti-slavery movement that declared each human being to be a self-owner. As with other abolitionists, the early feminists were individualists who drew inspiration from the *Declaration of Independence* and its principles of individual rights and responsibility.

With this vision of individualist feminism, *Liberty for Women* boldly explores a wide range of issues that confront the modern woman, including self-defense, economic well-being and employment, sex and abortion, the family, technology, and much more. This new feminism asserts the rights of consenting adults to their own sexuality, opposes censorship, and defends every woman's right to self-defence.

Education

The" Primacy of Women's Education-"If Government by the initial exclusion of the masses accentuated the segregation of the masses from the privileged few, by their initial restriction of their (educational) efforts to the male population, they brought a line of division where it had never existed before, within the household." While the movement for equal education for men and women began in Great Britain about a century ago with such serious thinkers as Frederick Maurice, who was a founder of Queen',, College for woman in 1848, and John Stuart Mill, whose "Subjection of Women" was published in 1869, it did not reach India until several decades later. Even today the inequality is evident. According to the statistics issued by the Indian Ministry of Education for 1945-46, there were six and a half times as many boys and men in secondary schools and colleges as there were girls.

The underlying habits of men and women are largely fixed in the early years, and these years are spent chiefly with I the mother. If she is open minded, inquiring and alert, looking behind rumour and tradition to find the facts, concerned with the course of events, informed about the nature of the world around her and interested in it, and acquainted with history and literature and enjoying them, then her children will learn these interests and attitudes from her. The educated, conscientious mother who lives and works with her children in the home is the best teacher in the world of cloth character and intelligence. Much of what she learned at school her children Yet unconsciously as second nature by living in her company. In a society made up of such homes children starting to school already have a background of information, understanding and culture which result in their getting more benefit from school than otherwise would be possible.

Marxist Feminism

Marxist feminism is a sub-type of feminist theory which focuses on the dismantling of capitalism as a way to liberate women. Marxist feminism states that private property, which gives rise to economic inequality, dependence, political confusion and ultimately unhealthy social relations between men and women, is the root of women's oppression in the current social context. It looks at the family in a very negative and critical way.

According to Marxist theory, the individual is heavily influenced by the structure of society, which in all modern societies mean a class structure; that is, people's opportunities, wants and interests are seen to be shaped by the mode of production that characterizes the society they inhabit. Marxist feminists see contemporary gender inequality as determined ultimately by the capitalist mode of production. Gender oppression is class oppression and women's subordination is seen as a form of class oppression which is maintained (like racism) because it serves the interests of capital and the ruling class. Marxist feminists have extended traditional Marxist analysis by looking at domestic labour as well as wage work in order to support their position.

Radical Women, a major Marxist-feminist organization, bases its theory on Marx' and Engels' analysis that the enslavement of women was the first building block of an economic system based on private property. They contend that elimination of the capitalist profit-driven economy will remove the motivation for sexism, racism, homophobia and other forms of oppression.

Production and Reproduction

Women born to feminist or non-traditionalist mothers are somehow only 'physically' female. They are not brought-up 'like women', and as a result they do not have a distinct, well-defined self-identity, and when they do, it is mainly an 'intellectual' self-identity. What is constantly conveyed to them—explicitly and implicitly—is that "there is no *difference* between men and women." While the life of men has remained more or less the same despite 'the Industrial Revolution,' women's life has undergone a radical change. A simple comparative glance at women's life, say rural and urban, or a grandmother and her grand-daughter, or a modern western woman and an ordinary eastern woman in a traditionalist, non-developed country, can give us some feeling of the kind of change women have gone through. Such a comparison can unfold the wide range of quantitative and qualitative changes that woman's life has undergone. This change is so extensive and immense that it might even bring to mind, that they are different species, or from different planets.

This drastic change of feminine identity has largely occurred in feminist families. In traditionalist families, however changes have been very gradual and largely as an after-effect or reflection of the transformations occurring in the outside world. Here what has changed and is changing gradually is largely the 'superstructure' and not the 'structure.'

Unlike 'modern' women, the traditionalist women are made conscious of their sexuality from early days of their childhood, and are reminded constantly—directly or indirectly, explicitly or implicitly and in thousand different ways—that they are different from men. In my country, for example, one of these 'thousand different ways,' is vestment. As it is now probably well-known to all, Islamic women, in addition to their ordinary clothes, are obliged to wear *chado,r* a special type of covering, which like every other aspect of our life, must have once had a *biological function,* in other words, a survival value that is now buried deep under its apparent 'religious function.'

In the traditional families, girls are supposed to start wearing *chador* from the age of religious puberty—which is nine for girls, but sixteen for boys (Notice the rather significant age difference). They should wear it in the presence of men with the exception of their fathers, brothers, grandfathers and uncles. This obligation would naturally and constantly remind them that they are different from boys, an allusion, not found as strongly in the life of non-traditionalist girls. Such reminders help a traditionalist woman to be constantly aware of her sexuality, i.e. her difference, a condition not shared by her 'modern' sisters. In fact, the sexual awareness in the latter is mainly only felt during her menstruation or when she falls in love, i.e. is sexually aroused. As we proceed we will see that this sexual awareness *if it does transform to a deeply rooted, constitutional part of our consciousness* is perhaps the most efficient means left for modern women to rediscover her lost forgotten womanhood. The means to develop a whole healthy personality.

In our modern world of Relativity, the only "relative absolute" for us mortals is Nature and her laws. And in Nature, men and women are different, a concept *totally distinct from equality*. This seems to be an important confusion we are suffering from. Socio—economic and legal equality, possessing similar mental faculties and abilities, does not imply similarity in nature. By the same token, biological differences do not rule out the existence of equally powerful mental abilities or equal economic, sociological and legal rights. This is one of the historical errors that we have perpetrated: to confuse equality of rights with equality of nature (i.e. psychosomatic constitutions).

What is really astonishing is the fact that although the emergence and further development of Women's Liberation Movement (WLM), coincides with the progressive predominance of the *scientific* 'materialistic' outlook—the outlook that everywhere looks and searches for 'molecules' and material basis of everything, including thoughts, emotions, feelings—there has been little scientific attempt to look for the probable physical or biological (hormonal) sexual differences that should naturally lead to psycho-mental differences between the sexes. Not only this sort of scientific endeavor has been rare, but it seems that there has been a conscious attempt to avoid, suspect and look down at such undertakings. It seems our past prejudiced deductions from such biological differences—for example, 'smaller and lesser weight of women's brains implying lesser intelligence', etc.—has scared us off further direct research in this field. In fact, it would not be very wrong to regard Feminism partly as a reaction against the 'abuses' of the discovery of such biological differences. Today however, all this belongs to the past, and we are now more capable than ever to carry out more realistic and less prejudiced researches in the field of biopsychology of men and women. But in order to reach non-biased conclusions this time, several points about 'women's' problem' need clarification. For this purpose, it is first necessary to review the history of Women's Liberation Movement, its causes and consequences and clear the probable misunderstandings and misjudgments that may have occurred due to the relevant prevalent theories (feminist and communist) up to now.

Class

The countless chores collectively known as "housework"–cooking, washing dishes, doing laundry, making beds, sweeping, shopping etc.–apparently consume some three to four thousand hours of the average housewife's year. As startling as this statistic may be, ir does not even account for the constant and unquantifiable attention mothers must give to their children. Just as a woman's maternal duties are always taken for granted, her never-ending toil as a housewife rarely occasions expressions of appreciation within her family. Housework, after all, is virtually invisible: "No one notices it until it isn't done–we notice the unmade bed, not the scrubbed and polished floor." Invisible, repetitive, exhausting, unproductive, uncreative–these are the adjectives which most perfectly capture the nature of housework.

The new consciousness associated with the contemporary women's movement has encourages increasing numbers of women to demand that their men provide some relief from this drudgery. Already, more men have begun to assist their partners around the house, some of them even devoting equal time to household chores. But how many of these men have liberated themselves from the assumption that housework is women's work"? How many of them would not characterise their housecleaning activities as "helping" their women partners?

If it were at all possible simultaneously to liquidate the idea that housework is women's work and to redistribute it equally to men and women alike, would this constitute a satisfactory solution? While most women would joyously hail the advent of the "househusband," the desexualisation of domestic labour would not really alter the oppressive nature of the work itself. In the final analysis, neither women nor men should waste precious hours of their lives on work that is neither stimulating nor productive.

One of the most closely guarded secrets of advanced capitalist societies involves the possibility – the real possibility – of radically transforming the nature of housework. A substantial portion of the housewife's domestic tasks can actually be incorporated into the industrial economy. In other words, housework need no longer be considered necessarily and unalterably private in character. Teams of trained and well-paid workers, moving from dwelling to dwelling, engineering technologically advanced cleaning machinery, could swiftly and efficiently accomplish what the present-day housewife does so arduously and primitively. Why the shroud of silence surrounding this potential of radically redefining the nature of domestic labour?

Because the capitalist economy is structurally hostile to the industrialisation of housework. Socialised housework implies large government subsidies in order to guarantee accessibility to the working-class families whose need for such services is most obvious. Since little in the way of profits would result, industrialised housework – like all unprofitable enterprises – is anathema to the capitalist economy.

Nonetheless, the rapid expansion of the female labour force means that more and more women are finding it increasingly difficult to excel as housewives according to the traditional standards. In other words, the industrialisation of housework, along with the socialisation of housework, is becoming an objective social need. Housework as individual women's private responsibility and as a female labour performed under primitive technical conditions, may finally be approaching historical obsolescence.

Although housework as we know it today may eventually become a bygone relic of history, prevailing social attitudes continue to associate the eternal female condition with images of brooms and dustpans, mops and pails, aprons and stoves, pots and pans. And it is true that women's work, from one historical era to another, has been associated in general with the homestead. Yet female domestic labour has not always been what it is today, for like all social phenomena, housework is a fluid product of human history. As economic systems have arisen and faded away, the scope and quality of housework have undergone radical transformations.

As Frederick Engels argued in his classic work on the *Origin of the Family, Private Property and the State*, sexual inequality as we know it today did not exist before the advent of private property. During early eras of human history the sexual division of labour within the system of economic production was complementary as opposed to hierarchical. In societies where men may have been responsible for hunting wild animals and women, in turn, for gathering wild vegetables and fruits, both sexes performed economic tasks that were equally essential to their community's survival. Because the community, during those eras, was essentially an extended family, women's central role in domestic affairs meant that they were accordingly valued and respected members of the community.

The centrality of women's domestic tasks in pre-capitalist cultures was dramatised by a personal experience during a jeep trip I took in 1973 across the Masai Plains. On an isolated dirt road in Tanzania, I noticed six Masai women enigmatically balancing an enormous board on their heads. As my Tanzanian friends explained, these women were probably transporting a house roof to a new village which they were in the process of constructing. Among the Masai, as I learned, women are responsible for all domestic activities, thus also for the construction of their nomadic people's frequently relocated houses. Housework, as far as Masai women are concerned, entails not only cooking cleaning, child-rearing, sewing, etc., but house-building as well. As important as their men's cattle-rearing activities may be, the women's "housework" is no less productive and no less essential than the economic contributions of Masai men.

Within the pre-capitalist, nomadic economy of the Masai, women's domestic labour is as essential to the economy as the cattle-raising jobs performed by their men. As producers, they enjoy a correspondingly important social status. In advanced capitalist societies, on the other hand, the service-oriented domestic labour of housewives, who can seldom produce tangible evidence of their work, diminishes the social status of women in general. When all is said and done, the housewife, according to bourgeois ideology, is, quite simply, her husband's lifelong servant.

The source of the bourgeois notion of woman as man's eternal servant is itself a revealing story. Within the relatively short history of the United States, the "housewife" as a finished historical product is just a little more than a century old. Housework, during the colonial era, was entirely different from the daily work of the housewife in the United States today.

Alienation

There is an urgent need for reconstructing models of property to make them more women-friendly. Women, now and in the past, have typically held less property than men, and sometimes, as in classical 'democratic' Athens, no property at all. (Dickenson 1997b) In both classical and liberal democratic theory, it is because women are propertyless that they are not construed as political subjects; it is because they are not accorded the status of subjects that they hold little or no property. Yet it is not enough to assume, as many feminists have done, that women have had no other relation to property than as its objects. As the legal theorist Carol Rose points out, there has been far more feminist interest in women as objects of property than as its subjects. (Rose 1994)

Women's relationship to property is stranger than that. Women are neither simple objects of property-holding, nor are they unqualified subjects whose property-holding may suffer under rectifiable practical handicaps. If liberalism cannot shed light on this dilemma, can Marxism help? Perhaps the Marxist concept of alienation might get at some of this strangeness. Many feminist theorists have picked up on the psychological aspects of alienation, but few have applied it to economics and technology.

Marriage and Family

Marriage in India is regarded as one of the most significant life-cycle rituals and is a familial and societal expectation for Hindus. In traditional Hindu society, marriage was considered a sacrament and not a contract and therefore was expected to be for life. It is important to point out that *vivaha* (wedding) is generally obligatory for all individuals. According to Kanailal Kapadia (1966), the primary aim of a Hindu marriage is *dharma praja* (progeny, particularly sons) and *rati* (pleasure). Furthermore, marriage is regarded not only as a union of two individuals, but also as the union of two families, making them almost like blood relatives. Marriages are religiously, economically, politically, and socially oriented and they are generally arranged by the elders and extended family members (Chekki 1996; Sureender, Prabakaran, and Khan 1998).

Even in contemporary Indian society, Hindus consider marriage as a social and cultural obligation and a contract for life. Marriage is not viewed as a means to attain personal happiness nor as a means of sharing your life with a person you love. Instead, the basic qualities of family unity, family togetherness, family harmony, family cohesiveness, and sharing of common family goals, values, and a way of life are of significant importance, and personal considerations are secondary. That the couple is not in love with each other or that the two partners are not physically attracted to one another or the possibility that the two do not have too much in common are not considerations because love is expected to come after marriage (Medora 2002). It is customary for individuals to marry within their religion, caste, and subcaste.

In India the family is the most important institution that has survived through the ages. India, like most other less industrialized, traditional, eastern societies is a collectivist society that emphasizes family integrity, family loyalty, and family unity. C. Harry Hui and Harry C. Triandis (1986) defined collectivism, which is the opposite of individualism as, "a sense of harmony, interdependence and concern for others" (p. 244). More specifically, collectivism is reflected in greater readiness to cooperate with family members and extended kin on decisions affecting most aspects of life, including career choice, mate selection, and marriage (Hui and Triandis 1986; Triandis et al. 1988).

The Indian family has been a dominant institution in the life of the individual and in the life of the community (Mullatti 1992). For the Hindu family, extended family and kinship ties are of utmost importance. In India, families adhere to a patriarchal ideology, follow the patrilineal rule of descent, are patrilocal, have familialistic value orientations, and endorse traditional gender role preferences. The Indian family is considered strong, stable, close, resilient, and enduring (Mullatti 1995; Shangle 1995). Historically, the traditional, ideal and desired family in India is the joint family. A joint family includes kinsmen, and generally includes three to four living generations, including uncles, aunts, nieces, nephews, and grandparents living together in the same household. It is a group composed of a number of family units living in separate rooms of the same house. These members eat the food cooked at one hearth, share a common income, common property, are related to one another through kinship ties, and worship the same idols. The family supports the old; takes care of widows, never-married adults, and the disabled; assists during periods of unemployment; and provides security and a sense of support and togetherness (Chekki 1996; Sethi 1989). The joint family has always been the preferred family type in the Indian culture, and most Indians at some point in their lives have participated in joint family living (Nandan and Eames 1980).

Radical Feminism

To radical feminists, women's oppression is the most fundamental form of oppression." It is the model for all other kinds of oppression. A prostitute, in their view, does not act out of free choice but is a victim of coercion in both its most subtle and direct forms. Because oppression is so entrenched in people's thinking, changes in the structuring of society alone are not sufficient to overcome it. The attitudes of men must be changed and a state of equality made manifest in the power dynamic between men and women. As in the case of the socialist feminist and the Marxist feminist, once equality has been achieved and the structuring of society corrected, prostitution as we know it will play a diminished role in society—if one at all. Liberal feminism and radical feminism contrast sharply in certain of their fundamental views. Liberal feminist thinking is a more reasoned, intellectual perspective than the radical feminist position, which has both emotional and political centering in its logical expressions.

It has been said of the radical feminists that their tactics and their philosophy are inseparable." This is understandable, since their focus is on widespread cultural awakening rather than on scholarly debate." Their political vibrancy comes in part from the fact that (1) they are saying something relevant and true about men that can almost universally be appreciated by women, and (2) their logical standards are predicated on politics rather than precise theory and thus they become the be-all and end-all for a diversity of people. While their central logic may be "unrefined" compared to the scholarly approach, it could ultimately command the widest base of political support given certain changes. Radical feminists tend to muddle their ideas, producing concepts that do not make finer distinctions of reality."

The oppression of women by men is assumed to be of the same intensity among all men, yet obviously as Imelda Whelehan has pointed out, "Men have different degrees of access to [the] mechanisms of oppression."" The distinction between rape and prostitution is obscure; its logic is tied to an abstract theory of degradation distant from representing the actual sense of the word "degradation." Radical feminism focuses on men as oppressors, yet says little about the possibility of the woman being an oppressor of other women or of men." Radical feminists do not view prostitution as a harmless private transaction. On the contrary, they believe that it reinforces and perpetuates the objectification, subordination, and exploitation of women." They see men as universally believing myths regarding their own sexuality. Two myths are: (1) that men need more sex than women and (2) that they are genetically the stronger sex and therefore should be dominant in relationships with women. Feminist writer Alison M. Jaggar describes the radical feminist view as one in which "almost every man/woman encounter has sexual overtones and typically is designed to reinforce the sexual dominance of men." To the feminist, a man's belief that he has no choice other than to respond to his sexual urges, creates a self-validating tautology of belief predicated on the notion that his aggressive behaviors are linked to his inherited traits.

The feminist sees otherwise, viewing the source of men's sexuality as deriving in part from the culture and not exclusively from biology. According to this line of thinking, prostitution and pornography as factors in male experience only exacerbate his self-serving belief in the primacy of his sexuality. His role as the "dominant" sex is reinforced in his mind as something very real, when in fact it is not. In this sense, influences such as prostitution and pornography can be viewed as degrading to all women, as acceptance of these events reinforces and perpetuates a cruel fantasy of women as weak and submissive. D. Kelly Weisberg, in Application of Feminist Legal Theory to Women's Lives, describes this process in the following way: "According to the radical feminist view, men are socialized to have sexual desires and to feel entitled to have those desires met, whereas women are socialized to meet those desires and to internalize accepted definitions of femininity and sexual objectification." As men cling to the idea that their sexuality is an absolute expression of their need and dominance, they prevent women from effecting new attitudes, self-realizations, and behaviors.

Gender

Gender comprises a range of differences between men and women, extending from the biological to the social. At the biological level, men and women are typically distinguished by the presence of a Y-chromosome in male cells, and its absence in female cells. At the social level, however, there is debate regarding the extent to which the various biological differences necessitate differences in social gender roles and gender identity, which has been defined as "an individual's self-conception as being male or female, as distinguished from actual biological sex." Historically, feminism has posited that many gender roles are primarily socially constructed, offering explanations in terms of unequal economic and other power relations, rather than in biology.

Patriarchy

Religious patriarchy works as a vehicle for encouraging women to accept gender oppression through religion, in order to maintain the cohesion of the male-dominated gender system in India. Religious patriarchy brings to the forefront many theoretical and political questions regarding the location of women in religion. Examining the politics of location also requires an exploration of the historical, geographical and cultural boundaries which provide the groundwork for political definition. The position of women in religion is actually based on multiple locations that have evolved through integration of complex configurations of language and power. In this presentation, the presenter likens the position of women in patriarchal religion to the control exerted over individuals during the colonial period and continuing during the imperialistic era.

Reproductive Technology

There is really no official Ecofeminist position on reproductive technologies. Some argue that the use of technology to manipulate human biology is dangerous because it allows patriarchal science to consume the only real trump card that women have. They also argue that the use of such technologies entrenches the mindset by which human manipulation of the natural environment is accepted, justifying environmental degradation and maintaining the incorrect assumption that humans are not interrelated with nature. Other Ecofeminists argue that women have a right to reproductive technology because their bodies belong to them. To control their wombs, they argue, is to oppress them and treat them as less than human. Much controversey surrounds the issue of reproductive technologies-the following list of websites provides a basis for researching all angles of the debate.

Motherhood

The act of giving birth is the only moment when both pain and pleasure converge in a moment of time. It is in the manner of the sharp point of a needle, astride upon that point are both pleasure and pain, simultaneously assailing the female that is undergoing the miracle of childbirth.This is the only instance where both pleasure and pain work in unison. also a miracle. This is the second miracle. Before the childbirth, the lady was a woman. After the childbirth, the woman is transformed into a mother. This is a revolutionary act; an evolutionary happening; in the manner of the silkworm getting transformed into some winged angel; a miracle. This is the third miracle.This experience of transformation into motherhood is a privilege reserved exclusively for women. Men do not undergo such miraculous transformation.Motherhood is another name of devotion. The selfless love and devotion towards the infant or child are grown from the seeds of innocence; no cunning, scheming, selfish motives here.

Socialist Feminism

Socialist feminism is a branch of feminism that focuses upon both the public and private spheres of a woman's life and argues that liberation can only be achieved by working to end both the economic and cultural sources of women's oppression. Socialist feminism is a dualist theory that broadens Marxist feminism's argument for the role of capitalism in the oppression of women and radical feminism's theory of the role of gender and the patriarchy.

Some contributors to this perspective have critiqued traditional Marxism for failing to find an inherent connection between patriarchy and classism. Marx and Engels were largely silent on gender oppression except to subsume it underneath broader class oppression.

Marx felt that when class oppression was overcome, gender oppression would vanish as well. According to socialist feminists, this view of gender oppression as a sub-class of class oppression is naive and much of the work of socialist feminists has gone towards separating gender phenomena from class phenomena.

Other socialist feminists, notably two long-lived American organizations Radical Women and the Freedom Socialist Party, point to the classic Marxist writings of Frederick Engels (Origin of the Family, Private Property and the State) and August Bebel (Woman and Socialism) as a powerful explanation of the link between gender oppression and class exploitation.

Division of Labour—Unifies and Dual System

The division of labour between men and women in crop production varies considerably from region to region and community to community. However, it is usually men who plough the fields and drive draught animals whereas women do the major share of sowing, weeding, applying fertilizer and pesticides, harvesting and threshing.Similarly, men tend to do the work of large-scale cash cropping, especially when it is highly mechanized, while women take care of household food production and small-scale cultivation of cash crops, requiring low levels of technology. This pattern is particularly pronounced in sub-Saharan Africa, where men and women customarily farm separate plots. Men tend to grow cash crops and keep the income, while women use their land primarily for subsistence crops to feed their families.

Women make an essential contribution to producing staple crops. In Southeast Asia, for example, it is women who provide up to 90 percent of the labour for rice cultivation. They do almost all the work of planting and transplanting, fertilizing, weeding, irrigating and harvesting. After the rice has been harvested, they also carry out the post-harvest tasks before the rice can be stored, marketed, cooked or eaten.

Women also play a big role in growing secondary crops, such as legumes and vegetables. In addition to providing essential nutrients, these crops are often the only food available during the lean season between harvests or when the main harvest fails. Home gardens, often tended almost exclusively by women, also claim precious labour-intensive time. Despite their often complementary roles in agriculture, studies have shown that in almost all societies, women tend to work longer hours than men. The difference in workloads is particularly marked for rural women, the world's principal food producers. Women are involved in every stage of food production and, although there is a gender-based division of labour, women do tend to shoulder the larger share. In addition to food production activities, women have the responsibility of preparing and processing the food while fulfilling their fundamental role of nurturing and caring for children and tending to elderly members of the household.

Exploitation

Trafficking in women and children is a gross violation of human rights. However, this does not prevent an estimated 800 000 women and children to be trafficked each year across international borders. Eighty per cent of trafficked persons end in forced sex work. India has been identified as one of the Asian countries where trafficking for commercial sexual exploitation has reached alarming levels. While there is a considerable amount of internal trafficking from one state to another or within states, India has also emerged as a international supplier of trafficked women and children to the Gulf States and South East Asia, as well as a destination country for women and girls trafficked for commercial sexual exploitation from Nepal and Bangladesh. Trafficking for commercial sexual exploitation is a highly profitable and low risk business that preys on particularly vulnerable populations.

Indian Women—Family, Caste, Class, Culture, Religion, Social System

The status of women in India has been subject to many great changes over the past few millennia. From a largely unknown status in ancient times through the low points of the medieval period, to the promotion of equal rights by many reformers, the history of women in India has been eventful.

There are very few texts specifically dealing with the role of women; an important exception is the *strIdharmapaddhati* of Tryambakayajvan, an official at Thanjavur around c.1730. The text compiles strictures on womenly behaviour dating back to the Apastamba sutra (c. 4th c. BCE). The opening verse goes:

> *mukhyo dharmah smrtishu vihito bhartrshu-shrushanam hi :*
>
> *the primary duty of women is enjoined to be service to one's husband.*

where the term *shushrusha* (lit. "desire to hear") covers a range of meanings from the devotee's homage to god, or the obsequieous service of a slave.

Scholars believe that in ancient India, the women enjoyed equal status with men in all fields of life. However, some others hold contrasting views. Works by ancient Indian grammarians such as Patanjali and Katyayana suggest that women were educated in the early Vedic period Rigvedic verses suggest that the women married at a mature age and were probably free to select their husband. Scriptures such as Rig Veda and Upanishads mention several women sages and seers, notably Gargi and Maitreyi.

Some kingdoms in the ancient India had traditions such as *nagarvadhu* ("bride of the city"). Women competed to win the coveted title of the *nagarvadhu*. Amrapali is the most famous example of a nagarvadhu.

According to studies, women enjoyed equal status and rights during the early Vedic period. However, later (approximately 500 B.C.), the status of women began to decline with the Smritis (esp. Manusmriti) and with the Islamic invasion of Babur and the Mughal empire and later Christianity curtailing women's freedom and rights.

Although reformatory movements such as Jainism allowed women to be admitted to the religious order, by and large, the women in India faced confinement and restrictions. The practice of child marriages is believed to have started from around sixth century.

The Indian woman's position in the society further deteriorated during the medieval period when Sati, child marriages and a ban on widow remarriages became part of social life in India. The Muslim conquest in the Indian subcontinent brought the purdah practice in the Indian society. Among the Rajputs of Rajasthan, the Jauhar was practised. In some parts of India, the Devadasis or the temple women were sexually exploited. Polygamy was widely practised esp. among Hindu Kshatriya rulers. In many Muslim families, women were restricted to Zenana areas.

In spite of these conditions, some women execeled in the fields of politics, literature, education and religion. Razia Sultana became the only woman monarch to have ever ruled Delhi. The Gond queen Durgavati ruled for fifteen years, before she lost her life in a battle with Mughal emperor Akbar's general Asaf Khan in 1564. Chand Bibi defended Ahmednagar against the mighty Mughal forces of Akbar in 1590s. Jehangir's wife Nur Jehan effectively wielded imperial power and was recognized as the real force behind the Mughal throne. The Mughal princesses Jahanara and Zebunnissa were well-known poets, and also influenced the ruling administration Shivaji's mother, Jijabai was deputed as queen regent, because of her ability as a warrior and an administrator. In South India, many women administered villages, towns, divisions and heralded social and religious institutions.

The Bhakti movements tried to restore women's status and questioned some of the forms of oppression. Mirabai, a female saint-poet, was one of the most important Bhakti movement figures. Some other female saint-poets from this period include Akka Mahadevi, Rami Janabai and Lal Ded. Bhakti sects within Hinduism such as the Mahanubhav, Varkari and many others were principle movements within the Hindu fold to openly advocate social justice and equality between men and women.

Shortly after the Bhakti movement, Guru Nanak, the first Guru of Sikhs also preached the message of equality between men and women. He advocated that women be allowed to lead religious assemblies; to perform and lead congregational hymn singing called Kirtan or Bhajan; become members of religious management committees; to lead armies on the battlefield; have equality in marriage, and equality in Amrit (Baptism). Other Sikh Gurus also preached against the discrimination against women.

Traditions such as sati, jauhar, and devadasi have been banned and are largely defunct in modern India. However, some cases of these practices are still found in remote parts of India. The purdah is still practiced by many Indian women, and child marriage remains prevalent despite it being an illegal practice, especially under current Indian laws.

In India, people learn the essential themes of cultural life within the bosom of a family. In most of the country, the basic units of society are the patrilineal family unit and wider kinship groupings. The most widely desired residential unit is the joint family, ideally consisting of three or four patrilineally related generations, all living under one roof, working, eating, worshiping, and cooperating together in mutually beneficial social and economic activities. Patrilineal joint families include men related through the male line, along with their wives and children. Most young women expect to live with their husband's relatives after marriage, but they retain important bonds with their natal families.

Despite the continuous and growing impact of urbanization, secularization, and Westernization, the traditional joint household, both in ideal and in practice, remains the primary social force in the lives of most Indians. Loyalty to family is a deeply held ideal for almost everyone.

Large families tend to be flexible and well-suited to modern Indian life, especially for the 67 percent of Indians who are farmers or agricultural workers or work in related activities. As in most primarily agricultural societies, few individuals can hope to achieve economic security without being part of a cooperating group of kinsmen. The joint family is also common in cities, where kinship ties can be crucial to obtaining scarce jobs or financial assistance. Numerous prominent Indian families, such as the Tatas, Birlas, and Sarabhais, retain joint family arrangements even as they work together to control some of the country's largest financial empires.

The joint family is an ancient Indian institution, but it has undergone some change in the late twentieth century. Although several generations living together is the ideal, actual living arrangements vary widely depending on region, social status, and economic circumstance. Many Indians live in joint families that deviate in various ways from the ideal, and many live in nuclear families—a couple with their unmarried children—as is the most common pattern in the West.

However, even where the ideal joint family is seldom found (as, for example, in certain regions and among impoverished agricultural laborers and urban squatters), there are often strong networks of kinship ties through which economic assistance and other benefits are obtained. Not infrequently, clusters of relatives live very near each other, easily available to respond to the give and take of kinship obligations. Even when relatives cannot actually live in close proximity, they typically maintain strong bonds of kinship and attempt to provide each other with economic help, emotional support, and other benefits.

As joint families grow ever larger, they inevitably divide into smaller units, passing through a predictable cycle over time. The breakup of a joint family into smaller units does not necessarily represent the rejection of the joint family ideal. Rather, it is usually a response to a variety of conditions, including the need for some members to move from village to city, or from one city to another to take advantage of employment opportunities. Splitting of the family is often blamed on quarrelling women—typically, the wives of coresident brothers. Although women's disputes may, in fact, lead to family division, men's disagreements do so as well. Despite cultural ideals of brotherly harmony, adult brothers frequently quarrel over land and other matters, leading them to decide to live under separate roofs and divide their property. Frequently, a large joint family divides after the demise of elderly parents, when there is no longer a single authority figure to hold the family factions together. After division, each new residential unit, in its turn, usually becomes joint when sons of the family marry and bring their wives to live in the family home.

Although many other nations are characterized by social inequality, perhaps nowhere else in the world has inequality been so elaborately constructed as in the Indian institution of caste. Caste has long existed in India, but in the modern period it has been severely criticized by both Indian and foreign observers. Although some educated Indians tell non-Indians that caste has been abolished or that "no one pays attention to caste anymore," such statements do not reflect reality. Caste has undergone significant change since independence, but it still involves hundreds of millions of people. In its preamble, India's constitution forbids negative public discrimination on the basis of caste.

However, caste ranking and caste-based interaction have occurred for centuries and will continue to do so well into the foreseeable future, more in the countryside than in urban settings and more in the realms of kinship and marriage than in less personal interactions.

Castes are ranked, named, endogamous (in-marrying) groups, membership in which is achieved by birth. There are thousands of castes and subcastes in India, and these large kinship-based groups are fundamental to South Asian social structure. Each caste is part of a locally based system of interdependence with other groups, involving occupational specialization, and is linked in complex ways with networks that stretch across regions and throughout the nation.

The word *caste* derives from the Portuguese *casta*, meaning breed, race, or kind. Among the Indian terms that are sometimes translated as caste are *varna* (see Glossary), *jati* (see Glossary), *jat*, *biradri*, and *samaj*. All of these terms refer to ranked groups of various sizes and breadth. *Varna*, or colour, actually refers to large divisions that include various castes; the other terms include castes and subdivisions of castes sometimes called subcastes. Many castes are traditionally associated with an occupation, such as high-ranking Brahmans; middle-ranking farmer and artisan groups, such as potters, barbers, and carpenters; and very low-ranking "Untouchable" leatherworkers, butchers, launderers, and latrine cleaners. There is some correlation between ritual rank on the caste hierarchy and economic prosperity. Members of higher-ranking castes tend, on the whole, to be more prosperous than members of lower-ranking castes. Many lower-caste people live in conditions of great poverty and social disadvantage.

According to the Rig Veda, sacred texts that date back to oral traditions of more than 3,000 years ago, progenitors of the four ranked *varna* groups sprang from various parts of the body of the primordial man, which Brahma created from clay (see The Vedas and Polytheism, ch. 3). Each group had a function in sustaining the life of society—the social body. Brahmans, or priests, were created from the mouth. They were to provide for the intellectual and spiritual needs of the community. Kshatriyas, warriors and rulers, were derived from the arms. Their role was to rule and to protect others. Vaishyas—landowners and merchants—sprang from the thighs, and were entrusted with the care of commerce and agriculture. Shudras—artisans and servants—came from the feet. Their task was to perform all manual labour.

Later conceptualized was a fifth category, "Untouchable" menials, relegated to carrying out very menial and polluting work related to bodily decay and dirt. Since 1935 "Untouchables" have been known as Scheduled Castes, referring to their listing on government rosters, or schedules. They are also often called by Mohandas Karamchand (Mahatma) Gandhi's term Harijans, or "Children of God." Although the term *Untouchable* appears in literature produced by these low-ranking castes, in the 1990s, many politically conscious members of these groups prefer to refer to themselves as Dalit (see Glossary), a Hindi word meaning oppressed or downtrodden. According to the 1991 census, there were 138 million Scheduled Caste members in India, approximately 16 percent of the total population.

The first four *varnas* apparently existed in the ancient Aryan society of northern India. Some historians say that these categories were originally somewhat fluid functional groups, not castes. A greater degree of fixity gradually developed, resulting in the complex ranking systems of medieval India that essentially continue in the late twentieth century. Although a *varna* is not a caste, when directly asked for their caste affiliation, particularly when the questioner is a Westerner, many Indians will reply with a *varna* name. Pressed further, they may respond with a much more specific name of a caste, or *jati*, which falls within that *varna*.

For example, a Brahman may specify that he is a member of a named caste group, such as a Jijotiya Brahman, or a Smartha Brahman, and so on. Within such castes, people may further belong to smaller subcaste categories and to specific clans and lineages. These finer designations are particularly relevant when marriages are being arranged and often appear in newspaper matrimonial advertisements.

Members of a caste are typically spread out over a region, with representatives living in hundreds of settlements. In any small village, there may be representatives of a few or even a score or more castes.

Numerous groups usually called tribes (often referred to as Scheduled Tribes) are also integrated into the caste system to varying degrees. Some tribes live separately from others—particularly in the far northeast and in the forested center of the country, where tribes are more like ethnic groups than castes. Some tribes are themselves divided into groups similar to subcastes. In regions where members of tribes live in peasant villages with nontribal peoples, they are usually considered members of separate castes ranking low on the hierarchical scale.

Woman is man's companion, gifted with equal mental capacities. She has the right to participate in the activities of man to the very minutest detail and she has an equal right to freedom and liberty as him. She is entitled to a supreme place in her own sphere of activity as man is in his.

This ought to be the natural condition of things and not just as a result of learning to read and write. By sheer force of a vicious custom, even the most ignorant and worthless men have been enjoying superiority over women which they do not deserve and ought not to have. Many of our movements stop halfway and much of our work does not yield appropriate results because of the condition of our women.

Man and woman are equal in status, but are not identical. They are a peerless pair each being complementary to the other; each helps the other, so that without the one the existence of the other can not be conceived. Therefore it follows as a necessary corollary from these facts, that anything that will impair the status of either of them will involve an equal ruin of both.

UNIT-III

Women's Education

Women's Education

The" Primacy of Women's Education—"If Government by the initial exclusion of the masses accentuated the segregation of the masses from the privileged few, by their initial restriction of their (educational) efforts to the male population, they brought a line of division where it had never existed before, within the household." While the movement for equal education for men and women began in Great Britain about a century ago with such serious thinkers as Frederick Maurice, who was a founder of Queen',, College for woman in 1848, and John Stuart Mill, whose "Subjection of Women" was published in 1869, it did not reach India until several decades later. Even today the inequality is evident. According to the statistics issued by the Indian Ministry of Education for 1945-46, there were six and a half times as many boys and men in secondary schools and colleges as there were girls.

The underlying habits of men and women are largely fixed in the early years, and these years are spent chiefly with I the mother. If she is open minded, inquiring and alert, looking behind rumour and tradition to find the facts, concerned with the course of events, informed about the nature of the world around her and interested in it, and acquainted with history and literature and enjoying them, then her children will learn these interests and attitudes from her. The educated, conscientious mother who lives and works with her children in the home is the best teacher in the world of cloth character and intelligence. Much of what she learned at school her children Yet unconsciously as second nature by living in her company. In a society made up of such homes children starting to school already have a background of information, understanding and culture which result in their getting more benefit from school than otherwise would be possible.

There cannot be an educated people without educated women. If general education had to be limited to men or to women, that opportunity should be given to women, for then it would most surely be passed on to the next generation.

The Education of Women as Women-General education for interesting and intelligent living and for citizenship in large part can be the same for men and women. We have heard frequent suggestions that women's education should run to pretty "accomplishments," such as drawing, painting or the like-skills which will enable well-to-do women to pass the' time harmlessly while their husbands do the really important work. This point of view should be obsolete. Women should share with men the life and thought and interests of the times. They are fitted to carry the same academic work as men, with no less thoroughness and quality. The distribution of general ability among women is approximately the same as among men.

Yet, though men and women are equally competent in academic work, and though many subjects are equally interesting and appropriate, it does not follow that in all things men's and women's education should be identical. Indian universities for the most part are places of preparation for a man's world. Little thought has been given to the education of women as women. Women must, share the same programme as men or go without. There are ways in which many women's interests or appropriate fields of work diverge from those of men, and educational programmes should take that fact into account.

In every country, no matter how far the "liberation" of women has gone, husbands and wives commonly play different parts. In general the man provides the income and the woman maintains the home. For many women who crave to achieve standards of excellence, the home provides an excellent setting.

For a woman to give the home design, beauty, order and character, without being herself a slave to home-keeping and without imposing onerous prohibitions and restrictions on the freedom of movement of children, is a high art. It will not be acquired by chance, and for many women its acquisition will be impossible, except through education.

Gender bias in Enrolment

A study group analyzed gender bias in school enrollment by developing a two-period model where women become part of extended families of their in-laws. Each family decides how many sons and daughters are sent to school and thus become skilled. Gender bias occurs due to failure of the families to internalize inter-household externalities. "Groom-specific" dowry worsens the situation. Under "bride-specific" dowry, bias exists if and only if the skill premium in the labour market is bigger than that in the marriage market. A specific discriminatory "food-for-education" policy is shown to reduce bias, but increase total enrollment.

Curriculum Content

Quality content includes relevant curriculum and learning materials developed in the context of national goals for education. A relevant curriculum is both a mirror of what goes on in the community and a window into the rest of the country, the world, and a better, more peaceful future for all people. It is relevant and sensitive to both boys and girls. The curricula and materials should ensure that learners can read, use numbers and be able to use life skills in real life. The latter should include knowledge about rights, gender, health, HIV/ AIDS prevention and peace. Quality content is appropriate to children's level of learning and in languages that both students and teachers understand. Governments should adopt relevant, student-centred and non-discriminatory curriculum plans that are easily understood by teachers.

Quality Content for Girls

Girls are often invisible in curriculum content and images. This means that girls may not find many illustrations or stories of girls and women in textbooks and other learning materials—especially not of notable, empowered girls and women.

It also means that girls are often told to take certain courses and not to take others. For example, girls may be told that they shouldn't take science or mathematics courses. If they are able to enroll in those courses, the textbooks and teaching are often geared to the boys. Learning to identify gender bias in the curriculum is a critical component of quality education for all.

Teaching girls skills for life—good decision-making and self-confidence, for example, and how to identify gender bias—is also crucial to empowerment. These skills will enable girls to better apply their knowledge throughout their lives.

Dropouts Negative Capability in Education

A dropout is considered, a student who for any reason other than death leaves school before graduation without transferring to another school.

Dropping out of school is a well documented social problem and often present daunting circumstances for adolescents. Dropping out is also associated with delinquency, and low school achievements.

One of the major reasons for children being kept out-of-school was the lack of education of parents. The public report on basic education (popularly referred to as the PROBE report) sought to find reasons for both dropouts and never-enrolment of children in five states (Rajasthan, Himachal Pradesh, Uttar Pradesh, Madhya Pradesh, and Bihar). It was found that parents' attitudes towards education have a major effect on education. It seems that when either of the parents is literate or especially when women are literate, they are more willing to send their children, especially girls, to the school.

"The huge dropout rates, however, indicate that children, girls more often than boys, are needed for other activities such as looking after other siblings, domestic work and help with farm work. Parents play a crucial role in keeping young people in school. The degree and nature of family support are determined by such factors as a stressful/unstable home life, socio-economic status, minority membership, siblings' completion of high school, single parent household, poor education of parents and primary language other than English" (Horn, 1992).

The girls who are denied educational opportunities disproportionately as compared to boys suggest clear cut discrimination in household behaviour. Parental and social attitudes in most Indian cultural context tend to perpetuate the stereotypes of girls being transient members of families on their journey to marriage and boys being the mainstay of support to ageing parents. The subordination of the adult women in the household runs parallel with a subordination of the girl child, socializing the latter into the pre-ordained role that she will assume as an adult. The implications of such unequal treatment result in limiting the opportunities and choices that girl children may have both in the present and in the future. To use Amartya Sen's felicitous phrase, "the capabilities of girls will be severely restricted by the denial of education. If freedom is the goal of development, it will be substantially restricted by the fact that illiterate girls will become illiterate women." One way to empower women would be to bring them out of the limiting boundaries of the household into the wider world of social and political relations. In order to equip women to deal as men do with that external world, education plays an important role. In contrast, the current policies of the state will perpetuate the confinement of women to their homes and hinder their progress and passage into the world of the 'city.'

Values in Education

Non-racism and Non-sexism

This value outlines the challenge of striving towards practices that treat everybody as equals in order to redress the imbalances of the past where people were oppressed or devalued because of their race or gender. From this value the policies of affirmative action flow.

Non sexism also means that female educators and students are not victims of sexual abuse or harassment in schools, and that females are not discouraged from completing their schooling because of abuse, harassment or pregnancy.

Ubuntu (Human Dignity)

Ubuntu has a particularly important place in our value system for it derives specifically from African customs: I am human because you are human. Out of the values of Ubuntu and human dignity flow the practices of compassion, kindness, altruism and respect which are at the core of making schools places where the culture of teaching and culture of learning thrive and of making them dynamic hubs of industry and achievement rather than places of conflict and pain. Ubuntu embodies the concept of mutual understanding and the active appreciation of the value of human difference. It requires you to know others if you're to know yourself within a multicultural environment. Ultimately, Ubuntu requires you to respect others if you are to respect yourself.

An Open Society

The South African Constitution as the supreme law lays the foundation for a democratic and open society in which government is based on the will of the people. Democracy and openness are interchangeable and interdependent values.

The Constitution is the route to an open society because we have the right to freedom of conscience, religion, thought, belief and opinion, the right to freedom of expression in relation to the press, artistic creativity, academic issues, scientific research, assembly and association. Our rights come with certain responsibilities: we may not exercise our rights to openness if they have the intention of inciting violence, propagandising war, or advocating hatred based on race, ethnicity, gender or religion. The value of openness cherishes debate, discussion and critical thought, for a society that knows how to talk and how to listen does not need to resort to violence.

It means, most of all, encouraging a culture of dialogue and debate that is often absent or discouraged in our schools. A culture of discussion out of which values and priorities are perpetually being reflected on, evaluated and reassessed should be cultivated.

Accountability (Responsibility)

Democratic tools such as the vote confirm and reinforce the values of accountability, responsiveness and openness. More specifically the public administration, which includes the school system, must be governed by the values and principles of professionalism, efficiency, equity, transparency, representivity and accountability. But accountability means that we are all responsible for the advancement of our nation through education and our schools and that we are responsible to others in the society for our individual behaviour. In the school situation this implies, among other things, constant contact with and reporting to parents.

The Rule of Law

South Africa is founded on the value of the supremacy of the constitution and the rule of law. The law is supreme in that there is a consensus of rules and regulations we must obey. All participants within the education system are subject to the law of the land. Administrators may not defraud school budget for personal gains, educators may not physically or sexually abuse their learners, learners may not carry illegal weapons, possess illegal narcotics, trash school property and intimidate educators. Non-violence might be the value that flows out of the constitutional principles of Ubuntu, equality and openness, but it is also one that is upheld by the rule of law.

Respect

School-based research on values and education conducted for the Department of Education shows that the two values people feel are most lacking in schools are respect and dialogue. Respect is an essential precondition for communication, for teamwork and for productivity. Learning cannot happen if there is not mutual respect between educators and learners.

The Convention of the Rights of the Child goes further: It calls for education to be directed to strengthening "the development of respect for the child's parents, for his or her own cultural identity, language and values, for the national values of the country in which the child is living, the country from which he or she may originate, and for civilisations different from his or her own". Education must also direct itself to "the preparation of the child for responsible life in a free society, in the spirit of understanding, peace, tolerance, equality of sex, and friendship among all peoples, ethnic, national and religious groups and persons of indigenous origin".

Reconciliation

Reconciling is more than merely being a question of saying sorry. It requires redress in other, even material, ways, as well. "Unity in Diversity" means accepting each other through learning, it means interacting with each other, and studying how we have interacted with each other in the past. It means accepting that South Africa is made up of people and communities with very different cultures and traditions, and with very different experiences of what it means to be South African, remembering that these experiences have often been violent and conflictual.

Vocational Education Recent Trends in Women's Education

The trend in contemporary K-12 vocational education is away from the use of the word *vocational* to label these programmes. Most states have selected a broader term, although a few use *vocational technical education.* A number of states have followed the lead of the national vocational education organizations and adopted the term *career and technical education.* Others use variations, such as career and technology education and professional-technical education, and several states include the word *workforce* in describing these programmes. The changes in terminology reflect a changing economy, in which technical careers have become the mainstay.

When the term *career education* first became popular in the 1970s, it was distinguished from vocational education by its emphasis on general employability and adaptability skills applicable to all occupations, while vocational education was primarily concerned with occupational skill training for specific occupations. That basic definition of career education remains appropriate today.

The purpose of career and technical education is to provide a foundation of skills that enable high school students to be gainfully employed after graduation-either full-time or while continuing their education or training. Nearly two-thirds of all graduates of career and technical programmes enter some form of postsecondary programme. Across the United States, career and technical education programmes are offered in about 11,000 comprehensive high schools, several hundred vocational-technical high schools, and about 1,400 area vocational-technical centers. Public middle schools typically offer some career and technical education courses, such as family and consumer sciences and technology education. About 9,400 postsecondary institutions offer technical programmes, including community colleges, technical institutes, skill centers, and other public and private two-and four-year colleges. In 2001 there were 11 million secondary and postsecondary career and technical education students in the United States, according to the U.S. Office of Educational Research and Improvement.

The subject areas most commonly associated with career and technical education are: business (office administration, entrepreneurship); trade and industrial (e.g., automotive technician, carpenter, computer numerical control technician); health occupations (nursing, dental, and medical technicians); agriculture (food and fiber production, agribusiness); family and consumer sciences (culinary arts, family management and life skills); marketing (merchandising, retail); and technology (computer-based careers).

Women Teacher Training Committees and Commissions on Education

NCERT: An Apex Resource Organization in School Education

The National Council of Educational Research and Training (NCERT) was set up by Government of India in 1961 as an autonomous organisation registered under Societies Registration Act (Act XXI of 1860) to advise and assist the Ministry of Human Resource Development, Government of India and Departments of Education in States/ UTs in formulation and implementation of their policies and major programmes in the field of education, particularly for qualitative improvement of school education. For realization of its objectives, the NCERT and its Constituent Units:

- Undertake, aid, promote and coordinate research on areasrelated to school education;
- Organize pre-service and in-service training of teachers;
- Organize extension services for institutions that are engaged in educational research, training of teachers or have extension services to schools;
- Develop and disseminate improved educational techniques, practices and innovations;
- Collaborate, advise and assist State Education Departments, Universities and other educational institutions;
- Act as a clearing-house for ideas and information to all matters relating to school education;
- Undertake the preparation and/or the publication of books, materials, periodicals and other literature to achieve its objectives;
- Act as a nodal agency for achieving goals of universalisation of elementary education.

In addition to research, development, training, extension, publication and dissemination activities, the NCERT acts as a major agency for implementing the bilateral Cultural Exchange Programmes with other countries in the field of school education. The NCERT also interacts and works in collaboration with international organizations, visiting foreign experts and delegations and offers various training facilities to educational personnel from developing countries.

Constituent Units

The major Constituent Units of the NCERT are:

1. National Institute of Education (NIE), New Delhi
2. Central Institute of Educational Technology (CIET), New Delhi
3. Paṇdit Sunderlal Sharma Central Institute of Vocational Education (PSSCIVE), Bhopal

4. Regional Institute of Education (RIE), Ajmer
5. Regional Institute of Education (RIE), Bhopal
6. Regional Institute of Education (RIE), Bhubaneswar
7. Regional Institute of Education (RIE), Mysore
8. North-East Regional Institute of Education (NE-RIE), Shillong

Adult Literacy and Non Formal Education for Women's Development

The problems of non-formal education and adult literacy have continued to receive high priority. The Conference of Education Secretaries held in July, 1976 discussed at length the concept and programmes of non-formal education and suggested strategies for their future development. The CABE Committee on Non-formal Education and the Standing Committee of CABE, which also met in July, 1976, discussed further the issue raised in the Education Secretaries Conference and made important recommendations. Along with selective programmes of non-formal education, emphasis was given to mass programmes of adult literacy through a larger involvement of students under NSS, and of teachers.

The Directorate of Non-formal (Adult) Education.-To provide technical support for the programmes of adult education, particularly to the State Governments and voluntary organisations, the Directorate of Non-formal (Adult) Education was established in 1971 by taking out the Department of Adult Education from the NCERT. Since then the Directorate has grown considerably in size and coverage and has expanded its activities to cover many aspects of adult education/literacy which were hitherto unexplored. It is now functioning as a national resource centre in the field of non-formal education and is providing useful assistance in planning programmes, training, preparation of teaching/teaming materials, and evaluation and monitoring. Among the activities of the Directorate the following deserve special mention:

(1) The Directorate helped the State Governments of Andhra Pradesh, Kerala and Tamilnadu in organising

training courses for their non-formal education workers at different levels.

(2) It prepared curricular guidelines for non-formal education programmes. The emphasis in these guidelines is on developing. methodology of curriculum preparation and promoting efforts in, developing diversified and need-based curricula with an inter-disciplinary approach.

(3) It undertook a project to compile information in respect of various non-formal education activities organised by various Ministries/Departments of the Government of India under their programmes. This is being brought out in the form of a compendium that will help in co-ordinating the efforts in this field.

(4) It brought out 34 publications on various topics relating to non-formal education under its normal publications programme. These publications helped in disseminating useful information and providing academic help in implementing the programmes.

(5) It processed and supplied learning materials worth Rs. 4 lakh to various adult literacy programmes run by NSS, Nehru Yuvak Kendras and other organisations.

(6) It provided professional guidance in planning and implementing the urban adult education programmes run by Shramik Vidyapeeths and Workers Social Education Institutes.

(7) It continued and strengthened its documentation service under which bibliographies, abstracts, etc. were issued. The service has been extended to cover over 300 information cells for non-formal education located with different agencies all over the country. In addition, the service has also been extended to about 80 other national and international agencies identified as resource centres for non-formal education programmes.

(8) It continued to function as an associate centre for the UNESCO's Asian Programme of Educational Innovations and Development.

In recognition of its contribution in the field of adult literacy' the Directorate was awarded an Honourable Mention of the Nadezhda K. Krupskaya Prize for 1976 by UNESCO.

Non-formal Education Programme for Youth in 15-25 Age. group.-Youth in 15-25 age-group constitute the most vital segment of the country's human resources. Since a majority of them are still illiterate or semi-literate, a comprehensive scheme of providing them non-formal education facilities was launched in 1975-76. The scheme which was expanded in its coverage and scope during the year, aims at providing functional literacy and non-formal education in the following areas:

(i) Society and environment-position of the individuals, their civic orientation and their rights and duties;

(ii) Employment and vocational development;

(iii) Food production, distribution and nutrition;

(iv) Health, hygiene and family welfare planning; and

(v) Home and family life.

The programme is being implemented on a sharing basis by the Central and State Governments. The Central Government financed the programme in 25 districts in 1975-76 and extended it to 50 districts during 1976-77, each district having 100 centres with an approximate enrolment of 30 in each centre. The programmes of the States covered about 100 districts. About 3 lakh youth have benefited from the programme during the year.

To provide academic support, to non-formal education programmes in the fields of training, material production, evaluation, etc., it is proposed to set up State Resources Centres in each State.

Three such centres, in Tamilnadu, Maharashtra and Rajasthan have already come into being and the Government of India have extended financial assistance to them.

Farmers' Functional Literacy Project: This project is a part of the integrated programme of Farmers Training and Functional Literacy being implemented jointly by the three Central Ministries, namely, the Ministry of Education & Social Welfare, the Ministry of Agriculture & Irrigation and the

Ministry of Information. & Broadcasting. The Ministry of Education and Social Welfare is responsible for the functional literacy component of the programme. The scheme had so far been confined to districts covered under high-yielding variety crop areas and covered 123 districts till 1975-76. During 1976-77, its coverage was extended to additional 21 districts. In each district the project is operated through 60 centres and each centre has an enrolment of about 30. The project covered about 2.5 lakh farmers during the year.

The scheme having demonstrated the benefits of an integrated approach to rural development, was diversified in its scope to provide linkages with other developmental programmes. In 1975-76 it was extended to cover one district under SFDA (Small Farmers' Development Agency) and during 1976-77 it was extended to cover one district under the drought prone areas programme and five districts under the integrated tribal development projects.

In operation for about a decade now, it has a fairly wide coverage. To evaluate the scheme and to advise on taking up similar other schemes, particularly in the context of the Sixth Five-Year Plan, a highpower committee of evaluation, under the chairmanship of Shri J. C. Mathur ICS (retd.) has been set up.

Non-formal Education for Urban Workers: Urban workers constitute an important segment of the population and their education is an important component of the overall efforts in adult education. Their educational programmes require to be linked with their economic activities, on the one hand, and social and cultural responsibilities, on the other. Two types of programmes have been in operation for them. The polyvalent adult education programme, which is offered through the three shramik vidyapeeths at Bombay, Delhi and Ahmedabad, aims at providing basic knowledge and skills to urban workers related directly to their jobs. The educational programmes in these vidyapeeths are more functional and related directly to the participants' work. The other programme is offered through the workers social. education institutes at Indore and Nagpur. The emphasis in these programmes is more on arousing a sense of social and civic responsibility and on stimulating a desire for knowledge in the working class.

To suggest future directions for the development and expansion of the urban adult education programmes and to reorient them in the light of past experience, a committee was set up to review the programmes of workers social education institutes, vis-a-vis, the programmes of the shramik vidyapeeths. The Committee, after studying different programmes offered by the two types of institutions, recommended a reorientation of workers' social education institutes on the pattern and approach followed by the shramik vidyapeeths. It further suggested that the social education aspect, expected to be the sole content of the workers' social education institutes, should be built into the shramik vidyapeeths and a network of such vidyapeeths should be set up all over the country in various urban and industrial centres.

Production of Literature for Neo-literates: To encourage the production of reading material for neo-literates, the Government of India organise each year a prize competition of manuscripts for neo-literates. The 19th competition was launched in 1976-77 and its scope was enlarged because the Department of Family Planning had decided to collaborate in that project. From 1976-77, 65 prizes will be awarded for outstanding manuscripts written on various topics in different Indian languages, 25 of them being earmarked for manuscripts written on family planning. Under the other part of the scheme, State Governments are provided grants-in-aid for producing and publishing better quality material for the neo-literates.

The Raja Rammohun Roy: Library Foundation, which was established to strengthen library movement in the rural areas, further expanded its activities and covered 5800 libraries in rural and semi-urban areas. The Foundation decided to set up a committee to evaluate its working and undertake a review of the present status of rural libraries.

Assistance to Voluntary Organisations Engaged in Adult Education Programmes: The voluntary organisations share a substantial part of the responsibility in the field of non-formal education and adult literacy. The Ministry of Education continued to extend financial and academic support to these agencies. Emphasis during the year was mostly on projects of an innovative nature and those which benefited the deprived sections of the society. Some of the voluntary agencies took up very significant projects which benefited particularly illiterate women, urban slum-dwellers and tribals. Over 50 voluntary agencies were assisted during the year and the total amount of assistance was nearly Rs. 20 lakh.

Cooperation with Unesco: Greater cooperation with Unesco has been achieved during the year. The Directorate of Nonformal (Adult) Education with the cooperation of Unesco undertook three experimental projects of preparing curricula under different socioeconomic settings. The emphasis was more on the development of methodology. The three projects involved preparation of curricula for rural women with the help of the Literacy House, Lucknow, for slum-dwellers with the help of Bengal Social Service League, Calcutta and for fishermen with the help of the Department of Adult Education, S. V. University, Tirupati. All the three projects were completed during the year and the report was submitted to Unesco.

The Government of India hosted the first phase of the Regional Mobile Field Operational Seminar organised by Unesco in November, 1976, with the active help of the Directorate of Non-formal Education in which 42 persons participated and also deputed its officers to participate in similar seminars organised in Iran and Afghanistan.

Exchange of Experience with Other Countries: Exchange of experience with other countries in the field of adult education was further strengthened during the year. A 5-member delegation of experts in adult education visited the Federal Republic of Germany in May, 1976 and studied the adult education programmes of that country for a period of two weeks. The Cultural Exchange Programme concluded by the Government of India with Hungary, USSR & Czechoslovakia inter alia, contained provisions for exchange of information, experience, personnel, etc. in the field of adult and non-formal education.

UNIT-IV

Women Resource and National Development

Concept of Work Productive and Non-productive Work—Use Value and Market Value

Work from home theory is fast gaining popularity because of the freedom and flexibility that comes with it. Since one is not bound by fixed working hours, they can schedule their work at the time when they feel most productive and convenient to them. Women benefit a lot from this concept of work since they can balance their home and work perfectly. People mostly find that in this situation, their productivity is higher and stress levels lower. Those who like isolation and a tranquil work environment also tend to prefer this way of working. Today, with the kind of communication networks available, millions of people worldwide are considering this option.

Women who want to be independent but cannot afford to leave their responsibilities at home aside will benefit a lot from this concept of work. It makes it easier to maintain a healthy balance between home and work. The family doesn't get neglected and you can get your work done too. You can thus effectively juggle home responsibilities with your career. Working from home is definitely a viable option but it also needs a lot of hard work and discipline. You have to make a time schedule for yourself and stick to it. There will be a time frame of course for any job you take up and you have to fulfill that project within that time frame.

There are many things that can be done working from home. A few of them is listed below that will give you a general idea about the benefits of this concept.

Baby-sitting

This is the most common and highly preferred job that women like doing. Since in today's competitive world both the parents have to work they need a secure place to leave behind their children who will take care of them and parents can also relax without being worried all the time. In this job you don't require any degree or qualifications. You only have to know how to take care of children. Parents are happy to pay handsome salary and you can also earn a lot without putting too much of an effort.

Nursery

For those who have a garden or an open space at your disposal and are also interested in gardening can go for this method of earning money. If given proper time and efforts nursery business can flourish very well and you will earn handsomely. But just as all jobs establishing it will be a bit difficult but the end results are outstanding.

Freelance

Freelance can be in different wings. Either you can be a freelance reporter or a freelance photographer. You can also do designing or be in the advertising field doing project on your own. Being independent and working independently will depend on your field of work and the availability of its worth in the market. If you like doing jewellery designing you can do that at home totally independently.

Internet Related Work

This is a very vast field and here sky is the limit. All you need is a computer and Internet facility. Whatever field you are into work at home is perfect match in the software field. You can match your time according to your convenience and complete whatever projects you get.

Diet Food

Since now a days women are more conscious of the food that they eat hence they prefer to have home made low cal food and if you can start supplying low cal food to various offices then it will be a very good source of income and not too much of efforts. You can hire a few ladies who will help you out and this can be a good business.

Thus think over this concept and go ahead.

Productive and Unproductive Labour

Productive and unproductive labour were concepts used in classical political economy mainly in the 18th and 19th century, which survive today to some extent in modern management discussions, economic sociology and Marxist or Marxian economic analysis. The concepts strongly influenced the construction of national accounts in the USSR and other Soviet-type societies.

Classical Political Economy

The classical political economists, such as Adam Smith and David Ricardo raised the economic question of which kinds of labour contributed to *increasing society's wealth*, as against activities which do not produce a vendible commodity which can be resold at a profit. They regarded human labour as the mainspring of wealth, and therefore they regarded the economical use of labour as highly important.

Within an enterprise, for example, there were many tasks which had to be performed, such as cleaning, record and bookkeeping or repairs, which did not directly contribute to producing and increasing wealth.

There were also whole occupations such as domestic servants, soldiers, schoolteachers etc. which, although necessary, did not seem "productive" in the sense of increasing the material wealth of a society. Part of the population consumed wealth but did not create it. To maximize economic growth, therefore, "unproductive costs" which consumed part of the total national income rather than adding to it should be *minimized*; productive labour had to be *maximized*.

The question was also looked at in terms of "earned" versus "unearned" income. In a market-based economy based on trade and exchange, people can obtain incomes from all manner of activities. Some of these incomes could be seen as making net *additions* to the national income, while others represented only a *transfer* of income. Some activities *created* new wealth, others only *transferred* wealth created somewhere else or *appropriated* wealth.

Many different economic and moral arguments were made to either justify or else criticise the incomes gained from different activities, on the ground that they were "productive" or "unproductive", "earned" or "unearned", "wealth-creating" or "wealth-consuming".

A Quote from Adam Smith

"There is one sort of labour which adds to the value of the subject upon which it is bestowed; there is another which has no such effect. The former, as it produces a value, may be called productive; the latter, unproductive labour. Thus the labour of a manufacturer adds, generally, to the value of the materials which he works upon, that of his own maintenance, and of his master's profit. The labour of a menial servant, on the contrary, adds to the value of nothing. Though the manufacturer has his wages advanced to him by his master, he, in reality, costs him no expense, the value of those wages being generally restored, together with a profit, in the improved value of the subject upon which his labour is bestowed. But the maintenance of a menial servant never is restored. A man grows rich by employing a multitude of manufacturers; he grows poor by maintaining a multitude of menial servants. The labour of the latter, however, has its value, and deserves its reward as well" (Andrew Skinner edition 1974, p. 429-430).

Neoclassical Economics

In neoclassical economics, the distinction between productive and unproductive labour was however rejected as being largely *arbitrary* and irrelevant. All the factors of production (land, labour and capital) create wealth and add value; they are all "productive".

If the *value* of a good is just what somebody is prepared to pay for it (or its marginal utility), then regarding some activities as value-creating and others not is a purely subjective matter; *any* activity which produces anything, or generates an income, could be considered *production* and *productive*, and the only question that remains is *how* productive it is.

This could be measured by striking a ratio between the monetary value of output produced, and the number of hours worked to produce it (or the number of workers who produce it). This is called a "output/labour ratio". The ratio "GDP per capita" is also used by some as an indicator of how productive a population is.

However, in calculating any output value, some concept of value is nevertheless required, because we cannot relate, group and aggregate prices (real or notional) at all without using a valuation principle. All accounting assumes a value theory, in this sense.

A persisting management preoccupation, particularly in large corporations, also concerns the question of which activities of a business are value adding. The reason is simply that value-adding activities boost gross income and profit margins (note that the "value-added" concept is a measure of the *net* output, or gross income, after deduction of materials costs from the total sales volume).

If the aim is to realise maximum shareholder value, two important valuation problems occur. Firstly, productive assets being used in production have no actual market price, being withdrawn from the market and not offered for sale. They have at best an historic cost, but this cost does not apply to inventories of new output produced. The current value of productive assets can therefore be estimated only according to a probable price that they would have, *if* they were sold, or if they were replaced. Secondly, there is the problem of what exactly the increases or decreases in the value of productive assets being held can be attributed to. In what has become popularly known as "value-based management", these problems are pragmatically tackled with the accounting concepts of market-value added (MVA) and economic value-added (EVA). This style of management focuses very closely on how assets and activities contribute to maximum profit income.

National Accounts

In national accounts and social accounting theory the concepts of productive and unproductive labour do survive to some extent. The first reason is that if we want to estimate and account for the value of the net new output created by a country in a year, we must be able to distinguish between sources of *new* value added and *conserved* or *transferred* value. In other words, we need a *value-theoretic principle* which guides us in relating, grouping and computing price-aggregates.

It is obvious that if products or incomes are merely *exchanged* or *transferred* between A and B, then the *total* product value, or total income, does not increase; all that has happened here is, that they have been shifted around, and *redistributed*. Total wealth has not increased, no new value was added. By implication, some activities add new value, others do not.

Secondly, it is necessary to create an operational statistical coverage of *production* itself, which can be used to allocate incomes, activities and transactions in the economy as either belonging to "production", or falling outside "production". Thus, some work *produces* something in the economic sense, other work does not.

In general, national accounts adopt a very wide definition of production; it is defined as any activity of resident "institutional units" (enterprises, public services, households) combining the factors of production (land, labour and capital) to transform inputs into outputs. This includes both market production as well as non-market production, if it recognisably generates an income. The advantage of the wide definition is, that practically all flows of production-related income can be captured (but at the same time a large amount of *unpaid* work-housework and voluntary work-is not accounted for).

Nevertheless, some incomes are ruled out of production and regarded as *transfers* of wealth. A transfer is defined basically as a payment made or income received without providing any good, service or asset in return, for example: government benefits. Some forms of interest on loans, some property rents, and most capital gains on financial assets and property are also excluded, they are effectively transfers (flows of income and expenditure are regarded as unrelated to production and to the value of new output) or intermediate expenditure.

Thirdly, national accounts will show the contribution of different *economic sectors* to the total national product or national income. These sectors are mainly output-defined (e.g. agriculture, manufacturing, business services, government administration). It is therefore possible to distinguish to some extent between "productive" activities *producing* some tangible product or service, and other commercial or government activities which do not (yet generate incomes).

A large amount of work done in society is not captured in national accounts, because it is unpaid voluntary labour or unpaid household labour. The monetary value of this work can be estimated only from time use surveys. Thus, national accounting definitions of "production" are strongly biased towards activities which yield a money-income.

Marx's Critique

Karl Marx regarded land and labour as the source of all wealth, and distinguished between *material* wealth and *human* wealth. Human wealth was a wealth in social relations, and the expansion of market trade created ever more of those. However, wealth and economic *value* were not the same thing in his view; value was a purely social category, a social attribution. Both in Das Kapital and in *Theories of Surplus-Value*, Marx devoted a considerable amount of attention to the concept of "productive and unproductive labour". He sought to establish what economic and commercial ideas about productive labour would mean for the lives of the working class, and he wanted to criticise apologetic ideas about the "productive" nature of particular activities. This was part of an argument about the source of surplus value in unpaid surplus labour. His view can be summarised in the following 10 points.

- work is not "naturally productive", both in the sense that it takes work to make work productive, and that productive work depends on tools and techniques to be productive.
- generally speaking, a worker is *economically* productive and a source of additional wealth to the extent that s/he can produce more than is required for his/her own subsistence (i.e. is capable of performing surplus-labour) and adding to a surplus product.
- the definition of productive and unproductive labour is *specific* to each specific type of society (for example, feudal society, capitalist society, socialist society etc.) and depends on the given relations of production.
- there exists no neutral definition of productive and unproductive labour; what is productive from the point of view of one social class may not be productive from the point of view of another.
- the only objective definition of productive labour is in terms of what is as a matter of fact productive within the conditions of a given mode of production.
- from the point of view of the capitalist class, labour is productive, if it increases the value of (private) capital or results in (private) capital accumulation.
- *Capitalistically productive labour* is therefore labour which adds to the mass of surplus value, primarily through profitably producing goods and services for market sale.
- no new value is created through acts of exchange only; therefore, although labour which just facilitates exchange is "productive" from the employer's point of view (because he derives profit from it), it is unproductive from the social point of view because it accomplishes only a transfer of wealth. This "unproductive" labour is accepted however because it reduces the costs of capital accumulation, or facilitates it, or secures it.
- the definition of productive and unproductive labour is not static, but evolving; in the course of capitalist

development, the division of labour is increasingly *modified*, to make more and more labour productive in the capitalistic sense, for example through marketisation and privatisation, value-based management, and Taylorism.

- whether work has been productive can really be known only "after the fact" in capitalist society, because commodity-producing living labour is in most cases definitely valued by the market only *after* it has been performed, when its product (a good or service) is exchanged and paid for.

Marx accordingly made, explicitly or implicitly 10 distinctions relevant to defining productive labour in a capitalist mode of production:

- commodity production, versus other production
- capitalist production versus non-capitalist production
- production versus circulation (exchange)
- production for profit, versus non-profit production
- productive consumption versus unproductive consumption
- material (tangible) production, versus non-material production
- production of use values, versus production of exchange-values
- production of value, versus appropriation of revenue
- production of income, versus distribution of income
- production versus destruction

In most cases, using these distinctions, it would be obvious whether the labour was capitalistically productive or not, but in a minority of cases it would be not altogether clear or controversial. In part, that is because the division of labour is not static but constantly evolving. The general criterion which Marx suggests is that:

"If we have a function which, although in and for itself unproductive, is nevertheless a necessary moment of [economic] reproduction, then when this is transformed,

through a division of labour, from the secondary activity of many into the exclusive activity of a few, into their special business, this does not change the character of the function itself" (Capital Vol. 2, Penguin ed., p. 209).

Obviously, functions falling outside capitalist production altogether would not be *capitalistically* productive.

Generally, Marx seems to have regarded labour as mainly unproductive from the point of view of capitalist society as a whole, if it involved functions which have to do purely with:

- the maintenance of a class-based social order as such (legal system, police, military, government administration).
- the maintenance and securing of private property relations (police, security, legal system, banking, accounting, licensing authorities etc.).
- operating financial transactions (in banking, financing, commercial trade, financial administration)
- insurance and safety.
- criminal activity.

This didn't necessarily mean that unproductive functions are *not socially useful* or economically useful in some sense; they might well be, but they normally did not directly *add* net new value to the total social product, that was the point, they were a (necessary) financial cost to society, paid for by a *transfer* of value created by the productive sector. Thus, they represented an appropriation or deduction from the surplus product, and not a net addition to it. In the division of labour of modern advanced societies, unproductive functions in this Marxian sense occupy a very large part of the labour force; the wealthier a society is, the more "unproductive" functions it can afford. In the USA for example, facilitating exchange processes and processing financial claims alone is the main activity of more than 20 million workers. Legal staff, police, security personnel and military employees number almost 5 million workers.

Productive Labour as Misfortune?

In the first volume of Das Kapital, Marx suggests that productive labour may be a misfortune:

> *"That labourer alone is productive, who produces surplus-value for the capitalist, and thus works for the valorisation of capital. If we may take an example from outside the sphere of production of material objects, a schoolmaster is a productive labourer when, in addition to belabouring the heads of his scholars, he works like a horse to enrich the school proprietor. That the latter has laid out his capital in a teaching factory, instead of in a sausage factory, does not alter the relation. Hence the notion of a productive labourer implies not merely a relation between work and useful effect, between labourer and product of labour, but also a specific, social relation of production, a relation that has sprung up historically and stamps the labourer as the direct means of creating surplus-value. To be a productive labourer is, therefore, not a piece of luck, but a misfortune."*

The idea here seems to be that being capitalistically "productive" effectively means "being exploited," or, at least, being employed to do work under the authority of someone else. Marx never finalised his concept of capitalistically productive labour, but clearly it involved both a technical relation (between work and its useful effect) and a social relation (the economic framework within which it was performed).

Ecological Critique

The ecological critique focuses on mindless "production for production's sake", attacking both the neoclassical notion and the Marxist concept of "productiveness". It is argued noeclassical economics can understand the value of anything (and therefore the costs and benefits of an activity) *only* if it has a *price*, real or imputed.

However, physical and human resources may have a value which *cannot* be expressed in price terms, and to turn them into an object of trade via some legal specification of property rights may be harmful to human life on earth. Activities may have *non-priced costs and benefits* which never feature on the balance sheet, at most in propaganda and advertising.

The Marxian view is also dismissed by ecologists, because it argues only human labour-time is the substance and source of economic value in capitalist society. Again, it is argued a very *restricted* idea of economic value is being operated with by Marxists. In part, this misses Marx's own point, namely that it was not him, but the growth of commercial trade which made labour-exploitation the fulcrum of wealth creation. Nevertheless, the ecological argument is that for the sake of a healthy future and a sustainable biosphere, a *new valuation scheme* for people and resources needs to be adopted.

The core of this critique is clearly an ethical one: all the existing economic theories *provide no healthy norms that would ensure correct stewardship for the environment* in which all people have to live. Markets provide no moral norms of their own apart from the law of contract. To develop a better concept of "productiveness" would require a new morality, a new view of human beings and the environment in which they live, so that harmful economic activity can be outlawed, and healthy alternatives promoted.

Ecologists typically distinguish between "good" and "bad" market trade and production. Some believe capitalism can "go green" (producing in an environmentally friendly way), and that capitalism is "cleaner" than Soviet-type socialism. Others think that capitalism *cannot* "go green" because of the nature of the beast; so long as human accounting is done in terms of private costs and private profits, many "external effects" (externalities) will be disregarded, and at most legal restrictions can limit the environmental damage somewhat.

Gender Division of Labour

Role-sharing and working conditions are not static, but are continually being redefined in the wake of processes of social change. Tasks, for example, that used to be done communally by the villagers are now done for pay-poorer villagers work for richer.

With labour becoming scarcer, cost-effectiveness grows in importance: buying processed rice to prepare meals can sometimes be more economical than the labour-intensive husking and cleaning of rice in the home. This is true, for example, when women can utilise the energy and time involved more cost-effectively in field work.

Division of Labour within the Family

As a result of a progressive disintegration in existing family structures, changes are also taking place on the level of the gender division of labour, often at the expense of women. The tendency is for women, besides their traditional household tasks-such as the time-consuming and strenuous fetching of water and firewood-to be more and more bound up in the sort of work for which men were formerly responsible.

How work is divided and organised by gender within the family is closely related to the size of the family and to the availability of, as well as the amount of work needing to be done in, women's own separate fields. The disintegration of the extended family and the transition to the nuclear family often results in a shortage of work capacity within the family, so that the woman's help in all aspects of field work is needed more. If the women have fields of their own, the men expect them, as a rule, to cultivate them alone or with the help of their children-although helping in the men's fields generally takes priority over this. The changes in family structure that have been outlined are accompanied by reduced willingness and capacity on the part of the men to act supportively.

For practical project work, information about who performs what tasks is needed for two reasons: first, it serves to identify the target group for project activities and, second, information about gender division of labour provides important indicators for determining the specific impacts that project activities have on women and men.

Processing

The production and processing of agricultural products are activities that in many countries are done separately and for which different persons can be responsible. Thus, in many West African countries the processing of manioc into gari (cassava flour) is typically the domain of small independent woman producers, for whom it is an important source of income.

By contrast, the cultivation of manioc is often men's business. Since, however, choice of variety, amount cultivated and production intensity can have impacts on subsequent processing (slight suitability of a variety for producing gari, longer distances/higher transportation volumes), women are competent and motivated dialogue partners for project activities in the production and processing sectors.

Regarding the social and gender division of labour, the following questions should be asked about tasks in the post-harvest sector.

- Who does what tasks as they come up?
  - o women
  - o men
  - o children and young people (boys/girls)
- Does work occur within or outside the family?
- On what terms are these tasks done?
  - o without pay
  - o payment in cash/kind
  - o work done in exchange for work
- How is each activity organised?
  - o individually
  - o collectively

Income-producing Activities

In many cases, women have other sources of income than do men. In order to secure or further develop specific income sources, limiting factors such as lack of capital, restricted mobility, or unclear market factors must be eliminated. To make it possible to include these parameters adequately in the project, the following questions need to be answered:

- By what activities is income earned locally/in the (project) region?
  - o by women
  - o by men *(differentiated by age, class and ethnicity)*
- By what activities is income earned outside the immediate locality/the project region?

- o income from entrepreneurial activities in agriculture
- o income from leasing
- o income from wage labour
- o income from non-agricultural activities
- o proportion agricultural/non-agricultural income
- o proportion cash/barter income
- o proportion migratory work income (temporary/ permanent migration)
- o income earning period (all year/seasonal)

- What unpaid activities are done by women and men locally?
  - o agricultural activities
  - o household activities
  - o honorary activities (village health care, associations, etc.)

Income-producing activities are highly significant for women because of their increasing financial obligations. This should be qualified by noting that these income-producing activities should not-as is frequently the case-be linked to increased workloads for women.

It should also be taken into consideration that sometimes negative side-effects, such as effects on health or the level of education, accompany income-producing activities.

Modes of Production

It has to be admitted-if only hypothetically-that there is a close correlation between the modes of economic production and the role given to the individual in society. Consequently, one must also undoubtedly admit that fluctuations which economic mechanisms experience, whether these are cycles, crises, stagnation phenomena, or inversely, rapid development, have a marked influence on the processes of individuation, it therefore follows that these processes of individuation do not follow a uniform trajectory, and that they may be regressions of individuation just as there exist economic discontinuance and involutions. Thus, for example, one may juxtapose the economic cycles which have marked the history of the Islamic lands between the 10th and 15th centuries with the almost parallel cycles of emergence or, according to the case, effacing of the individual.

However, the main issue is not to look at the individual in society in broad general terms, but to individuals as they related to the process of economic change. For example, what is the relationship between investment and individual prestige in society? There is no need to analyse modes of production in terms of economic cycles and economic theory, but in terms of specific themes related to the individual, i.e. have a set of concrete questions to put forward to historians, anthropologists and others.

Women in Organized and Unorganized Sector—Training, Skills and Income Generation

In India, a major chunk of labour force is employed in the unorganized sector. The unorganized/informal employment consists of causal and contributing family workers; self employed persons in un-organized sector and private households; and other employed in organized and unorganized enterprises that are not eligible either for paid, sick or annual leave or for any social security benefits given by the employer.According to the results of the National Sample Survey conducted in 1999-2000, total work force as on 1.1.2000 was of the order of 406 million. About 7 % of the total work force is employed in the formal or organized sector (all public sector establishments and all non-agricultural. Thus, the unorganized sector plays a vital role in terms of providing employment opportunity to a large segment of the working force in the country and contributes to the national product significantly. The contribution of the unorganized sector to the net domestic product and its share in the total NDP at current prices has been over 60%. In the matter of savings the share of household sector in the total gross domestic saving mainly unorganized sector is about three fourth. Thus unorganized sector has a crucial role in our economy in terms of employment and its contribution to the National Domestic Product, savings and capital formation.

In the manufacture of *gari* (cassava flour produced by fermentation of cassava), smoke and heat are produced, as are prussic acid fumes. This is true even of the many larger production plants in which the furnaces are not properly constructed. Since *gari* is to a large extent produced by women, they-and their infants, which they carry on their backs-are especially liable to health damage.

In the chop-bars of Kumasi, young girls are often employed in order to reduce expenses. Although this does offer them the chance to improve their income and with it their family's overall economic situation, on the other hand, it nevertheless prevents them for the time from gaining further education.

These aspects must be taken into consideration at the project level when formulating conceptions for income-producing activities.

Trade

In West Africa, trade-especially in agricultural products-plays a prominent role with respect to women's chances to earn an income.

In Mali and Burkina Faso, women attach great significance to raising small animals and to small-scale trade (*petite commerce*) as commercial activities. Three are three main forms:

- sale of raw products (millet, peanuts, rice, beans, peas, butter nuts, néré kernals, onions, spices)
- sale of processed products (millet beer, shea butter, soumbala, peanut butter and cake, tobacco, spun cotton, woven mats, etc.)
- sale of cooked dishes (rice with sauce, fried rice, fritters, biscuits, pastries, boiled or roasted peanuts/peas)..

The sale of processed products and cooked dishes predominates. In Burkina Faso, Dolo production is particularly intense-not least due to the numerous well-drilling projects and the consequent improvement in the water supply. In Mali, by contrast, these activities are of secondary importance, primarily for sociocultural reasons. In both countries, the sale of raw products tends to play a subordinate role.

In many African regions, the marketing of field crops is a good opportunity for women to earn an income. Taro, for example, rejected by men on account of its allegedly negative effect on their fertility, is nutritionally more valuable than many other products-including cassava, for example-(taro can be used as food for children or sick persons). Women can benefit from this by creating a market for taro products.

Unpaid Activities

Measures that save time and reduce work in the area of unpaid activities (elimination of hand-grinding of grain through introduction of mills, lessening time and effort spent seeking firewood through use of energy-saving stoves, etc.) can enable women to engage in more income-producing activities. However, the extent to which this in fact really happens depends in turn-apart from the possibilities at hand-principally on the social status of women and men, and is also a question of gender-determined relative strength. The introduction of work-saving technologies can also have a counterproductive impact, as the following example from Senegal shows.

The Mill

As she hears the announcement on the radio, Maimouna remembers with what enthusiasm she had formerly spoken to the women of her village, how convinced she had been that they should join in the project, her project. She believed that the millet mill would mean they could sleep another hour and take a literacy course. The water pump would give them time for a chat and they would be able to meet more often under the kapok tree to do each other's hair.

Maimouna would have more time for her vegetable garden and her little field. At night, she reckoned up the additional income in her head and imagined all the things she would do with it. She wanted to begin modestly, because the first earnings would surely not be all too plentiful. First, the garden fence was to be repaired and the children were to get new clothes. But then,, when the vegetable garden and the larger field returned larger yields, she would buy the silver bangles she had always wanted and would go to Dakar. Dakar, city of lights. In Dakar she would visit her aunt, who would be astonished at the many presents her niece would bring her, and that she could read the newspaper now! Her aunt would be sorry she had left the village so soon.

Time has passed, and Maimouna no longer pounds millet. Nor does she have to walk for kilometres any more to get firewood and water. Instead, her husband now makes her work in his fields, digging weeds and watering his vegetables. She has not been able to enlarge her own field. The council of elders has given her to understand that she has no claim to land, that she can be well-satisfied with what she has received from her husband.

Still, she now has the most beautiful garden in the village and has even been congratulated on it by the project and the prefect. But nobody has asked her what has happened to the money from the vegetables it produced, and if they did,.she wouldn't have had anything good to report. Since she has a few pennies more, Karim won't buy schoolbooks and clothing for the children anymore. He won't even pay for the spices in the couscous now. That is so embarrassing to Maimouna that she can hardly admit it even to herself. Lately Karim even thinks she should also buy his tobacco and cola nuts. Thanks to Maimouna, he has saved a lot of money, so he can marry a second wife sooner than planned-the ox has already been bought.

But why complain. The whole village is full of praise for Maimouna's courage and energy. She is held to be an example for all women who are not content with their lot. The broth boils over. Maimouna forgets her dreams; she must wake the children. In her village they say that there are only two possibilities for women: "Mut mba moot"-submit or go. But where?

New Economic Policy and its Impact on Women's Employment—Globalization

The principle of gender equality has been basic to Indian thinking for over a century; i.e., even in the pre-independence period a thought was given to this principle through various social reformers like Rajaram Mohan Roy, Vidhyasagar, Pandita

Ramabai, Mahatma Phule, Agarkar, Ranade, Veeresalingam Pantalu, Sri Narayana Guru, etc. It was in 1931 that the Indian National Congress adopted gender equality as a guiding principle in the Fundamental Rights Resolution. The Constitution of India adopted in 1950, not only grants equality to women, but also empowers the State to adopt measures of affirmative discrimination in favor of women and it also imposes a fundamental duty on every citizen to uphold the dignity of women, which, in reality is still an illusion.

Despite the above provision within the Constitution it was not until 1971 that the Govt. of India gave much thought in actuality towards the principle of gender equality and even this, only after the request from the U.N. The Govt. of India appointed a Committee on the Status of Women in India (CSWI) to examine the position of women in the changing socio-economic context. The Committee in its report (1975) entitled "Towards Equality" recommended and stressed the need for special temporary measures to transform the de-jure equality guaranteed by India's Constitution into de-fact equality. As a consequence one could see that the shift in recognition to women and the welfare measures regarding women were reflected in the VI Five Year Plan (1980-85). In 1985, under the Human Resource Development Ministry, a separate Department of Women and Child Welfare was set up.

The year 1993 witnessed two constitutional amendments i.e., 73rd and 74th, which guaranteed 1/3rd representation to women at Local Self-Government (Rural as well as Urban). Despite the efforts of the Government in leading the women into the national development process, there are still many problems like marginal employment, low level of skill, problem of being excluded from decision making, poverty, lack of education, training and information, patriarchal impact etc. With such challenges the women's movement has been asking for more space in the decision making process at all levels: economic, social as well as political. In this context it is important to highlight three important issues undertaken by the Government of India, i.e., (1) The new economic policy, highlighting the impact on women. (Economic status), (2) The

Uniform Civil Code, discussing what is it that is being asked for? (Social status), (3) The proposal of 1/3 reservation for women in the House of People and State Legislative Assemblies, (Political status).

New Economic Policy

The New Economic Policy (N.E.P) was introduced primarily due to the 1990's fiscal position of the Central Government which came under severe strain because of sustained borrowing over several years. The worsening fiscal deficits of 1980's had weakened the micro-economic situation, and the Gulf War of 1990 precipitated the balance of payment crisis. The growing political instability at the turn of the decade into the 1990's further contributed towards the collapse of international confidence in the ability of Government to manage the economy. This led to a drying up of the market for external commercial loans in 1990/1991 and capital outflow of Non-Resident Indian (NRI) deposits.

Despite emergency borrowing from Reserve Tranche and the compensatory contingency financing facility of the International Monetary Fund (IMF), the level of foreign exchange reserves dropped precipitously to a little over $4 billion in June 1991, barely sufficient to finance imports for a fortnight. All these factors compelled the Congress Ministry to formulate a new economic policy on Ist June 1991. With the introduction of new economic reforms the Government of India accepted liberalization, privatization and globalisation. Basically, in the reformed economic system, liberalization broadly meant reducing import duties, giving more scope for foreign investment, lessening the control, reducing the 'Quantitative' restrictions on the imports, privatization, lessening state intervention and making the economic system more free.

Taking into consideration the period prior to the entry of the new economic policy, the State played an important role concerning the problems of women. Most of the gender issues pertained 'to oppression within the family or outside to which redress was sought through the intervention of the State. Legal reforms in criminal law, particularly against dowry, rape, domestic violence and of recent regarding the property rights along with laws for equal wages, maternity protection, etc. led to considerable progress. Although the progress achieved was not up to the expectations of the women's movement, the very actual existence of the rights and guarantees meant that an appeal could be made to an enforcing authority. Thus prior to 1990 state intervention led to much progress in the status of women although not as anticipated. The prereform model of development, although supported by a number of policies, was too half-heartedly established, e.g., subsidies took care of the poorer but not always all the poor; eradication of poverty was never achieved, despite wide network of schools and Public Health Centres; basic health services remained unattended and complete literacy is miles away.

With the process of liberalisation and privatisation of the economy, it is argued by the feminist that the new policies will further marginalise the majority of women through reduction in their employment, reduction in their family resources, withdrawal of subsidised food, and abandonment of preferential and affirmative policies like lower interest rates for the unorganised sectors and poor women. Besides, with privatisation of educational and health institutions, the high cost would deprive a large number of women and poor of education and health facilities. Female labour would be exploited by the free market economy in areas where women are at a disadvantageous position. With such an economy, can a women avail herself of and afford education with the tremendous cost that goes along with it? Although the old policy was not so good either, from the point of view of the poor and women, it did achieve a few things for both of these categories.

Securities and guarantees are given in the organised sectors where one can find only 6% of women working. The organized sector has done much to draw women out of the family and household circumstances. It has also given a sort of independence to women under this sector but they meet with problems regarding their future career advancement. Further rapid changes in technology, automation and curtailment of employment has immensely reduced the opportunities of women to work in an organised sector. Transportation, communication, and financial services are areas, besides insurance, post-telegraph, tourism, industries, and banks, where women find opportunities. But here it seems to be open only to women with education. Women are also concentrating on information handling, secretarial and clerical jobs. This being a small group they do not enjoy the same status with their male counterparts in the trade unions or associations. Most of the union or association movements have systematically neglected the women's interest e.g., the insensitivity of trade unions towards women problems has forced some of the activists to move and establish their own organizations like SEWA (Self Employed Women's Association) split from the textile labour association of Ahmedabad (Gujarat).

Taking into consideration the above two areas, women had a ray of hope in the organised sector under the public enterprises with a definite scope for educated women to enter into the work force and be a part of national development in the economic front. In the unorganised sector, with a large number of women toiling in traditional roles, women are going to face acute insecurity in the era of privatization. The 6% women workforce in the organized public sector under the old economic policy is going to face a sharp decrease under the New Economic Policy. With the free trade, particularly in the agricultural field as construed in the GATT, denial of freedom to small farmers follows as a natural concomitant, but it will also hit the women hard. The GATT policies are aimed at further marginalizing the household and domestic food economies in which women play a significant role. It also leads to setting up multilateral trade organizations with which World Bank and IMF (International Monetary Fund) will form the centre of world governance.

The GATT is the platform where the capitalist patriarchy's notion of freedom as the unrestrained right of men with economic power to own, control, and destroy life is articulated as 'free-trade.' But for the Third World, and for women, freedom has different meanings. In what seems the remote domain of international trade, these different meanings of freedom are a focus of contest and conflict. Free trade in food and agriculture is the concrete location of the most fundamental ethical and economic issues of human existence of the present times. It is here that Third World women have a unique contribution to make because in their daily lives they embody the three colonizations on which modern patriarchy is based, the colonization of nature, of women and of the Third World?

Impact on Employment

The impact of N.E.P. on employment at rural as well as urban areas is clear enough from the data. The male unemployment as well as female unemployment rate seems to have,increased in 1993-94 as compared to the status in 1990-91. This impact is seen at both levels i.e., at urban as well as rural.

The percentage of women as per rate of employment in agriculture, mining and quarrying manufacturing, utilities, construction, and total non-agricultural areas, has been declining in the post-reform period, i.e., 1993-94 as compared to the 1987-88 pre-reform period, indicating the visible adverse impact of New Economic policy. Even in case of overall employment during the period 1983-91, it increased by 1.6%, while during 1990-98 it increased only by 1.17 which clearly indicates a decrease in employment percentage in the post reform period.

Another important result that needs mention is women's reservation policy in the public sector undertaking. Owing to privatization, there is considerable cut in governmental expenditure in public sectors. A number of public undertakings have turned into sick units and this is going to make the reservation policy of 33% for women meaningless. There has already been a deep impact on Scheduled Caste and Scheduled Tribe reservation which shows decline in percentage share after 1991.10 The Govt. budget cuts on government programmes for women e.g., expenditure on,DWCRA (Development of Women and Children in Rural Areas) was down by 21% while Nutrition Programme declined to 11 % in post reform period.

Poverty and N.E.P.

Poverty in the rural sector is another problem the N.E.P has failed to address effectively. There was a steady decrease in poverty rate from 56.4% in 1973 to 34.4% in 1989. But in the post reform period particularly in 1990-91 it decreased to 35% while in 1992-93 it increased again to 44%.12 Thus overall, the N.E.P. seems to have a negative impact on the developmental scope of women in India.

The massive increase in rural poverty, by over 60 millions during 1990-92 was, to a large extent, a direct result of stabilization and structural adjustment policies. 13 Comparatively, if one considers the 1983-91 situation, the 'Below Poverty Line' percentage decreased by 3.1% while during 1990-98 it increased by 2.7%. The comparison between pre-reform and post-reform situation, clearly indicates the negative impact of the NEP on the status of women 14.

Globalization, Gender Relations and the Situation of Women

Among the distinct groups of society upon whom globalization's impact has been most telling, women clearly stand out. Few observers will deny that the general issue of gender relations globally, and the question of women's human rights specifically, has undergone significant transformation. Spurred on by the various international conferences, declarations and, most significantly, by the Convention on the Elimination of All Forms of Discrimination against Women, the respect for and recognition of women's human rights has made significant advances worldwide. Needless to say, while much has been achieved, there remains a considerable amount yet to be accomplished. The phenomenon of globalization adds greater complexities to this quest, particularly in the economic arena, but also within the context of culture and politics.

Women have entered the workforce in large numbers in States that have embraced liberal economic policies. One United Nations survey concludes that "[i]t is by now considered a stylized fact that industrialization in the context of globalization is as much female-led as it is export led". The overall economic activity rate of women for the age group 20-54 approached 70 per cent in 1996. The highest absorption of women has been witnessed in the export-oriented industrial sector. This is especially the case in export processing zones (EPZs) and Special Economic Zones (SEZs), and in those labour-intensive industries that have relocated to developing countries in search of cheap labour. Investors have demonstrated a preference for women in the "soft" industries such as apparel, shoe-and toy-making, data-processing and semi-conductor assembling industries that require unskilled to semi-skilled labour. Such industries are also labour intensive, service oriented and poorly paid. Thus, according to the Women's Environment and Development Organization (WEDO) women bear the disproportionate weight of the constraints introduced under the yoke of globalization.

The process of economic liberalization has also spawned a huge growth in the informal sector and increased female participation therein. The participation of women in the informal sector is found to be typically higher than in the formal sector as it provides better opportunities of combining paid-work with household chores. The reasons for the idealization of what is perceived to be a docile labour force are not hard to unearth. In many countries, workers in EPZs find unionization and collective bargaining nearly impossible. As part of the "race to the bottom" to attract foreign direct investment (FDI), some countries have either exempted EPZs altogether or relaxed existing national labour safeguards vis-à-vis EPZs. Needless to say, such actions are in complete violation of International Labour Organization (ILO) standards encapsulated in the Declaration on Fundamental Principles and Rights at Work (1998).

The growth of the informal sector also means that traditional employment-related benefits and mechanisms of protection are not available to those employed in that sector. Aside from the demand for cheap labour, the loss of jobs held by men and the consequent reduction in traditional family income has also contributed to the large influx of women into the labour market. Those women who cannot find factory work, or whose family circumstances do not make factory work possible, have had to seek work in the informal sector under labour conditions worse than in export-oriented industries. TNCs also find subcontracting and hiring part-time or temporary labour more cost-effective. The net result is poorer quality labour opportunities. Under these circumstances underemployment seems to be as big a problem as open unemployment.

Deregulation and the privatization of State enterprises have been key components of structural adjustment programmes (SAPs) introduced by multilaterals as conditionalities attached to aid packages to developing countries. As Lim notes:

> *"Labour market deregulation has been an important feature of structural adjustment programmes. There has been explicit deregulation, whereby formal regulations have been eroded or abandoned by legislative means; and implicit deregulation, whereby remaining regulations have been made less effective through inadequate implementation or systematic bypassing. Such deregulation has been based on the belief that excessive government intervention in labour markets-through such measures as public sector wage and employment policies, minimum wage fixing, employment security rules-is a serious impediment to adjustment and should therefore be removed or relaxed. Deregulation might mean more employment for women, but the danger is that such employment would tend to be on less favourable terms. The question is whether the market can be left almost entirely to determine the price of female labour and the conditions of female employment."*

The same author also points to the causal connection between the liberalization of trade and the preference for cheap labour-almost always provided by women-in the quest to realize comparative cost advantages. Similarly, States around the world, but particularly in the geopolitical South have felt compelled to ease labour standards, modify tax regulations, and to generally relax standards of scrutiny and oversight in the bid to attract FDI in a mercilessly competitive global economic system. This "race to the bottom" has seen developing States engage in a perverse competition to provide the best investment environment by progressively lowering, *inter alia*, labour standards.

The phenomenon of quantitatively increased employment opportunities accompanied by low-quality conditions of work is manifested especially in the EPZs. It is estimated that at the turn of the last century, 93 developing countries had EPZs, compared with 24 in 1976. In a few countries such as Malaysia, the Philippines, the Republic of Korea and Sri Lanka it is the main employer of women. Women provide up to 80 per cent of labour requirements in EPZs.

Women also comprise the largest segment of migrant labour flows, both internally and internationally. Large numbers of rural women, often young and poorly educated, migrate to the metropolis in search of employment. In some countries this migration is largely to urban-based EPZs and SEZs. The vulnerability of these women makes them easy prey for exploitation, both economically and sexually. They are often willing to work under less suitable conditions of work than are acceptable to both men and to poor urban women.

In Asia, in particular, the migration of large numbers of female workers to the Middle East from, for example, West Asia, and South-East Asia, has had a strong impact both socially and economically. It has been estimated, for example, that the ratio of females to males who comprise migrant labour is 12:1 among Filipinos migrating to Asian destinations; 3:1 among Indonesians and 3:2 among Sri Lankans. Many of these women work as domestic workers, seamstresses, nurses, assistants in retail shops and restaurants, and as entertainers (oftentimes in the sex industry).

While most women have the opportunity of earning higher wages than at home, labour conditions and mechanisms of both social and physical security in receiving countries seem to be perilous at best. More often than not, receiving States tend not to observe even minimal labour standards with regard to migrant workers, particularly women. Heavy economic dependence of the sending States on the inward monetary remittances of migrant workers has inhibited them from demanding fair labour conditions and protection from receiving States, thereby further weakening the position of such workers.

Women in the agricultural sector have also been adversely affected by the promotion of export-oriented economic policies, trade liberalization and TNCs' activities in agriculture-related industries. Emphasis on export crops has displaced women workers in certain countries from permanent agricultural employment into seasonal employment. Subsistence farming has been severely affected in the new economic environment, leaving women farmers to seek seasonal employment. Aside from the tenuous and low economic returns of seasonal agricultural employment, the Food and Agriculture Organization of the United Nations (FAO) has noted that the destruction of subsistence farming, increased industrial pollution and the loss of land to large commercial ventures, often financed by TNCs, have given rise to grave problems relating to food security and the health of the rural poor.

Globalization also affects women who may not be integrated into the formal sector. Under the yoke of the SAPs that have been in vogue in most African countries since the early 1980s, women whose work is outside the arena of the globalized market in goods and services have been adversely affected. Rendered invisible by concepts such as "efficiency", "stabilization", and "cost-effectiveness", the labour of African women becomes the shock absorber of the processes of adjustment and the social costs that result therefrom. Unfortunately, the so-called social "safety nets" that have subsequently been introduced to "alleviate" the situation of these women have done little to fundamentally mitigate the crisis.

The United Nations Secretary-General has pointed to adverse labour conditions as a major factor contributing to the increased feminization of poverty. The logical expectation that the demand for female labour will improve their bargaining position and drive up wages has not been realized. The very opposite appears to be taking place. Women are concentrated in "footloose" industries which can relocate their processes or components of production easily across frontiers into countries that provide a "better" investment environment, i.e. one that observes lower labour standards and more deregulation. The possibility of easy relocation for these light industries acts as a major disincentive to the raising of wages. This phenomenon affects labour forces in both developed and developing economies. It has been pointed out, for example, that after the adoption of the North American Free Trade Agreement (NAFTA), employers in the United States were able to stave off demands for higher wages by indicating the possibility of moving production offshore to an environment with a cheaper labour force. In this context, it is important to pay heed to the call in the Beijing Platform for Action to review and modify macroeconomic policies and development strategies to ensure that they promote the rights of women.

In dealing with the issue of poverty eradication, especially among women, the Secretary-General acknowledges that "[f]iscal policy should avoid compression of expenditure on health, education and skill formation, even under conditions of budgetary constraints At the international level, a main objective of development assistance should be to support national efforts for sustained human capital formation In the interested countries, the 20/20 initiative is particularly relevant in this regard." The report goes on to emphasize the need for social safety nets to allow people weather adverse conditions created by slow growth and crisis (such as that in Asia), acknowledging that fast growth per se does not guarantee equitable distribution or social protection. Interestingly, the IMF is among the institutions that have contributed to the compilation of the report, despite its largely deleterious role in fostering the Asian crisis in the late 1990s, and its only partial admission of culpability for the crisis.

Structural Adjustment Programmes

Structural adjustment is a term used to describe the policy changes implemented by the International Monetary Fund (IMF) and the World Bank (the Bretton Woods Institutions) in developing countries. These policy changes are conditions (Conditionalities) for getting new loans from the IMF or World Bank, or for obtaining lower interest rates on existing loans. Conditionalities are implemented to ensure that the money lent will be spent in accordance with the overall goals of the loan. The Structural Adjustment Programmes (SAPs) are created with the goal of reducing the borrowing country's fiscal imbalances. The bank from which a borrowing country receives its loan depends upon the type of necessity. In general, loans from both the World Bank and the IMF are claimed to be designed to promote economic growth, to generate income, and to pay off the debt which the countries have accumulated.

Through conditionalities, Structural Adjustment Programmes generally implement "free market" programmes and policy. These programmes include internal changes (notably privatization and deregulation) as well as external ones, especially the reduction of trade barriers. Countries which fail to enact these programmes may be subject to severe fiscal discipline. Critics argue that financial threats to poor countries amount to blackmail; that poor nations have no choice but to comply. Since the late 1990s, some proponents of structural adjustment such as the World Bank, have spoken of "poverty reduction" as a goal. Structural Adjustment Programmes were often criticized for implementing generic free market policy, as well as the lack of involvement from the country. To increase the borrowing country's involvement, developing countries are now encouraged to draw up Poverty Reduction Strategy Papers (PRSPs). These PRSPs essentially take the place of the SAPs. Some believe that the increase of the local governments participation in creating the policy will lead to greater ownership of the loan programmes, thus better fiscal policy. The content of these PRSPs has turned out to be quite similar to the original content of bank authored Structural Adjustment Programmes. Critics argue that the similarities show that the banks, and the countries that fund them, are still overly involved in the policy making process.

Conditions

Some of the conditions for structural adjustment can include:

- Cutting social expenditures, also known as austerity,
- Focusing economic output on direct export and resource extraction,

- Devaluation of currencies,
- Trade liberalization, or lifting import and export restrictions,
- Increasing the stability of investment (by supplementing foreign direct investment with the opening of domestic stock markets),
- Balancing budgets and not overspending,
- Removing price controls and state subsidies,
- Privatization, or divestiture of all or part of state-owned enterprises,
- Enhancing the rights of foreign investors vis-a-vis national laws,
- Improving governance and fighting corruption.

These conditions have also been sometimes labeled as the Washington Consensus.

UNIT-V

Human Entrepreneurships

Concept and Meaning

Entrepreneurship according to Onuoha (2007) is the practice of starting new organizations or revitalizing mature organizations, particularly new businesses generally in response to identified opportunities. Entrepreneurship is often a difficult undertaking, as a vast majority of new businesses fail. Entrepreneurial activities are substantially different depending on the type of organization that is being started. Entrepreneurship ranges in scale from solo projects (even involving the entrepreneur only part-time) to major undertakings creating many job opportunities. Many "high value" entrepreneurial ventures seek venture capital or angel funding in order to raise capital to build the business. Angel investors generally seek returns of 20-30% and more extensive involvement in the business. Many kinds of organizations now exist to support would-be entrepreneurs, including specialized government agencies, business incubators, science parks, and some NGOs. Lately more holisitc conceptualizations of entrepreneurship as a specific mindset (see also entrepreneurial mindset) resulting in entrepreneurial initiatives e.g. in the form of social entrepreneurship, political entrepreneurship, or knowledge entrepreneurship emerged.

Importance of Entrepreneurship

There are many differing views on what makes someone an entrepreneur and what an entrepreneurial venture is. In a sense the definition itself is evolving as the field itself comes into the mainstream of American business. While we speak of many of the originators of businesses in the past as entrepreneurs, it was not until the mid1970's that the concept became a prevalent enough part of our economy that definitions even were necessary. Consequently, we see in the literature a wide variety of possibilities for what this field of endeavor really is.

Looking online, the Webster's Revised Unabridged Dictionary from 1913 defined an entrepreneur as "one who creates a product on his own account." That sounds a trifle stuffy, is very limited and doesn't fit for many of the people widely known as entrepreneurs. The meaning of the word entrepreneur has certainly evolved since 1913.

Does just creating a product make you entrepreneurial if you never do anything with it? What if you take someone's product and make it a success? That is not entrepreneurial? Investorwords, a set of definitions of financial terms, defines an entrepreneur as "an individual who starts his/her own business." At what point then are you no longer an entrepreneur? When are you no longer starting up? From the Merriam-Webster Online comes a more current definition: "one who organizes, manages, and assumes the risks of a business or enterprise." Assuming risk certainly fits most entrepreneurs. This definition is definitely richer, but still lacks the sense of innovation that one usually associates with entrepreneurs.

Moving from formal definitions, Ashoka, an organization which promotes social change, calls for "social entrepreneurs," people who open up major new possibilities in education, health, the environment, and other areas of human need, "just as business entrepreneurs lead innovation in commerce, social entrepreneurs drive social change." The concept of business entrepreneurs leading innovation is appealing because it denotes more than just starting a business. An entrepreneur herself, Daile Tucker, provides her thoughts on what it takes to be an entrepreneur in Are You an Entrepreneur? She defines an entrepreneur as "a person who has decided to take control of his future and become self-employed whether by creating his own unique business or working as a member of a team, as in multi-level marketing." She identifies work ethics and several character traits of successful entrepreneurs, ending with "Entrepreneurs compete with themselves and believe that success or failure lies within their personal control or influence." This begins to touch on motivational aspects for being an entrepreneur which may distinguish the type of person drawn to being an entrepreneur.

Mark Hendricks takes Tucker's definition a step further, acknowledging innovation, but also providing alternatives. Hendricks suggests that to be an entrepreneur you don't particularly have to be daring. Many entrepreneurs are perfectly content to sell tried-and-true products, bringing a steady income without the intensity of launching a new product. He labels these lifestyle entrepreneurs. They want to be their own boss and make a good living, but they don't need to be on the cutting edge, which entails living where one wants, working with people one likes, and doing work one wants to do.

Entrepreneurial Traits—Factors Contributing to Women Entrepreneurship

Women Entrepreneurs may be defined as the women or a group of women who initiate, organize and operate a business enterprise. Government of India has defined women entrepreneurs as an enterprise owned and controlled by a women having a minimum financial interest of 51% of the capital and giving at least 51% of employment generated in the enterprise to women. Like a male entrepreneurs a women entrepreneur has many functions. They should explore the prospects of starting new enterprise; undertake risks, introduction of new innovations, coordination administration and control of business and providing effective leadership in all aspects of business.

Push-Pull Factors and Women in Business

Women in business are a recent phenomenon in India. By and large they had confide themselves to petty business and tiny cottage industries. Women entrepreneurs engaged in business due to push and pull factors. Which encourage women to have an independent occupation and stands on their on legs. A sense towards independent decision-making on their life and career is the motivational factor behind this urge. Saddled with household chores and domestic responsibilities women want to get independence Under the influence of these factors the women entrepreneurs choose a profession as a challenge and as an urge to do some thing new. Such situation is described as pull factors. While in push factors women engaged in business activities due to family compulsion and the responsibility is thrust upon them.

Problems of Women Entrepreneurs in India

Women in India are faced many problems to get ahead their life in business. A few problems cane be detailed as;

1. The greatest deterrent to women entrepreneurs is that they are women. A kind of patriarchal – male dominant social order is the building block to them in their way towards business success. Male members think it a big risk financing the ventures run by women.
2. The financial institutions are skeptical about the entrepreneurial abilities of women. The bankers consider women loonies as higher risk than men loonies. The bankers put unrealistic and unreasonable securities to get loan to women entrepreneurs. According to a report by the United Nations Industrial Development Organization (UNIDO), "despite evidence that women's loan repayment rates are higher than men's, women still face more difficulties in obtaining credit," often due to discriminatory attitudes of banks and informal lending groups (UNIDO, 1995b).
3. Entrepreneurs usually require financial assistance of some kind to launch their ventures-be it a formal bank loan or money from a savings account. Women in developing nations have little access to funds, due to the fact that they are concentrated in poor rural communities with few opportunities to borrow money (Starcher, 1996; UNIDO, 1995a). The women

entrepreneurs are suffering from inadequate financial resources and working capital. The women entrepreneurs lack access to external funds due to their inability to provide tangible security. Very few women have the tangible property in hand.

4. Women's family obligations also bar them from becoming successful entrepreneurs in both developed and developing nations. "Having primary responsibility for children, home and older dependent family members, few women can devote all their time and energies to their business" (Starcher, 1996, .The financial institutions discourage women entrepreneurs on the belief that they can at any time leave their business and become housewives again. The result is that they are forced to rely on their own savings, and loan from relatives and family friends.
5. Indian women give more emphasis to family ties and relationships. Married women have to make a fine balance between business and home. More over the business success is depends on the support the family members extended to women in the business process and management. The interest of the family members is a determinant factor in the realization of women folk business aspirations.
6. Another argument is that women entrepreneurs have low-level management skills. They have to depend on office staffs and intermediaries, to get things done, especially, the marketing and sales side of business. Here there is more probability for business fallacies like the intermediaries take major part of the surplus or profit. Marketing means mobility and confidence in dealing with the external world, both of which women have been discouraged from developing by social conditioning. Even when they are otherwise in control of an enterprise, they often depend on males of the family in this area.
7. The male-female competition is another factor, which develop hurdles to women entrepreneurs in the business

management process. Despite the fact that women entrepreneurs are good in keeping their service prompt and delivery in time, due to lack of organisational skills compared to male entrepreneurs women have to face constraints from competition. The confidence to travel across day and night and even different regions and states are less found in women compared to male entrepreneurs. This shows the low level freedom of expression and freedom of mobility of the women entrepreneurs.

8. Knowledge of alternative source of raw materials availability and high negotiation skills are the basic requirement to run a business. Getting the raw materials from different souse with discount prices is the factor that determines the profit margin. Lack of knowledge of availability of the raw materials and low-level negotiation and bargaining skills are the factors, which affect women entrepreneur's business adventures.

9. Knowledge of latest technological changes, know how, and education level of the person are significant factor that affect business. The literacy rate of women in India is found at low level compared to male population. Many women in developing nations lack the education needed to spur successful entrepreneurship. They are ignorant of new technologies or unskilled in their use, and often unable to do research and gain the necessary training (UNIDO, 1995b). Although great advances are being made in technology, many women's illiteracy, strucutural difficulties, and lack of access to technical training prevent the technology from being beneficial or even available to females ("Women Entrepreneurs in Poorest Countries," 2001). According to The Economist, this lack of knowledge and the continuing treatment of women as second-class citizens keeps them in a pervasive cycle of poverty ("The Female Poverty Trap," 2001). The studies indicates that uneducated women donot have the knowledge of measurement and basic accounting.

10. Low-level risk taking attitude is another factor affecting women folk decision to get into business. Low-level education provides low-level self-confidence and self-reliance to the women folk to engage in business, which is continuous risk taking and strategic cession making profession. Investing money, maintaining the operations and ploughing back money for surplus generation requires high risk taking attitude, courage and confidence. Though the risk tolerance ability of the women folk in day-to-day life is high compared to male members, while in business it is found opposite to that.
11. Achievement motivation of the women folk found less compared to male members. The low level of education and confidence leads to low level achievement and advancement motivation among women folk to engage in business operations and running a business concern.
12. Finally high production cost of some business operations adversely affects the development of women entrepreneurs. The installation of new machineries during expansion of the productive capacity and like similar factors dissuades the women entrepreneurs from venturing into new areas.

Women Entrepreneurs may be defined as the women or a group of women whr initiate, organize and operate a business enterprise. Government of India has defined women entrepreneurs as an enterprise owned and controlled by a women having a minimum financial interest of 51% of the capital and giving at least 51% of employment generated in the enterprise to women. Like a male entrepreneurs a women entrepreneur has many functions. They should explore the prospects of starting new enterprise; undertake risks, introduction of new innovations, coordination administration and control of business and providing effective leadership in all aspects of business.

Push-Pull Factors and Women in Business

Women in business are a recent phenomenon in India. By and large they had confide themselves to petty business and tiny cottage industries. Women entrepreneurs engaged in business due to push and pull factors. Which encourage women to have an independent occupation and stands on their on legs. A sense towards independent decision-making on their life and career is the motivational factor behind this urge. Saddled with household chores and domestic responsibilities women want to get independence Under the influence of these factors the women entrepreneurs choose a profession as a challenge and as an urge to do some thing new. Such situation is described as pull factors. While in push factors women engaged in business activities due to family compulsion and the responsibility is thrust upon them.

Gender Issues in Micro-enterprise Development

In many countries, at all levels of development, women's access to the labour market is consistently more difficult than men's. Employment opportunities as wage workers are often denied to women because of their family responsibilities, lack of skills, social and cultural barriers or lack of wage employment. In this context, self-employment or the setting up of their own enterprise-generally a micro-enterprise-may constitute the only possibility for women to get access to employment and to earn an income. This is more so since the private sector is more and more taking precedence over the public sector in terms of employment creation. An increasing number of women have come to realise this and have launched some kind of economic activity.

As a result, in many countries-especially in developing and transition economies-women represent the majority of entrepreneurs in micro-enterprises and the informal sector. However, policies and programmes relating to micro-enterprise development, when they exist, are still often based on the implicit assumption that entrepreneurs are mostly men.

The rationale for supporting the development of women-headed micro and small enterprises is two-fold. First, it contributes to poverty alleviation. Second, it contributes to women's economic and social empowerment. More generally, it is now widely recognised that the main vehicles for economic growth are the micro and small enterprises therefore, as a matter of economic efficiency, it is important to ensure that potential women entrepreneurs are not left out of any development process.

The unprecedented increase of international trade and the rapid pace of technological change that are commonly referred to as globalization, while offering new opportunities to the economies, constitute a formidable challenge for women-headed micro and small enterprises, as well as for all those interested in equality issues.

Micro Enterprises Gender and Technology

While there is no universal definition of micro and small enterprises, there is some agreement as to their general characteristics in developing countries: very small scale of operation, low level of technology, low access to credit and lack of managerial capacity. Further description of these enterprises is related to their considerably low level of productivity and income, as well as to their strong tendency to operate in the informal sector where they have few linkages with the modern economy and do not comply with government registration.

The size of an enterprise may be defined according to various criteria, including: the number of workers, the volume of output or sales, the value of assets, the use of energy, etc. The criterion of the number of workers is the most widely used, because of its apparent simplicity and because data on the other criteria are generally lacking. For operational purposes, it is often agreed that micro-enterprises include self-employed persons and enterprises with up to 10 workers (including apprentices and paid and unpaid family workers); small enterprises comprise between 10 and 50 workers. These "definitions" have to be adapted to specific conditions prevailing in various countries.

The Entrepreneur

It is often stressed that the human being should be at the centre of any economic activity. Given the human dimension of the enterprise, it is hence of utmost importance to mention the role of the entrepreneur. The report of the 1997 ILO Conference on *General conditions to stimulate job creation in small and medium-sized enterprises* defines an entrepreneur as "one who surveys the potential of his or her business environment, identifies opportunities to improve it, marshals resources, and acts to maximize operational opportunities". Another important characteristic is risk taking.

Entrepreneurs are usually assimilated with owners and managers of registered enterprises. Since many women are self-employed, they are seldom recognised as entrepreneurs, not even by themselves. This lack of visibility and recognition may result in women entrepreneurs being overlooked by institutions and programmes interested in enterprise development.

Key Gender Issues in Entrepreneurship Development for Women

Constraints

Women face constraints at almost every stage of their business operation (start-up, survival, diversification, growth). While some of the constraints are also experienced by male entrepreneurs, women have additional, gender specific constraints. These constraints and barriers can be summarized as follows:

- behavioural barriers, e.g. women have little self-confidence and a negative self-image;
- role barriers, e.g. conflicting role demands and time constraints;
- social and cultural barriers, e.g. negative attitudes towards women in business; the fact that women are supposed to fulfil other roles; restrictions as to the choice of sector; lack of family support; lack of mobility; etc.
- educational barriers, e.g. women have relatively lower education levels, have received a biased education and usually have limited access to vocational training opportunities. Even in transition economies where

women have a good educational level, they frequently have problems in accessing relevant vocational training;

- occupational barriers, e.g. women have fewer opportunities in the formal sector of the economy for skill development;
- infrastructural barriers, e.g. access to credit, technology, support services, land, information is systematically more difficult for women;
- legal barriers, e.g. independent legal action is limited for women.

It can be assumed that most of these constraints have a socio-cultural origin and, as such, require fundamental attitudinal changes in the socio-cultural environment, which is a long-term process.

Characteristics of Women-headed Micro-enterprises

Women who do manage to set up their enterprise in spite of all the above mentioned constraints often set up micro-enterprises rather than small, medium or large enterprises. Therefore, female businesses disproportionately concentrate in the micro-enterprise sector of the economy.

Because of the variety of constraints and their different socio-economic levels, women entrepreneurs do not constitute an homogeneous group. They may have different motivations, interest and potentials. An increasing number of women have had access to education and are willing to make use of their skill and experience not only as wage workers-where their carrier is often hampered by the *glass ceiling* and where they may lack the flexibility required to combine their multiple roles-but also as self-employed and entrepreneurs. Many more women are engaged in entrepreneurial activities, even without a proper educational background, out of sheer necessity.

Over and above their differences, women-headed micro-enterprises generally display some common features:

- They are set up with existing skills (evolving around the domestic sphere) and little capital.
- They are most of the time unregistered and operate in the informal sector of the economy.

- In many cases, production takes place at home. In some cases, women sit at the market place while producing (i.e. basket weaving), selling, as well as cooking and looking after the children.
- They rely heavily upon family workers (paid or unpaid).
- They tend to concentrate in the least rewarding sectors. Production usually covers a fairly narrow range of consumer goods (garments, woven goods, processed food) and handicrafts. Most of the time, these sectors are related to the tasks traditionally performed by women.
- As the economic activity is most often undertaken in addition to household chores and, in rural areas, to agriculture, women are not able to dedicate continuous attention to it. There is a lack of clear-cut division between household and business, both in terms of time allocation and financial flows (re-investment is often subject to prior fulfilment of the family's basic needs). The total work load is heavy.
- The owner/operator performs all the functions herself. The marketing and managerial functions are embryonic.
- Output is marketed locally (this is usually the case for local consumer goods) or intended for the tourist and, rarely, the export markets (this is usually the case for handicrafts).
- Depending on the socio-cultural environment and transport facilities, women may market directly their production, or use intermediaries: male members of the household or traders (including money lenders).
- Depending on the socio-cultural and legal environment, women either may or may not fully control revenues from their economic activities. In many situations, the male members of the household have control over these revenues. Usually, women loose some control whenever they cannot market their own output. However, women in trading activities are more likely to control the revenues from their business.

It must be emphasized that women-headed enterprises cannot be envisaged in isolation to the economic and socio-cultural environment in which they evolve. This environment may or may not be conducive to entrepreneurship development for women. Such societal practices as undervaluation of women's economic role, sex-role stereotyping, women's limited access to certain types of vocational training, policies, legislation, etc., may prevent women from engaging in business, sustaining or expanding their current business, or may even exclude them from important segments of the micro and small enterprise sector (e.g. enterprises with a high growth potential).

Technology and Production

Radical innovations transform existing markets, create new markets, and stimulate economic growth. This study investigates how the experience, education, and prior knowledge of technology entrepreneurs relate to innovation radicalness. Findings from a sample of 145 technology entrepreneurs operating within university-affiliated incubators suggest that general and specific human capital are both vital to innovation outcomes. Innovation radicalness was positively associated with formal education and prior knowledge of technology, but negatively associated with prior knowledge of ways to serve markets. This suggests a counterintuitive conclusion—the less technology entrepreneurs know about ways to serve a market, the greater their chances of using technology knowledge to create breakthrough innovations within it. Finally, we discuss configurations of human capital that are likely to bestow unique advantages in the construction of radical innovations.

Innovation is of central importance to entrepreneurship (Covin & Miles, 1999; Schumpeter, 1942) and of immense interest, given that it is the primary instrument of competition for many firms (Baumol, 2002). Arguably, the most common way of defining innovation involves using an incremental versus radical framework. Pavitt (1991) describes radical innovations as revolutionary or discontinuous changes, while incremental innovations are conventional or simple extensions in a line of historical improvements. In economic terms, the impact of radical innovation is considerably more dramatic. They can transform existing markets, create new ones, and make an enormous economic contribution (Leifer et al., 2000). Although radical innovation outcomes have been empirically linked to entrepreneurship at a macro level (e.g., Baumol, 2002), how this is accomplished at a micro level of analysis is poorly understood.

Understanding how individuals create breakthrough innovations has rich theoretical and practical implications for entrepreneurship. Entrepreneurship, as a scholarly field, seeks to understand how, by whom, and with what effects opportunities to create future goods and services are discovered and exploited (Shane & Venkataraman, 2000). A number of studies provide evidence that aspects of an individual' s human capital facilitate the recognition or development of an opportunity (Davidsson & Honig, 2003; Shane, 2000; Shepherd & DeTienne, 2005). Human capital theory posits that individuals with more or higher quality human capital will reap more desirable outcomes (Becker, 1964). However, the question of how human capital contributes to the process of enacting radical innovation has eluded most scholars. This research endeavors to fill that void by investigating how aspects of individual human capital are linked to the recognition of opportunities bearing radical innovation outcomes.

To investigate human capital and its relationship to radical innovation, we draw on prior entrepreneurship research that examines both general and specific human capital (e.g., Corbett, 2007; Dimov & Shepherd, 2005). In doing so, this article makes a number of contributions. First, we increase our understanding of the characteristics of technology entrepreneurs by examining three types of general human capital that are associated with innovation radicalness—experience depth, experience breadth, and formal education. Second, we examine specific human capital by investigating technology entrepreneurs' prior knowledge. We demonstrate how differences in prior knowledge of markets, customer problems, ways to serve markets, and technology at opportunity recognition systematically influence the radicalness of subsequent products and services.

We then explore which combinations of general and specific human capital are associated with radical innovation. By examining the configurations of technology entrepreneurs' human capital associated with high innovation versus low innovation, we hope to increase understanding about which characteristics are associated with radicalness. Further, we believe that differences in prior knowledge at opportunity recognition form knowledge configurations or gestalts that bestow unique advantages. Such configurations provide a more holistic picture of the factors that influence opportunity recognition. By examining knowledge configurations, we can see which elements of prior knowledge are most likely to be associated with radical innovation and learn how multivariate combinations of human capital can be used to understand the subsequent outcomes of technology entrepreneurs.

To summarize, this study investigates the types of general and specific human capital that are associated with radical innovation outcomes and how configurations of human capital might be linked to higher levels of innovation radicalness. The paper unfolds along the following lines. In the next section, we briefly review literature surrounding innovation outcomes and the entrepreneur. We then present a theoretical argument for why aspects of individual human capital will influence differences in innovation outcomes. Hypotheses related to general and specific human capital and its effects on innovation radicalness are proposed. We then report the methods and results of our empirical examination. A discussion follows and the paper concludes with implications for research and practice.

The Entrepreneur and the Radical Innovation Advantage

Entrepreneurial ventures and small businesses contribute about two and a half times more innovations per employee than do large firms (Acs & Audretsch, 2003) and are responsible for the bulk of radical innovations in the economy (Baumol, 2002, 2006). Radical innovation lies at the core of new business development and long-term wealth creation (Ahuja & Lampert, 2001; Kirchhoff, 1991). Despite the fact that large firms have the competencies to manage the development of new offerings, they languish in terms of emergent technology ventures and their ability to create innovation breakthroughs. Utterback (1994) and Christensen (2000), among others, have noted how firms that dominate one generation of technology often fail to maintain leadership in the next because they have turned their attention to incremental improvements and, as a consequence, diminished their capacity to create truly new breakthroughs (Benner & Tushman, 2002; Leifer et al., 2000).

Yet radical or breakthrough innovations are chief among the competitive weapons that enable firms to launch entrepreneurial ventures. Although large businesses account for nearly three-quarters of U.S. expenditure on research and development, independent entrepreneurs are more likely to account for the most fundamentally novel innovations (Baumol, 2006). Most revolutionary new business ideas, it can be argued, have been, and are likely to continue to be provided by the independent entrepreneur.

What gives individual entrepreneurs a radical innovation advantage? One explanation may be that opportunities to create radical innovation depend more on individual knowledge and initiative than on organizational processes. Baumol (2006) showed that among the most radical innovations within the last two centuries, the majority have emerged from individual entrepreneurs. Similarly, in a study of 12 radical innovation projects in large established firms, it was an individual scientist or an engineer who discovered the critical breakthrough in each case (O'Connor & Rice, 2001). Although we cannot assume the process of creating radical innovation is the same within large organizations as it is within the start-up context, the extant research suggests there is much to learn from the independent technology entrepreneur.

We believe it is the human capital attributes of technology entrepreneurs that enable them to generate the breakthrough insights that lead to radical innovations. Becker (1964) identified knowledge and experience as the major components of human capital. Technology entrepreneurs are individuals who recognize and exploit opportunities by leveraging technology knowledge and experience to create new value through the venture creation process. To shed light on how radical innovations are created, we use the lens of human capital theory to set forth a model of general and specific human capital and its effects on innovation radicalness.

Literature Review and Hypothesis Development

The objective of this section is to review the literature and derive hypotheses that link aspects of technology entrepreneurs' human capital to the radicalness of their innovations. First, human capital theory is discussed as well as why such theory is of use in enhancing our understanding of how some individuals recognize opportunities to innovate. Well-known aspects of general human capital are reviewed and hypotheses are put forward. We then discuss specific types of knowledge shown to influence opportunity recognition and provide hypotheses specific to the prior knowledge framework used to examine technology entrepreneurs' specific human capital.

Technology Transfer

Several studies have focused on individual scientists and entrepreneurs in the context of university technology transfer, but few have examined the influence of human capital on the propensity to patent (Link & Siegel, 2007). We review below aspects of that focused literature, and this review motivates our subsequent hypotheses and empirical analysis. But, because patenting activity at universities is related to university spin-offs (Shane, 2004; Wright, Birley, & Mosey, 2004), selected key papers that emphasize star scientists or university researchers are also overviewed. Audretsch (2000) examined the extent to which entrepreneurs at universities are different than other entrepreneurs. He analyzed a dataset on university life scientists in order to estimate the determinants of the probability that they will establish a new biotechnology firm, and he found that university entrepreneurs tend to be older and more scientifically experienced. Audretsch offered no explanation for this finding, although it is consistent with our theory (below) that age approximated the absorptive capacity of faculty.

Whittington and Smith-Doerr (2005) examined gender differences in the patenting productivity of academic scientists.

They studied a sample of life science PhDs who had been involved in a university research programme that had received a National Institute of General Medical Sciences research service award, and these scientists were matched to the National Bureau of Economic Research Patent Citation Date File. Their analysis suggests that academic females patent less than males but that the commercial value of their patents, measured in terms of citations, is equal to or greater than males.

Wright, Vohora, and Lockett (2004) examine, through case studies of U.K. university spinout formations, the efficacy of joint venture spinout (JVSO) companies. A JVSO is a new venture in which technology is assigned or licensed into a new company that is jointly owned by the university and the industrial partner. JVSOs may provide a faster, more flexible, less risky and less costly business venturing route to commercializing university intellectual property in comparison to venture backed university start-ups.

In a sense, faculty patenting activity with industry is a form of a joint venture research relationship, and one that may be more efficient than sole academic patenting or sole industry patenting. This is not a point tested empirically in this paper, but rather a topic for future study.

More broadly, Zucker and Darby, and their various collaborators, explored the role of star scientists in the life sciences on the creation and location of new biotechnology firms in the United States and Japan. Zucker, Darby, and Armstrong (2000) assessed the impact of these university scientists on the research productivity of U.S. firms. A star scientist is defined as a researcher who has discovered over 40 genetic sequences, and affiliations with firms are defined through co-authoring between the star scientist and industry scientists. Some of these scientists resigned from the university to establish a new firm or kept their faculty position, but worked very closely with industry scientists. Research productivity is measured using three proxies: (1) number of patents granted, (2) number of products in development, and (3) number of products on the market. They found that ties between star scientists and firm scientists have a positive effect on these three dimensions of research productivity, as well as other aspects of firm performance and rates of entry in the U.S. biotechnology industry (Zucker, Darby, & Armstrong, 1998; Zucker, Darby, & Brewer 1998).

Zucker and Darby (2001) also examined detailed data on the outcomes of collaborations between star university scientists and biotechnology firms in Japan. Similar patterns emerged in the sense that they found that such interactions substantially enhanced the research productivity of Japanese firms, as measured by the rate of firm patenting, product innovation, and market introductions of new products. However, they also reported an absence of geographically localized knowledge spillovers resulting from university technology transfer in Japan, in contrast to the United States, where they found that such effects were strong. The authors attributed this result to the following interesting institutional difference between Japan and the United States in university technology transfer. In the United States, it is common for academic scientists to work with firm scientists at the firm's laboratories; in Japan, firm scientists typically work in the academic scientist's laboratory. Thus, according to the authors, it is not surprising that the local economic development impact of university technology transfer appears to be lower in Japan than in the United States.

The unit of analysis in Bercovitz and Feldman (2004) was also the individual faculty member. They analyzed the propensity of U.S. medical school researchers at Duke University and Johns Hopkins University to file invention disclosures, a potential precursor to technology commercialization. The authors found that three factors influence the decision to disclose inventions: norms at the institutions where the researchers were trained and the disclosure behaviors of their department chairs and peers, respectively. These authors ignored human capital measures and only emphasized institutional effects.

Appropriate Technology

Appropriate technology (AT) is technology that is designed with special consideration to the environmental, ethical, cultural, social and economical aspects of the community it is intended for. With these goals in mind, AT typically requires fewer resources, is easier to maintain, has a lower overall cost and less of an impact on the environment compared to industrialized practices.

The term is usually used to describe simple technologies suitable for use in developing nations or less developed rural areas of industrialized nations. This form of appropriate technology usually prefers labour-intensive solutions over capital-intensive ones, although labour-saving devices are also used where this does not mean high capital or maintenance cost. In practice, appropriate technology is often something described as using the simplest level of technology that can effectively achieve the intended purpose in a particular location. In industrialized nations, the term *appropriate technology* takes a different meaning, often referring to engineering that takes special consideration of its social and environmental ramifications.

Background and Definition

The term *appropriate technology* came into some prominence during the 1973 energy crisis and the environmental movement of the 1970s. The term is typically used in two arenas: utilizing the most effective technology to address the needs of developing areas, and using socially and environmentally acceptable technologies in industrialized nations.

Appropriate Technology Founders

In the modern world appropriate technology is supposed to commence from Mahatma Gandhi who advocated rural technology during 1920s to help India's village to become self reliant and hence could help in the freedom struggle against British. To Gandhi self reliance was very strongly tied to freedom. E. F. Schumacher who was very strongly influenced by Gandhi's philosophy took his village development further and coined "intermediate technology" in early 1970s. It is Schumacher's book Small is Beautiful that really started the appropriate technology movement.

Appropriate Technology Practitioners

Some of the wellknown practitioners of the appropriate technology-sector include: M K Ghosh, Chaman Lal Gupta, Sen Kapadia, B.V. Doshi, Buckminster Fuller, William Moyer (1933–2002), Satish Kumar (1936–present), Anil K. Rajvanshi, Amy B. Smith, Amory Lovins, Sanoussi Diakité, Victor Papanek, Johan Van Lengen and Arne Næss (1912–present)

Appropriate Technology in Developing Areas

The term has often been applied to the situations of developing nations or underdeveloped rural areas of industrialized nations. The use of appropriate technology in these areas seeks to fill in the gaps left by conventional development which typically focuses on capital-intensive, urban development.

Appropriate technologies are not necessarily "low" technology, and can utilize recent research, for example cloth filters which were inspired by research into the way cholera is carried in water. A type of high-efficiency, white LED lights is used by the Light Up the World Foundation in remote areas of Nepal to replace more traditional forms of lighting that cause health problems associated with kerosene lamps or wood fires.

Intermediate Technology

Coined by E. F. Schumacher, the term intermediate technology is similar to appropriate technology. It refers specifically to tools and technology that are significantly more effective and expensive than traditional methods, but still an order of magnitude (one tenth) cheaper than developed world technology. Proponents argue that such items can be easily purchased and used by poor people, and according to proponents can lead to greater productivity while minimizing social dislocation. Much intermediate technology can also be built and serviced using locally available materials and knowledge. This intermediate technology is conducive to decentralization, compatible with the laws of ecology, gentle in its use of scarce resources, and designed to serve the human person instead of making him the servant of machines.

Appropriate Hard and Soft Technologies

According to Dr. Maurice Albertson and Faulkner, appropriate hard technology is "engineering techniques, physical structures, and machinery that meet a need defined by a community, and utilize the material at hand or readily available. It can be built, operated and maintained by the local people with very limited outside assistance (e.g., technical, material, or financial). it is usually related to an economic goal." Some have explored the use of classroom projects for university-level physics students to research, develop and test appropriate hard technology .

Albertson and Faulkner consider Appropriate soft technology as technology that deals with "the social structures, human interactive processes, and motivation techniques. It is the structure and process for social participation and action by individuals and groups in analyzing situations, making choices and engaging in choice-implementing behaviors that bring about change."

Appropriate Technology in Developed Countries

The term *appropriate technology* is also used in developed nations to describe the use of technology and engineering that results in less negative impacts on the environment and society. E. F. Schumacher asserts that such technology, described in the book *Small is Beautiful* tends to promote values such as health, beauty and permanence, in that order.

Often the type of appropriate technology that is used in developed countries is "Appropriate and Sustainable Technology" (AST); or appropriate technology that, besides being functional and relatively cheap (though often more expensive than true AT), is also very durable and lasts a long time.

Parallel to this theory, British architect interested in human settlements and development, John F. C. Turner (co-author and editor of the book Freedom To Build and author of the book Housing By People), has said that truly appropriate technology is technology that ordinary people can use for their own benefit and the benefit of their community, that doesn't make them dependent on systems over which they have no control. This definition focuses on the idea that technology typically creates dependencies and thus to truly be appropriate, technology should enhance the local or regional capacity to meet local needs, rather than creating or amplifying dependencies on systems beyond local control.

Emerging Technologies—Information Technology

Emerging technologies and converging technologies are terms used to cover various cutting-edge developments in the emergence and convergence of technology.

Emerging technologies are those which represent new and significant developments within a field; converging techologies represent previously distinct fields which are in some way moving towards stronger inter-connection and similar goals.

Overview

Over time, new methods and topics are developed and opened up. Some arise due to theoretical research, others due to commercial research and development or new tools and discoveries. Technological growth includes incremental developments, and disruptive technologies. An example of the former was the gradual roll-out of DVD as a development intended to follow on from the previous optical technology Compact Disc. By contrast, disruptive technologies are those where a new method replaces the previous technology and make it redundant, for example the replacement of horse drawn carriages by automobiles.

Emerging technologies is a general term used to denote significant technological developments that in effect, broach new territory in some significant way in their field. Examples of currently emerging technologies include nanotechnology, biotechnology, cognitive science, robotics, and artificial intelligence.

Converging technologies are a related topic, signifying areas where different disciplines are converging and to an extent merging or developing broad links, towards a common direction. Thus as computers become more powerful, and media becomes digitized, computing and media are described as being converging technologies.

Debate Over Emerging Technologies

Many writers, including computer scientist Bill Joy, have identified clusters of technologies that they consider critical to humanity's future. Advocates of the benefits of technological change typically see emerging and converging technologies as offering hope for the betterment of the human condition. However, critics of the risks of technological change, and even some advocates such as transhumanist philosopher Nick Bostrom, warn that some of these technologies could pose dangers, perhaps even contribute to the extinction of humanity itself; i.e., some of them could involve existential risks.

Much ethical debate centers on issues of distributive justice in allocating access to beneficial forms of technology. Some thinkers, such as environmental ethicist Bill McKibben, oppose the continuing development of advanced technology partly out of fear that its benefits will be distributed unequally in ways that could worsen the plight of the poor. By contrast, inventor Ray Kurzweil is among techno-utopians who believe that emerging and converging technologies could and will eliminate poverty and abolish suffering.

Acronyms

NBIC, an acronym standing for Nanotechnology, Biotechnology, Information technology and Cognitive science, is currently the most popular term for emerging and converging technologies, and was introduced into public discourse through the publication of *Converging Technologies for Improving Human Performance*, a report sponsored in part by the U.S. National Science Foundation.

Various other acronyms have been offered for essentially the same concept such as GNR (Genetics, Nanotechnology and Robotics). Journalist Joel Garreau in *Radical Evolution: The Promise and Peril of Enhancing Our Minds, Our Bodies — and What It Means to Be Human* uses "GRIN", for Genetic, Robotic, Information, and Nano processes, while science journalist Douglas Mulhall in *Our Molecular Future: How Nanotechnology,*

Robotics, Genetics and Artificial Intelligence Will Transform Our World uses "GRAIN", for Genetics, Robotics, Artificial Intelligence, and Nanotechnology. Another acronym coined by the appropriate technology organization ETC Group is "BANG" for "Bits, Atoms, Neurons, Genes".

Impacts of Women's Development

ITDGPractical Action's intervention in Eastern Sudan started in 1993, following an investigation into the needs of poor people in the area, the potential to expand the productive sector, and the possibilities for intervention byITDGPractical Action. The eastern region was identified as the neediest area for programme activities because of its broad span of productive technologies, accessibility to local markets, and the relatively large numbers of poor and unemployed people who frequently migrate to the area.

ITDGPractical Action launched the Women's Development Associations (WDAs) Project as a food processing training project in April 1994. The project covered the areas of Kassala and Gedarif states, targeting poor women-headed households, including marginalized women. In the second phase of the project, 2000-2003, the objectives and purpose evolved to include poverty alleviation through the empowerment of women. The project aimed at strengthening WDAs as active civil society organizations in Eastern Sudan.

ITDGPractical Action provided support by equipping WDAs with necessary knowledge and skills, which have enhanced the members' income-earning opportunities and improved their overall living conditions. It also helped WDAs to communicate with each other, and create links with potential supporters such as credit institutions and related authorities.

An evaluation has now been carried out to assess the extent to which the project goal and purpose have been achieved. The evaluation team adopted participatory methodology to ensure the involvement of stakeholders and partners in this learning process.

UNIT-VI

Eye Opener to Women Health Education

Gender in Health

Gender refers to those characteristics of women and men that are socially and culturally determined; whereas sex refers to biological differences between women and men. Gender combines powerfully with other health determinants, such as poverty, age, ethnicity and other markers of social exclusion, to produce particular patterns of inequity, or unfair differences. The case for taking gender inequity seriously in health policy, planning and delivery encompasses rights based, effectiveness and sustainability arguments. The goals of gender equity and poverty eradication are interlinked and often interdependent.

Gender shapes vulnerability to illness and ability to protect and maintain health. For instance, high HIV prevalence rates amongst young women in sub-Saharan Africa reflect the multiple challenges girls and young women face in negotiating sexual relationships. Gender affects access to health services and the quality of care received.

For example, shockingly high rates of maternal mortality remain in part due to the barriers many poor women face in accessing relevant services. In many contexts, this is exacerbated by limited availability of quality services to meet women's needs. Gender also affects burdens of ill-health, as women and girls frequently carry out the caring role at household and community levels.

There is an urgent need for action within and beyond the health sector. Gender and health interactions are part of a broader context of institutionalised gender inequity in social and economic relationships, which goes beyond the provision of health services. The Millennium Development Goals recognise that access to education and decision-making at all levels, and to financial resources strongly affects the health status of women.

Gender and Health Definition

Society prescribes to women and men different roles in different social contexts. There are also differences in the opportunities and resources available to women and men, and in their ability to make decisions and exercise their human rights, including those related to protecting health and seeking care in case of ill health. Gender roles and unequal gender relations interact with other social and economic variables, resulting in different and sometimes inequitable patterns of exposure to health risk, and in differential access to and utilization of health information, care and services. These differences, in turn have clear impact on health outcomes".

Mortality and Morbidity Factors Influencing Health

Mortality

Mortality rate is a measure of the number of deaths (in general, or due to a specific cause) in some population, scaled to the size of that population, per unit time. Mortality rate is typically expressed in units of deaths per 1000 individuals per year; thus, a mortality rate of 9.5 in a population of 100,000 would mean 950 deaths per year in that entire population. It is distinct from morbidity rate, which refers to the number of individuals in poor health during a given time period (the prevalence rate) or the number who currently have that disease (the incidence rate), scaled to the size of the population.

One distinguishes:

1. The crude death rate, the total number of deaths per year per 1000 people. The crude death rate for the

whole world is currently about 8.23 per 1000 per year according to the current CIA World Factbook.

2. The perinatal mortality rate, the sum of neonatal deaths and fetal deaths (stillbirths) per 1000 births.
3. The maternal mortality rate, the number of maternal deaths due to childbearing per 100,000 live births.
4. The infant mortality rate, the number of deaths of children less than 1 year old per 1000 live births.
5. The child mortality rate, the number of deaths of children less than 5 years old per 1000 live births.
6. The standardised mortality rate (SMR)-This represents a proportional comparison to the numbers of deaths that would have been expected if the population had been of a standard composition in terms of age, gender, etc..
7. The age-specific mortality rate (ASMR)-This refers to the total number of deaths per year per 1000 people of a given age (e.g. age 62 last birthday).

Infant mortality rate: *total:* 32.31 deaths/1,000 live births.
Male: 36.94 deaths/1,000 live births

Female: 27.12 deaths/1,000 live births (2008 est.)

Year	Infant mortality rate	Rank	Percent Change	Date of Information
2003	59.59	59		2003 est.
2004	56.29	56	-5.54 %	2004 est.
2005	56.29	55	0.00 %	2005 est.
2006	54.63	55	-2.95 %	2006 est.
2007	34.61	73	-36.65 %	2007 est.
2008	32.31	72	-6.65 %	2008 est.

In developing countries, reproductive morbidity commonly affects the quality of women's lives. This form of ill health has largely been ignored by the policy makers, health planners as well as researchers. The reproductive morbidity includes the obstetric and gynaecological conditions of ill health related to the reproductive process during and outside the childbearing episodes. The obstetric morbidity encompasses the conditions during pregnancy, delivery and post partum period and gynaecological morbidity includes the conditions outside pregnancy related events. In this part, the reproductive morbidity refers to gynaecological morbidity of ill health unrelated to pregnancy.

There are three methods for the diagnosis of gynaecological morbidity such as self reported symptoms, clinical examination and laboratory tests. Appropriate laboratory testing is considered as the "Gold standard" for the precise detection of reproductive morbidity and accurate measurement of prevalence of diseases. However, such tests have limited applicability in developing countries because they are expensive and present logistical difficulties. Health facilities at the community level are poorly equipped to deal with reproductive morbidity, since they do not have diagnostic facilities, drugs, supply of blood or surgical equipment to treat the diseases. Even, service providers are not well acquainted to detect the morbidity or to provide counselling.

Information about reproductive morbidity in developing countries is scanty. Although a few studies have been conducted in this field, but most of them are based on information obtained from clinics or hospitals. Large proportion of women does not visit health facilities unless the disease becomes serious. So, the results from hospitals or clinics do not reflect the magnitude of the disease burden.

The statistics provided by the hospitals are based on biomedical causes only, but information on social, economic, demographic and behavioural determinants are rare. In fact, a search of literature reveals that knowledge about reproductive morbidity and its determinants in Bangladesh and also in the sub-continent are almost non-existent. A few studies in this area showed a varying prevalence of reproductive morbidity and these mainly considered the adult women of reproductive age. Adolescent reproductive health has been ignored. Concerted efforts are needed to provide useful information for health planners and policy makers.

So, the appropriate strategies to be designed to bring about improvement in the reproductive health of women. With these objectives in view, the present study on self reported reproductive morbidity among adolescents was undertaken.

Materials and Methods

This was a cross sectional study conducted in both rural and urban areas of Bangladesh. The female adolescents aged 10-19 years irrespective of their marital status constituted the study population. A multistage cluster sampling technique was adopted to select the sample. Both quantitative and qualitative data on reproductive morbidity were collected. A total of 2883 adolescents were selected. They were also inquired about their health care seeking behaviour for their problems. Both uni-variate and bi-variate analyses were performed. Multivariate logistic regression analysis was used to identify the socio-economic and demographic factors which were significantly related to reproductive morbidity and care seeking behaviour. Data analysis was performed using Statistical Package for Social Science (SPSS, version 11.0). To substantiate the results of quantitative study, a series of focus group discussions were also conducted among the adolescents. In the present study, the analysis on quantitative data was presented.

Results

The mean age of the respondents was 16.3±1.8 years with a range of 10 to 19 years. Among the respondents, 34.9% were unmarried and 65.1% were married. The mean years of schooling was 4.7±3.3 years. Among them 23.6% were illiterate, 33.1% had 1-5 years of schooling and the rest had 6 and above years of schooling. Regarding parental education, more than two fifths (43.7%) of the adolescents' fathers were illiterate as against more than two thirds (69.9%) of mothers were illiterate indicating that mothers were more illiterate than fathers. The mean family size was 5.2 persons. About one third (29.6%) of the adolescents were currently engaged in different income generating activities other than household work. Overwhelmingly majority of the respondents were Muslims (89.0%) and only 11.0% were non-Muslims. About three fifths of the adolescents (57.3%) were from nuclear families and the rest from joint/ or extended families (42.7%). The median family income was Tk.2500.0 and about three fifths (58.1%) of the families had income less than Tk. 3000.0.

Nutrition and Health

Nutritional health provides a foundation for optimum fitness, performance, and overall health. Excellent nutrition results in more energy, better athletic performance, and less risk of illness. Poor nutrition can cause poor performance, low energy, mental and physical stress, and greater incidence of injuries. A balanced diet is achieved by eating healthy foods, plentiful nutrients, and adequate calories. Reaching this balance can be challenging, as calorie requirements and weight maintenance are a concern to most women. This is complicated by a confusing number of "miracle" diet and nutrition plans, which can be misleading and unhealthy.

As an active, athletic woman, your body often needs more nutrients than it receives. Most girls and women do not eat enough calcium and also have diets that lack enough iron, zinc, and vitamins D, E, and B, including folate. By knowing your potential deficiencies, you can correct them. You can design your own eating plan with a healthy balance of nutrients, vitamins, minerals, fluids, and adequate calories to enjoy the best food, health, and fitness.

Food Content

The building blocks of foods are carbohydrates, proteins, and fats; however, very few foods are "pure" carbohydrate, protein, or fat. Both natural foods, such as milk, and prepared foods, such as a cheeseburger, are combinations of protein, carbohydrate, and fat. Foods also contain vitamins and minerals, which function in the body as enzymes and regulators of organ and muscle function. Vitamins and minerals are in highest concentration and absorbed best by the body when eaten as they occur naturally in foods. Balanced nutrition requires eating a wide variety of healthy foods to meet all your needs. Unfortunately, many prepared foods and meals are not well balanced and are high in fats or sugars and low in fiber, vitamins, and minerals. The nutrition profile of the average athletically active female is low in carbohydrates, milk products, red meat, fruits, and vegetables. Understanding the value of these foods or their nutritional equivalents will allow you to correct these deficiencies.

The body needs carbohydrates, proteins, fats, vitamins, minerals, water, and electrolytes on a daily basis to function most effectively. Amounts of carbohydrates, proteins, and fats are measured in grams; one gram is about the weight of a paper clip. Vitamins and minerals are measured in micrograms (mcg), milligrams (mg), or international units (IU). The Food and Drug Administration, through much nutritional research, has standardized Reference Daily Intakes (RDI). Formerly called Recommended Daily Allowances (RDA), these guidelines help to set standards for meeting your nutritional needs to optimize health.

Carbohydrates

Carbohydrates are the best fuel source for muscles, brain, and blood. They are broken down by the digestive system into glucose, which is either stored or released directly into your bloodstream to provide energy for the body. Sugars are the simplest forms of carbohydrates; simple sugars include glucose, sucrose, and fructose. More complex carbohydrates, including starches and fibers, are simple sugars that are bonded with each other. Fiber is an important carbohydrate nutrient; insoluble fiber is not digested but is essential for transporting waste out of the body.

Foods that are primarily carbohydrates include fruits and vegetables, breads, pasta, cereal, and "fat-free" desserts and candy. Reading the food label of a package gives you information about total grams of carbohydrates, including the breakdown of sugar and fiber content. Carbohydrates contain four calories per gram; one gram equals about a quarter teaspoon of sugar.

The Importance of Carbohydrates to Athletes

Glucose is stored in the liver and muscles as glycogen. When the body needs fuel and does not have enough glucose in the bloodstream, it converts this stored glycogen to glucose, which travels in the blood to where fuel is needed. Glycogen is always the first source of energy, and for athletes, is the optimal source of energy, especially during competition or an event. The glycogen-to-glucose breakdown is a simple, quick body process. To improve performance, athletes try to maximize the amount of glycogen their body has available. Glycogen storage can be increased before an event by "carbo-loading". The total body storage capacity of glycogen is about 1,500 to 2,000 calories (Kcal)—basically enough energy to live off of for one inactive day or to carry you through 60 to 90 minutes of intense aerobic exercise. It is recommended that girls and women eat at least 55 percent of their calories as carbohydrates, which can be obtained from healthy servings of fruit, vegetables, bread products, and whole grains or beans. Dairy products also contain carbohydrates. Like all foods, however, there are best, good, and poor types of carbohydrates. Best types of carbohydrates are broken down to glucose more slowly and also contain healthy fiber.

Lately, high-carbohydrate diets have received bad press due to the popularity of "high-protein/low-carbohydrate" diets. This is unfortunate. Research in medicine, nutrition, and exercise physiology repeatedly shows that carbohydrates provide the best fuel for life and athletic performance. Diet plans have been compared, and over the long term, weight is best maintained with high-carbohydrate diets.

The Glycemic Index

Glycemic index, or GI, is an index given to mostly carbohydrate foods based on how quickly they raise blood sugar levels. The index is a number from 0 to 100; the higher the number, the quicker the food reaches the bloodstream as glucose. Sugar has the highest glycemic index (100); soybean one of the lowest (18). Foods with a high glycemic index are often processed, starchy, and sugary foods, although some natural foods, such as honey and watermelon, have high indexes. Foods that contain fat or fiber along with the sugar have lower indexes because the fat and fiber slow the release of glucose. Athletes in particular can use the glycemic index of foods to determine which types of carbohydrates provide the best fuel before and during events and training. High glycemic index food products such as GU or Cliff Shotz or drinks such as Gatorload or Endurox provide quick sources of energy and are useful in long endurance events in which the body has depleted its glycogen supply. High glycemic index carbohydrates need to be eaten frequently during endurance events lasting more than two hours to maintain blood glucose levels and provide energy. Before competition, low to medium glycemic index foods are recommended to promote steady blood glucose over the next one to two hours.

Research has recently suggested that people who regularly eat high glycemic index diets have a greater risk of diabetes, obesity, and heart disease due to a tidal wave of high and low blood sugar levels. High GI foods send a sudden flood of glucose into the blood, which causes the pancreas to release a large amount of insulin, the hormone that transfers blood glucose from the blood and into storage as glycogen or fat. The amount of insulin released corresponds to the amount of blood glucose; high levels of both glucose and insulin can be dangerous to body organs and increase the risk of diabetes. Also, there is a rebound of low blood sugar, which can cause sleepiness, moodiness, irritability, and, in diabetics, coma. Hunger is felt again sooner after high glycemic index foods are eaten due to this low blood sugar.

In contrast, low and medium glycemic index foods cause a slow release of glucose into the bloodstream. Normal amounts of glucose circulate and low amounts of insulin are released in a steady stream. This keeps blood glucose levels stable and protects the body and brain from the dangerous effects of unstable blood sugars. Mood is also stabilized, as brain glucose supplies are constant. In people at risk of diabetes, with a family history or a history of (gestational) diabetes in pregnancy, eating a low to moderate glycemic index diet will reduce the risk of developing diabetes later in life.

The Benefits of Low Glycemic Index Foods:

- Fewer hunger pangs
- Stable energy levels
- Steady blood sugars
- Less fatigue
- Stable mood
- Less insulin requirements

Learning to prevent large swings in blood sugars to improve a sense of well-being and performance is a valuable lesson in nutrition. A food's glycemic index can sometimes be surprising: white flour, white bread, and white rice have a high glycemic index, but whole-wheat flour, whole-wheat bread, and brown rice have a lower index. Starchy foods such as white potatoes, corn, and carrots also have a high glycemic index, although sweet potatoes, peas, and celery do not. The best way to incorporate the glycemic index into your lifestyle is to purchase a book that lists common foods (refer to "Resources" at the end of this book). The glycemic index of foods can also be lowered by eating them with foods that slow their digestion, specifically fat, protein, or fiber. For example, eating corn with butter or potatoes with meat lowers the glycemic index. You can also lower glycemic index of pastas and rice by cooking them al dente (firm, not overcooked, and mushy). The following is a chart of some common foods. Basically, low glycemic index foods have GIs less than 55, medium are 55 to 74 and high are 75 to 100.

Low GI Foods	Medium GI Foods	High GI Foods
Oatmeal 46	Power Bar 58	Jelly beans 80
Yogurt, sweetened 34	Ice cream 61	French bread 95
Meat ravioli 39	Raisins 64	Waffles 76
Soybeans 18	Sweet corn 55	Short-grain white rice 76
Milk 30	White rice 60	Corn flakes 87
Black beans 31	Pizza 62	Baked potato 90
Grapefruit 26	Wheat bread 71	French fries 78
Apple 39	Macaroni and cheese 67	Corn chips 76
Sweet potato 46	Croissant 70	Donut 78
Sponge cake 47	Banana 56	Pretzels 85
Fettucini 34	Chocolate 51	Rice cakes 80
Orange 46	Oatmeal cookie 58	Sugar, honey, 100
Peanuts 15	Popcorn 58	Bagel 75
Thin spaghetti 47	Pita bread 57	Watermelon 75

Fiber

A high-fiber diet has been recognized for years for its health benefits. Dietary fiber content is very important to long-term health. In fact, it has been identified as a necessary diet nutrient by the Food and Drug Administration (FDA). Fiber is a natural plant product that helps slow digestion, lowering glycemic indexes of foods. Fiber has also been identified for its many health prevention benefits, particularly reduced risk of breast cancer, colon cancer, diabetes, heart disease, constipation, diverticulosis, stroke, hypertension, and obesity.

The Reference Daily Intake (RDI) for fiber, based on a 2,000-calorie diet, is 25 grams/day. This should be your minimum. Because large amounts of fiber, especially if your digestive system is not used to it, can cause bloating, stomach upset, and diarrhea, increasing the overall amount of fiber in your diet should be done gradually with fiber distributed evenly throughout meals and snacks. Products such as Beano can help with gas and bloating if that is a problem. Eating various sources of fiber daily—such as popcorn, fresh and dried fruits, vegetables, nuts, beans, and whole grains is also recommended. You should also drink plenty of water with fiber, because this will make your stomach feel full for longer. Because of the cleansing effect fiber has on the digestive tract and bowels, avoid high-fiber products the night before, morning of, and during events, unless your body is used to a high-fiber diet.

The Health Benefits of a High-Fiber Diet:

- Decreases breast cancer
- Decreases colon cancer
- Decreases cholesterol
- Prevents and manages diabetes
- Prevents heart disease
- Prevents constipation
- Prevents diverticulosis
- Helps prevent stroke
- Prevents high blood pressure
- Helps prevent obesity
- Helps you feel full longer

Proteins

Proteins are essential for the body to build and repair muscle and tissues and produce enzymes and hormones, which keep the body regulated. Proteins are made up of combinations of several of the 20 types of amino acids. Some of these amino acids can be reused by the body, but almost half of them must be eaten on a regular basis; these are called "essential amino acids." Although proteins are best used by the body as building blocks for muscle tissue and hormones, they can also serve as an energy source if glycogen levels are low. They provide four calories per gram.

Vegetarians, especially vegans (who do not eat dairy, eggs, or fish) tend to have lower protein in their diets, sometimes lacking essential amino acids. In order to fully meet their protein needs, they can obtain complete proteins by combining grains (corn and wheat) and legumes (nuts, beans, and seeds) in their diet. These foods have additional benefits of having cancer-and disease-fighting properties. Vegetarian diets are quite healthy if followed intelligently to make sure protein (and calcium) needs are not neglected. Vegetarians who do not eat fish, dairy, or eggs should eat at least two servings daily from each of these food groups: legumes, grains, and nuts and seeds.

Vegans Must Eat at Least Two Servings Daily of Each of the Following

- Legumes—dried beans and peas, soybeans, tofu, peanuts, peanut butter
- Grains—cereals, breads, pasta, corn, rice, wheat
- Nuts and seeds—cashews, almonds, sunflower seeds, walnuts, pumpkin seeds

There are benefits to meat, poultry, and dairy sources of protein, as they have other valuable nutrients. Red meat is the most optimal source of iron, an essential mineral often deficient in active women. It also contains B vitamins, zinc, folic acid, and complete proteins. Actually, many of the nutrients in meat (iron, folic acid, vitamin B6, and zinc) are the same that are lacking most in women's diets. Red meat and fish also contain creatine, a building block of energy molecules. Fish is an excellent protein, as it contains healthy omega-3 fatty acids, which reduce heart disease and stroke, and is recommended to be eaten twice weekly.

Good Sources of Protein

- Red meat
- Eggs
- Poultry
- Legumes, tofu

- Fish
- Nuts and seeds
- Dairy products
- Certain whole grains

There has been some controversy regarding contaminants such as hormones, antibiotics, and bacterial or viral diseases associated with meat, poultry, and fish sources of protein. Hormones are fed to some chicken and cattle to increase size and decrease fat, and antibiotics are used liberally to prevent diseases. There are no specific dangers to eating these foods in small amounts, but there are some theories that in large quantities they can lead to food allergies or interfere with growth in younger children. If you are concerned about these risks, purchase meats and dairy products labeled "organic"; these are required to be free of hormones and antibiotics. Many milk, egg, and meat products are now labeled specifically as hormone-free or antibiotic-free.

Fish, although one of the healthiest proteins, can also be harmful especially to women planning pregnancy. Certain types of large fish, including swordfish, tilefish, large tuna steaks, and mackerel should not eaten more than once monthly due to their higher mercury content, which interferes with brain development in unborn and young children. These fish should be avoided for the first year prior to planning a pregnancy. Raw fish and shellfish can also transmit parasites and hepatitis A.

Food preparation is another concern. Fully cooking meats is recommended to kill any potential bacteria or diseases and is always recommended when preparing poultry. Eating blackened food is not recommended, as the charring has been linked to stomach and intestinal cancer.

Most girls and women actually eat enough protein, as it is found in many sources other than meat or fish. Tofu, nuts, peanut butter, cheese, milk, yogurt, and dried peas and beans are good sources of proteins. Some whole-grain breads and pastas also have protein. Many food and energy bars now contain protein as well. Athletic and active women require 1.4g to 1.8g/kg/day (.7 to .9 g/lb/day) to make up 20 to 25 percent of the diet. For an average 140-pound woman, this equals 100 to 126 grams of protein daily. (A three ounce serving of chicken contains 30 grams.)

Because most women's protein needs are easily met, there is no need for protein or amino acid supplements. These are expensive, put a strain on the kidneys, and cause dehydration and bone loss. They are also often combined with other chemicals, which can be dangerous.

The Pitfalls of Protein and Amino Acid Supplements

- Overload kidneys
- Cause dehydration
- Cause calcium loss
- Are expensive
- Are ineffective
- Are often combined with other unhealthy ingredients

Fats

Fats are a necessary building block of nutrition and are broken down into fatty acids. The most essential fatty acids that must be supplied by foods are linoleic and linolenic acid, essential for transporting the fat-soluble vitamins A, D, E, and K. Fatty acids also help in energy production, the chemical balance of hormones, and nerve and brain function. In the body, fat cushions vital organs, including the eyes, liver, and heart, and also provides insulation against heat loss. Fat is also a very efficient long-term storage site for fuel, providing nine calories per gram.

Fat's bad reputation comes from its high calorie content, which can lead to obesity if eaten in large amounts. Saturated fats found in meat and poultry have a legitimately bad reputation because they contain harmful cholesterol. What contains "bad" cholesterol, however, seems to change almost daily. It used to be thought that eggs, high-fat cheese, and butter fats were very bad for the heart, blood vessels, and arteries. Now these products have been found to also contain healthy fatty acids that are beneficial when eaten in moderation (one egg and one or two servings of butter fat foods a day). The greatest risk of "bad" fats are due to trans-fatty acids and saturated fats, which increase risk of cardiovascular (heart and blood vessel) disease and stroke. Trans-fatty acids found in stick margarine, shortening, and many snack foods are processed oils that become unhealthy in the chemical processing they go through. Saturated fats are found in high amounts in fatty meats, especially pork fat and rinds, beef fat and lard, and chicken fat and skin. Processed meats, including sausages, hot dogs, and pepperoni, should be avoided as much as possible, as they not only contain very high amounts of saturated fats, but also nitrates, a cancer-causing chemical.

Saturated fats can be avoided by choosing lean cuts of meat (sirloin and tenderloin), avoiding poultry skin and fat, and avoiding foods made with lard or beef, pork, or chicken fat. Full-fat dairy products should be eaten in moderation due to their higher content of saturated fats. Butter is somewhat controversial. Because it is a saturated animal fat, until recently, butter was considered unhealthy, and stick margarine was thought to be a healthier alternative. However, current research reveals that stick margarine is actually the worst type of spread (it is a trans fat). In contrast, butter has been found to contain conjugated linoleic acid, a healthy essential fatty acid. Therefore, eating a serving of butter a day is fine and is a much healthier choice than stick margarine. For those with high cholesterol and heart disease, using soft "buttery spreads" containing monounsaturated or polyunsaturated fats is the best choice, especially soft spreads containing plant products that assist in lowering cholesterol. (Take Control, Benecol, Smart Balance).

The most important research has shown that healthy fats, such as omega-3 fatty acids and monounsaturated and polyunsaturated fats, actually protect the heart from disease by raising the level of the good cholesterol, HDL. This makes certain fats some of the heart-healthiest foods. Heart-healthy fats include peanut butter, avocados, nuts, olive and peanut oil, and fish oil. Omega-3 fatty acids have also been shown to prevent some cancers.

Cutting all fats out of your diet is never recommended, especially for active athletic women, because fats are an essential part of hormone functioning, vitamin transport, and disease protection. Fats also promote a feeling of fullness and satisfaction from meals, reduce cravings for unhealthy foods, and allow carbohydrates to be digested more slowly, stabilizing blood sugar levels. Fat-containing foods such as meat, poultry, and dairy products provide natural sources of necessary nutrients especially important to women: iron, folate, and B vitamins in meats and calcium in dairy products. Fats should make up 20 to 30 percent of your regular diet.

HIV and AIDS Control Programme

In India, after the first case of HIV was detected in Chennai in 1986, the virus spread rapidly across the nation in both urban and rural areas. Since then, the HIV epidemic has travelled a long way, establishing itself with the greatest speed in the six high prevalence states of Andhra Pradesh, Maharashtra, Manipur, Nagaland, Karnataka and Tamil Nadu. The natural history of the HIV epidemic has played out in various forms-from the injecting drug use-driven epidemic of the North East seen in Manipur and Nagaland, to the sex work-driven epidemic of the south of India.

Since, every country and every government needs to have a solution to deal with such an issue; the government formulated the National AIDS Control Programme. Here are more details about this programme.

- National AIDS Control Programme: Phase I, Phase II, Phase III
- Current Scenario
- Key Achievements under NACP
- Combating HIV

Phases of National AIDS Control Programme:

Phase-I (1992-1999) was implemented across the country with objective to slow the spread of HIV to reduce future morbidity, mortality, and the impact of AIDS by initiating a major effort in the prevention of HIV transmission.

Phase-II (1999-2006) was aimed at reducing spread of HIV infection in India and strengthen India's capacity to respond to HIV epidemic on long term basis.

Some of the significant achievements of NACP-I & II are:

- Scaling up PMTCT and VCCTC services especially in the high prevalence states.
- Increasing access to free ARV is one of the major achievements of NACP-II. The national programme for ARV provision has motivated other State Governments (Kerala and Delhi) to announce provision of free ARV from the State Exchequer which is also a good sign.
- Recognizing the need of care and support for people living with HIV and AIDS and scaling up of Community Care Centers.
- The effectiveness of the condoms as one of the safest methods to prevent and control the spread of HIV and other STIs has been well established.
- Initiating the process for developing draft legislation on HIV and AIDS.

With the growing complexity of the epidemic, there have been changes in policy frameworks and approaches of the NACP. Focus has shifted from raising awareness to behaviour change, from a national response to a decentralized response and an increasing engagement of NGOs and networks of people living with HIV/AIDS. The National AIDS Prevention and Control Policy and the National Council on AIDS (NCA), chaired by the Prime Minister, provide policy guidelines and political leadership to the response.

Phase-III (2007-2012)is based on the experiences and lessons drawn from NACP-I and II, and is built upon their strengths. Its priorities and thrust areas are drawn up accordingly and include the following:

- Considering that more than 99 percent of the population in the country is free from infection, NACP-III places the highest priority on preventive efforts while, at the same time, seeks to integrate prevention with care, support and treatment.
- Sub-populations that have the highest risk of exposure to HIV will receive the highest priority in the intervention programmes. These would include sex

workers, men-who-have-sex-with-men and injecting drug users. Second high priority in the intervention programmes is accorded to long-distance truckers, prisoners, migrants (including refugees) and street children.

- In the general population those who have the greater need for accessing prevention services, such as treatment of STIs, voluntary counselling and testing and condoms, will be next in the line of priority.
- NACP-III ensures that all persons who need treatment would have access to prophylaxis and management of opportunistic infections. People who need access to ART will also be assured first line ARV drugs.
- Prevention needs of children are addressed through universal provision of PPTCT services. Children who are infected are assured access to paediatric ART.
- NACP-III is committed to address the needs of persons infected and affected by HIV, especially children. This will be done through the sectors and agencies involved in child protection and welfare. In mitigating the impact of HIV, support is also drawn from welfare agencies providing nutritional support, opportunities for income generation and other welfare services.
- NACP-III also plans to invest in community care centres to provide psycho-social support, outreach services, referrals and palliative care.
- Socio-economic determinants that make a person vulnerable also increase the risk of exposure to HIV. NACP-III will work with other agencies involved in vulnerability reduction such as women's groups, youth groups, trade unions etc. to integrate HIV prevention into their activities.

The strategic objectives of NACP-III are:

- Prevent infections through saturation of coverage of high-risk groups with targeted interventions (TIs) and scaled up interventions in the general population.
- Provide greater care, support and treatment to more people living with HIV/AIDS.

- Strengthen the infrastructure, systems and human resources in prevention, care, support and treatment programmes at District, State and National levels.
- Strengthen the nationwide Strategic Information Management System.

The specific goal of this phase is to reverse and stabilize the spread of AIDS by reducing the rate of incidence by 60 per cent in high prevalence States and by 40 per cent in vulnerable States.

Current Scenario: HIV situation in the country is assessed and monitored through regular annual sentinel surveillance mechanism established since 1992.As per the recent estimates using the internationally comparable Workbook method and using multiple data sources namely expanded sentinel surveillance system, NFHS-III, IBBA and Behavioural Surveillance Survey, there are 1.8-2.9 million (2.31 million) people living with HIV/AIDS at the end of 2007. The estimated adult prevalence in the country is 0.34% (0.25%-0.43%) and it is greater among males (0.44%) than among females (0.23%). The overall HIV prevalence among different population groups in 2007 continues to portray the concentrated epidemic in India, with a very high prevalence among High Risk Groups-IDU (7.2%), MSM (7.4%), FSW (5.1%) & STD (3.6%) and low prevalence among ANC clinic attendees (Age adjusted-0.48%).

Key Achievements under NACP:

- Promotion of voluntary blood donation has enabled reducing transmission of HIV infection through contaminated blood from about 6.07% (1999), 4.61% (2003), 2.07% (2005), 1.96% (2006) to 1.87% (2007).
- The number of integrated counseling and testing centres increased from 982 in 2004, 1476 in 2005, 4027 in 2006, 4567 in 2007 and 4817 in 2008 (till September, 2008). The number of persons tested in these centres has increased from 17.5 lakh in 2004 to 37.9 lakhs in 2008-09 (August, 2008).
- In the year 2007, a total of 3.2 million pregnant women accessed PPTCT services at ICTCs across the country

of which 18449 pregnant women were diagnosed to be HIV +ve. Of these 11460 (62%) pregnant women and the infants born to them received prophylactic single dose Nevirapine to prevent parent to child transmission of HIV.

- The number of STI clinics being supported by NACO has increased from 815 in 2005 to 895 in 2008. The reported number of patients treated for STI in 2005 was 16.7 lakh, in 2006, 20.2 lakh and in 2007, it has increased to 25.9 lakh.
- As of September 2008, 5,61,981 patients have been registered at ART centers and 1,77,808 clinically eligible patients are receiving free ART in Govt. & inter-sectoral health sector. This is achieved through 179 ART centers across 31 states. Total 159 Community Care Centers are established across country of providing Care & Support Services to PLHA's.
- The Targeted Intervention (TI) projects aim to interrupt HIV transmission among highly vulnerable populations. Such population groups include-commercial sex workers, injecting drug users, men who have sex with men, truckers and migrant workers. As on date, 1132 Targeted Interventions are operational in various states and UTs in the country.

Combating HIV

It is easy to fight against HIV/ AIDS if people lead by example. Also, we need to inform others about AIDS and empower them, so that they make safe choices.

People who may be infected with HIV need society's support and protection. They are not a threat to society. They have the right to live their life with dignity and continue with their jobs without losing their earning power. Every Indian needs to uphold the dignity of people living with HIV so that they can live secure harmonious lives.

The countrywide response to the National AIDS Control Programme of the Government has been constructive and yielded positive results. This shows the way forward in controlling the spread of this disease and soon making the country AIDS free.

On CMP Health and Population Policy Initiatives

Over the last fifteen years India has witnessed a sharp decline in the state's commitment to public health. Thus today our country has the fifth lowest public health expenditure in the world. As the National Health Policy admitted, this is, at 0.9 per cent of the GDP, lower than the average in even Sub Saharan Africa. Along with decreasing state spending on health, increasingly policy measures have encouraged the growth of the private sector in health care so that today we have the largest and least regulated private health care industry in the world. Evidence from across the country indicates that access to health care has declined sharply over this period. The policy of levying of user fees has impacted negatively upon access to public health facilities, especially for poor and marginalized communities and to women. As health care costs have increased sharply, it is not surprising that medical expenditure is emerging as one of the leading causes of indebtedness. At the same time, this has been accompanied by policies that have reduced access of the poor to public distributions systems of food so that per capita availability of food has shown an alarming decrease.

It is thus not surprising that in addition to starvation deaths, the huge load of preventable and communicable diseases remains substantially unchanged. Infant and Child mortality take an unconscionable toll of the lives of 22 lakh children every year. We are yet to achieve the National Health Policy 1983 target to reduce the Infant Mortality Rate to less than 60 per 1000 live births. More serious is the fact that the rate of decline in the Infant Mortality Rate, which was significant in the 1970s and 80s, has remarkably decelerated in the 1990s. 130,000 mothers die during childbirth every year. The NHP 1983 target for 2000 was to reduce Maternal Mortality Rate to less than 200 per 100,000 live births. However, 407 mothers die due to pregnancy related causes, for every 100,000 live births even today. As per the National Family Health Surveys in the last decade, the MMR has increased from 424 to 540 maternal deaths per 100,000 live births. Partially as a result of population policies, the disincentives and the two-child norm contained in them – at variance with the National Population Policy (2000) and the commitments made at the ICPD in Cairo – there is a massive shortfall of girls in the 0-6 years age group due to Sex Selective Abortions (SSA). Violence against women has grown, and taken many new forms, including a huge increase in so-called "honour killings". Indeed it would be no exaggeration to state that population policies have added to this violence.

It is thus with hope that we looked forward to the United Progressive Alliance government to initiate policy measures to arrest these trends. Although the Common Minimum Programme was committed to a substantial increase in health spending, this is not evident in the financial allocations made: the budget outlay for 2004-05, adjusted for inflation, shows no increase in the outlay for health and an 11.9 per cent increase for family planning, clearly indicating skewed priorities.

However, more alarmingly, the single line, "A sharply targeted population control programme will be launched in the 150-odd high-fertility districts", from the CMP has been acted upon to unveil policy measures for 209 districts in the country. This is a truly unfortunate move, with grave consequences for thousands of women and children from the poor, marginalized communities, especially dalits and adivasis, who along with deprivation, suffer higher levels of morbidity and mortality, and a high unmet need for health and family planning services.

These 209 districts in which the "sharply targeted population control programme" are to be launched are precisely the same districts with poor indicators for social development, especially female literacy, infant and child survival, maternal morbidity and mortality and other indicators of human and gender development. Instead of a package of health and development measures, what is being proposed is concentrating on a sharply targeted population control programme in these districts in five states. This profoundly regressive policy relies on targets for sterilization, coercive incentives and disincentives, and massive subsidies to the private sector, recalling the worst days of India's family planning history. Not only do such measures violate basic human rights, they have also been shown to be demographically unnecessary in bringing down population growth rates.

The declining Child Sex Ratio(CSR) is one deeply worrying indicator of the outcomes of such short-sighted population policies. Between 1991 and 2001, in urban areas, the CSR has declined from 935 to 903 and in rural areas from 948 to 934. More ominously, between January and June this year, in Delhi the Sex Ratio at Birth indicates 819 females being born for every 1000 males; in the prosperous and educated South Delhi zone, where demographic transition has by and large been completed, only 762 females were born for every 1000 males. A recent study by the Ministry of Health also indicated the dolorous outcome of the imposition of the two-child norm for contesting elections. A large majority of those disqualified on this ground were dalits, the adivasis and women from poor families, defeating the very purpose of democratic decentralization. Further, the study indicated that this norm had acted as an incentive for SSA. Clearly then population stabilization in this form cannot be the goal since it leads to profoundly unbalanced populations.

We therefore demand that the programme measures for these 209 districts be unreservedly scrapped. We cannot have a population policy that does not hinge on equity and gender justice. There should thus be no National Population Mission. Issues concerning women's health and reproductive rights can only be part of a larger package of a health and social development policy.

We welcome the UPA's commitment to increasing state spending on health, but this should be entirely devoted to strengthening the universal and comprehensive primary health care (PHC) system. Increasing state spending cannot become the vehicle to increasing public subsidy to the private or NGO sectors, which in fact require regulation. It is evident from the CSRs that the private sector has played a deeply regressive role in health care provision.

The Tenth Plan proposals for health and nutrition need to be reviewed keeping epidemiological priorities in mind. A basket of technologically determined vertical programmes cannot substitute for a systematic strengthening of a comprehensive, universal, integrated PHC system.

Ten years after Cairo, if the commitments made there have to have meaning, it is clear that we cannot have RCH without PHC; nor indeed can we have gender-just population policies without the enabling conditions of health and development. What we have demanded is the minimum and non-negotiable. We are still hopeful that the UPA government promises something new.

National Health and Population Policies and Programmes—Maternal and Child Health (MCH) to Reproductive and Child Health Approaches

In the absence of a basic questioning of women's status and role in society, birth control, abortions-and even maternal health care end up merely replacing an old set of traditions with new ones. Do maternal and child health services as they exist today have the potential to emancipate a woman or to further bind to her traditional roles, albeit in subtler ways? This article contends that the entire primary health programme reflects social attitudes towards women that view them primarily as mothers or potential mothers.

It is no longer a disputed fact that working class women participate in production with men and, like men, are alienated from the means of production. What makes their position still worse is that women participate more actively in reproduction than men do, and yet, unfortunately, are alienated from the means of reproduction as well. Juliet Mitchell (1971) argues that as in capitalist production where the social product is confiscated by capitalists, in reproduction the child is snatched away from a woman. Perhaps this is not strictly so. In patriarchal societies, the child, a result of physiological and emotional interaction, is seen as property, and male property at that. Concepts of illegitimacy and patriarchal lineage are examples. A child, created so actively by a woman, grows up in a capitalist and sexist milieu, and alienation occurs through the conditioning and values that she or he absorbs from infancy. Physical alienation does not usually occur because both women and children are conditioned socially not to question or to rebel inside the family. When women do so, physical alienation does occur in the form of custody in divorce, since custody is more often than not in favour of the male.

The changing role of the family further determines the newer roles that a woman performs within and outside the family. The institution of marriage too, on the exterior, becomes destabilised, say for example through, a divorce or the voluntary rejection of marriage by a sexually involved couple. However, the psychological and sociological functions and the grip of the family remain the same—they create the masculine and the feminine', resulting in a 'man's world' and a 'woman's world'. They also condition the newly born infant to-accept and appreciate the security and stability' that the bourgeois family has to offer.

The prescribed relationship between the husband, wife and child determines and influences the roles that men and women perform within and outside the family. As an example, one may quote the doctor-nurse-patient relationship as being analogous to the man-woman-child hierarchical familial triangle. Looking deeper these role models, by virtue of their predetermined status, define the extent of food, health facilities, education and employment opportunities that men and women will receive in relation to each other. Therefore, even though women do enter the production force with vigour and compulsion, they inevitably land up doing jobs that are qualitatively and thus economically inferior to those performed by men.

The wage system continues to be structured according to the assumption that a woman's wage is only supplementary. Women are thus seen as economic attachments to men, not as free labourers who participate equally (Rowbotham, 1973). Women are thus financially compelled to stay with their men even in the face of unmasked oppression. Separation, and consequently alone or with the children and without a man, often means a drastic drop in a woman's standard of living, if not abject impoverishment.

With enforced backwardness, it is also easier to push women out of the labour force than men, whether because of automation unemployment or omnipresent and omnipotent reproductive duties. Women thus become a reserve army, which will work, at half pay and who will-be re-absorbed by the family if there 'is' unemployment (Rowbotham, 1973). Underpaid outdoor work, invisible domestic labour and conjugal duties therefore leave a woman vulnerable to be doubly exploited. The condition of working class women is ideal for the creation of a powerful political force. Unfortunately their realisation of exploitation dissipates instead of being sharpened. The shunting from reproduction to production and back to reproduction acts as a safety valve to smoothen conflict.

The changing role of the family also determines the reproductive potential of the woman. The family in turn is governed by historical inevitability, market compulsions and often by the prevailing political will, where reproduction is concerned. In peasant households with considerable landholdings, it might be desirable to have as many extra pairs of hands as possible; similar may be the case in not so advanced capitalism, where the quantity of workers needs to be maintained at a high level so that their exploitation through underpayment is possible. However, with the decline of labour-intensive industry and with the emergence of capital-intensive industrialisation, the main economic task of the family would no longer be to produce a large number of children, since quality rather than quantity would be important in the labour market (Peggy Morton, quoted in Mitchell, 1971). The family adapts itself accordingly, and in turn monitors the reproductive ability of the woman to suit the requirements of the contemporary wage market.

The woman, therefore, is only seemingly liberated to become a wage earner. In truth, however, she holds no real power in either structure; in fact, forces that are alien, incomprehensible and beyond her control monitor her, both inside and outside the family. In the existing context, birth control, abortion or even good maternal health cares, in the absence of the basic questioning of a woman's role in society, end up merely replacing an old set of traditions with new ones. Not only does the woman perform the necessary functions that the traditional orthodox set-up demands from her, but she also faces the 'consequence' of being the modern, sexually liberated, bohemian woman.

It is in the light of this framework that we have to view the ideology of maternal and child health (MCH) services, whether they do liberate a woman even marginally, say from the risk of maternal and child mortality; whether a healthy pregnancy and childbirth coupled with birth spacing gives her more choice and more control over her body-or whether the existing MCH programme, in form and content, ends up merely making her a more healthy and well-programmed baby-making machine. In short, whether MCH, as it exists today, has the potential to emancipate or to further bind woman to her traditional role begs examination.

MCH-Sexist Bias in Planning

In a patriarchal world, it is no great surprise that male hegemony exists in all aspects of health care at the policy level, at the implementation stage and throughout the delivery of this care. Women as a group, therefore, have to receive health care that is designed in their own favour. Effective health care provided free of cost and accessible to all, especially to women during pregnancy delivery and the post-partum period should be considered a fundamental right. We must fight to see that no woman or child is at risk of dying, especially during these crucial months. But we must also emphasise that mere MCH will not do. 'Motherhood is only one of the roles that a woman may voluntarily, wish to perform during her lifetime. She may accept or reject it and, in spite of opting out of motherhood or marriage she is a full human being. Health services must be available to women irrespective of their child-bearing role.

The entire primary health programme reflects social attitudes towards women, viewing them primarily as mothers or potential mothers. In fact health services for women have been termed MCH services (ICSSR/ICMR, 1981). The same report notes that there is positive evidence to conclude that the health status of Indian women has declined over the past 35 years in spite of improved MCH programmes, mainly due to the fact that women are more 'at risk' nutritionally, and yet they utilise health services less than men do. They are of interest to the health services only when they conceive or when they have reached she upper limit of child bearing permitted by the government's Family Planning programme.

The infant mortality rates are also highly unimpressive (114 per, 1,000 live births in 1980 as compared to 129 in 1971). There has been no appreciable improvement in the nutritional level of children, in spite of programmes directed towards them, and even primary education has not become universal.

To shift resources towards women as a group, it is necessary for policy makers to be convinced that women contribute greatly towards world production-within the family, in the agricultural sector, in traditional as well as modern industries and also in commerce. An estimate of 18-30 per cent of the world's families are solely supported by, women while in many, others the woman's financial contribution is a substantial component (Wayne, 1985). Statistics unfortunately miss family and informal sector activities, resulting in this contribution being overlooked. Within the health care system factors that contribute towards women's ill-health are not considered-their socio-economic status, total workload the daily and seasonal pattern of activity, access to health care, etc.; neither are problems which affect women more severely such as malnourishment anaemia and occupational hazards, or those, which affect women specifically, such as abortion or spouse abuse.

MCH activities began informally in India around the turn of the nineteenth century-mostly voluntary efforts ranging from enrolling women students in medical colleges to training midwives and Lady Health Visitors. The transition to official control in MCH began in 1938. In 1953, following the introduction of training courses for Auxiliary Nurse Midwives (ANMS) and public health nurses, most voluntary health schools closed down (Iyer and jesani, 1995) (Sethna, 1978).

The Indian government's official MCH package includes antenatal, peri-natal and post-natal care, the Integrated Child Development Services scheme (ICDS), National Programme for Control of Blindness, and programmes for the Control of Diarrhoeal Diseases and Family Planning.

Undoubtedly, there exists a role, however limited, that MCH can play in a woman and child's life, provided it is universally available and of high quality. However, in the absence of a women's control over her own reproduction, a culturally and socially conditioned inability within her to be able to vocalise her gynaecological problems to a health worker, especially male, and the latter's reluctance to bridge the communication gap by demystifying pregnancy, make the MCH a watered-down programme, reduced to a mechanical distribution of iron and folic acid tablets, a mindless target-oriented approach towards immunisation and the endless weighing of children to identify the 'at risk' individuals in an already malnourished population.

The lack of control over one's own body is experienced by many women in the clinical approach to pregnancy and childbirth. Most often, questions that bother a woman deeply remain unasked. The concept that pregnant women should swallow tablets or receive injections for their own benefit without any active participation reveals the ambiguity and myth of 'people's participation' so loftily considered the basis of the Family Welfare Programme in India. In fact, passivity is a fundamental feature of the relationship between the providers and users of maternity services (Graham and Oakley 1981).

Growth charting accepted so enthusiastically, by our health care system, is yet another instance of mystification. When less than, 10 per cent of children under five in deprived sections are nutritionally normal, expensive growth monitoring is unnecessary. If 50 per cent of under-fives in India amounting to 55 million children were to be covered through growth monitoring charts, this activity of weighing and charting alone would require 110,000 workers annually, and would incur an expenditure of US $27.5 million for salaries, $20.0 million for Salter scales (1 for every 100 under-fives) and additional expenditure for repairs, replacements, maintenance, transport and new growth charts (Gopalan and Chatterjee, 1985).

Such activity, in fact detracts from motivational and educational work, which is of primary importance in child health and nutrition programmes (Srilatha, 1984). In a country with limited sources for child care, a social group that faces a high nutritional problem's needs to be identified and standard intervention is necessary for all their members (Nabarro, 1984).

MCH and Population Control

The scope of the already small package of MCH services is further reduced by making it a screen to achieve family planning targets. There is constant talk of integration of MCH and family planning' and, under this euphemistic slogan, a curriculum for undergraduate students of medicine and interns has been prepared by an expert committee. The training, programme has already been adopted by three teaching colleges. In one three courses were conducted, attended by nine teams of 27 professors (GOI, 1985: 125).

In the minds of policy-makers. MCH figures not as an independent programme but as a means to reduce fertility. The Annual Report (1984-85) of the Ministry of Health and Family Welfare (MHFW) states that:

To reach a couple protection rate (CPR) of 60.0 per cent of eligible couples by AD 2000, it is essential that the younger group of eligible couples be motivated to accept spacing and the small family norm. Moreover, the use of spacing, methods has a significant impact not only on curbing, population growth, but also on the health of the mother and child. (GOI, 1985: 116, emphasis added).

The Ministry's own assessment states that the crude birth rate (CBR) at the end of 1984 should have been 32.6 per cent per 1.000 population, whereas actually it was slightly higher—33.6 per cent. While 29.4 per cent of the couples were "protected" by the end of 1984 (sterilisation's accounted for 23.7 per cent of these), a CPR of 60.0 per cent is desired by the turn of the century. To give the family planning programme a boost, especially in backward areas, partial assistance from DANIDA, ODA (UK), UNFPA, USAID and the World Bank has been received to cover 63 districts in 14 states as 'Area Projects' for the intensive development of health and family welfare. 'The objectives are reduction of fertility and reduction of maternal and child mortality' (GOI 1985: 150). The government has introduced the concept of net reproduction rate unity (NRR one) in its Family Welfare (FW) Programme:

> After considerable experience in this regard [need to control population growth], the country has set before itself the long-term demographic goal of achieving NRR unity by AD 2000, with a birth rate of 21.0, death rate of 9.0 (life expectancy at birth being 64.0 years) and an infant mortality rate less than 60.0. In order to achieve this goal, the national family welfare programme has been and will be strengthened. It is a voluntary programme. (GOI, 1985: 164)

In the context of these new goals set by the Indian government the stranglehold of family planning over MCH can be fully understood. In fact, the first UN Advisory Mission as early as 1966, had gone as far as to insist that ANMs should be relieved from other responsibilities such as MCH and nutrition so as to concentrate their efforts on family welfare. This mission stated that 'this recommendation is reinforced by the fear that the [FP] programme may be otherwise used in some states to expand the much needed and neglected maternal and child welfare services. (UN Advisory Mission, 1966).

The first double-edged tool within the family welfare programme came in the form of the Medical Termination of Pregnancy (MTP) Act in the early 1970s. Regarded by feminists as a much-desired means to control one's fertility, the legalisation of abortion is, in itself, welcome. However, the government's interest in this legalisation becomes clear when one notes that by the end of March 1984, 4,553 institutions were rendering MTP services (as compared to 4,170 at the end of March 1983). In Bombay City alone, 50,000 MTPs are registered annually (Karkal, personal communication).

The official acceptance of NRRI by the government is especially sinister because, in lay person's terms, it suggests that only one daughter should replace her mother. Thus, female foeticide through sex determination (amniocentesis, chorionic villi biopsy) or through sex pre-selection (Ericsson-Japanese method) is in-built within the government's population control policy.

The government's emphasis on 'Child survival rings another ominous bell. Welcome in itself, the slogan is reduced to, spacing methods'. The MHFW states that 'since child survival is amongst the foremost factors which induce the couple to adopt the two child norm, the MCH programme has been given due importance' (GOI, 1985: 107.)*. The strategy becomes clearer when along with the slogan of 'child survival', the government has markedly increased its budget for family planning in the seventh Five Year Plan period, and the emphasis will now be on spacing methods for women. It is estimated that by 1990 spacing methods will account for 20.0 per cent of 'protected' couples, against the present level of 5.5 per cent. A contraceptive marketing organisation has been registered to promote methods (GOI. 1985: 101).

The Government now admits that one-third of all intra-uterine devices (IUDS) ever inserted are removed,' and one-fifth are expelled. The officially accepted drop-out rate for IUDS therefore is 53.3 per cent (GOI. 1986). Naturally, the proponents of population control would be desperate to design a and foolproof system that leaves little or no control in the hands of the woman to withdraw the contraceptive, and it is in context that the importance of injectable contraceptives implants should be understood. Though ICs do not as yet a part of the family planning programme, a programme introductory study on Net-En, an injectable contraceptive at primary health centres (PHCS) attached to 15 medical colleges is under way. Based on the results of this pilot project, it is that this spacing method will be introduced soon. In fact, according to official plans, it was to be introduced in The Indian Council for Medical Research is also conducting studies with Norplant—an implant for women. An appropriate version of this contraceptive was to be available by the end of 1985 to start programme introduction studies at the PHCs (GOI 1985: 107).*

Motivation: Distortion of Human Relationships

The state's emphasis on women targets and women motivators is a cause for concern among feminists because of the distortion in human relations brought about by the coercive, target-oriented campaign. When motivators are women, be they health staff or primary school teachers, they are constantly threatened with dire consequence such as job transfers, sexual harassment, humiliation and delayed salaries if they fail to fulfil their targets. Dangerous limits are reached when these women are the major or only source of livelihood for their families, when they are single, living in an alien village and are unable to meet targets.

These women, with the proverbial sword of Damocles hanging over their heads, are forced to see every other woman in the village as a potential target. All their conversations whether at the doorstep or at the village well, invariably ends with motivation for Family Planning. It is not surprising, therefore, that village women resent these motivators and consider them scheming nags. The entire fabric of woman-to-woman relationships is eroded in this situation with each party out-smarting the other whenever possible and harbouring mutual, deep-rooted resentment.

This distortion of basic human relations and support systems has dangerous political consequences. Sexist bias, international conspiracy and the government's population control policy are responsible for the inhuman family planning campaign. Targets are planned outside the micro-environment in, which the masses live. Dangerous contraceptives are dumped by ruthless, profit hungry multinationals. Yet, all these are invisible to the rural working class. The only visible oppressor they see is a poor ANM, most often from their own class and a victim of the present system as well. The anger directed towards another helpless victim help's the ruling class through a divide and rule strategy.

Not only does it break two working class solidarity, but it also diverts the issues, allowing the real enemy to escape without confrontation. It makes the rulers seem like the paternal and benevolent Caliphs of the Arabian Nights.

As regards the delivery of health services, the 'integration' of FP with primary health care has in fact had an adverse effect on the utilisation of health care at PHCs. A substantial majority of the rural population utilises a private practitioner in times of illness. The major reason for the non-utilisation of government services is the absurd emphasis of the latter on family planning. Women still prefer to be delivered at home by traditional dais or relatives, one reason being that any peri-natal or post-partum contact with a woman is immediately seized for target completion in the PHC. Immunisation camps suffer because covertly, many such camps are used to gather young mothers for copper-T insertions.

The shadow of the population control programme over all other essential public health services is resented by people and results in the poor utilisation of these basic services. It is annoying that public health services, especially, maternal and child services are used as a bait to lure people towards reducing population growth, without any consideration towards the existing socio-economic conditions or the helplessness and inability of the oppressed sections to rebel. In fact coercion thrives on these very conditions, and it is only a conscious organised working class that can focus on contradictions, unearth the intricate conspiracies and then demand that the health services be geared towards their own interests.

The conspiracy of the ruling class and the inhuman strategies employed by them-often in sugar-coated pills such as maternal and child health or as emancipation through birth control works to control the lives of an already exploited population. Patriarchy, which has the art of adapting itself to new situations, in fact of moulding new situations to suit its ends, prevails in policy-making research, medicine and science. Our own demands, be they of safe deliveries, of our children's survival and their well-being, or birth control, abortions and the like are snatched away and given back to us blunted.

Under the guise of giving us the choice, we are made spectators of our own oppression, be it through dangerous contraception, female foeticide, sex selection, surrogate motherhood or the perpetual tight-rope walk where our productive and reproductive duties are concerned. It is, therefore, necessary to constantly expose this design and build strong women's movement that attacks both class and patriarchal control over the various institutions that govern our lives. We have to relate the personal to the political; and should constantly question our role as women within and outside the family.

Coordinated Approach to Child Health: From Research to Practice

"Healthy People at Every Stage of Life: All people, and especially those at greater risk of health disparities, will achieve their optimal lifespan with the best possible quality of health in every stage of life." —Overarching CDC Healthy People Goal

CDC is changing to meet the challenges of public health in the 21st century. To address the shifting landscape of public health, the CDC has established four Health Protection Goals focusing on healthy people, healthy places, preparedness, and global health.

CDC's Healthy People goals encompass the unique health issues and risk behaviors that affect the quality of health in every stage of life. This broadcast of Public Health Grand Rounds focuses on Healthy People and the importance of establishing healthy behaviors during childhood instead of attempting to change unhealthy behaviors in adulthood. Major research initiatives and school and community based interventions to prevent and reduce unhealthy behaviors that cause and exacerbate chronic diseases is discussed.

The Case Study

Recent studies of children, adolescents, and young adults have demonstrated the close link of blood cholesterol level, blood pressure level, smoking, and obesity with the extent and severity of atherosclerosis among people well below 20 years of age.

This broadcast highlights the Coordinated School Health Programme Model (CSHP) to aid schools and communities in preventing and reducing chronic diseases. A CSHP consists of eight interactive components, which can help schools create programmes that help students establish healthy habits.

Researchers designed and tested a school health programme called Coordinated Approach to Child Health (CATCH) to help children improve their diet and increase their amounts of physical activity. CATCH, which now reaches more than half a million children in more than 1,200 schools in Texas, started as a clinical trial and is currently an effective public health intervention programme. The case study features Travis County which includes a large, heavily populated school system in Austin, TX.

In 2001, the Texas state legislature passed a bill authorizing the state Board of Education to require all school systems in Texas to provide 30 minutes per day of school-based physical activity and to implement a coordinated school health curriculum. Schools and communities, in particular, have a critical role to play in promoting the health and safety of young people and helping them establish lifelong healthy behavior patterns. Work with community partners continues to further the adoption and implementations of CATCH and similar behavioral change programmes across the nation.

Goal

This programme will seek to increase knowledge and awareness of how the CATCH programme gives schools and communities the tools they need to help children improve their diet and increase the amount of physical activity they engage in. By addressing chronic disease risk factors at a young age, we can begin to prevent and reduce the chronic disease burden in the U.S.

Objectives

1. State at least three reasons why it is important to implement evidence-based public health interventions designed to promote healthy lifestyle habits in a person's early years.,
2. Describe the Coordinated Approach to Child Health (CATCH) programme and how it has been implemented and disseminated in a school district and an organization that serves youth (Austin Independent School District, Austin, Texas, and the Young Men's Christian Association (YMCA) clubs, Rochester, New York).

3. Describe how federal, state, and local health and education agencies, legislators, universities, and community-based organizations can work together to improve health outcomes and leverage resources to implement successful and proven interventions.
4. Describe how a coordinated school health programme (CSHP) can improve health outcomes, specifically cardiovascular health, across the life stages.

Audience

Public health leaders; managers and professionals from local and state health departments, hospitals, community-based health organizations, boards of health, private physician practices, federal agencies, and academic institutions; and others who are concerned about preventing and reducing chronic disease across the life stages.

Issues of Old Age Women and Environment

We all want to age in a healthy way. Unfortunately, the quality of life of many older women, particularly in the South, leaves much to be desired. Older women form a forgotten group in the health and social policies of many governments. Almost everywhere in the world, women outlive men, but their rights to inheritance and to pensions are not generally well provided for. Health care is often not geared to their needs.

At the same time, older women fulfil important roles in society. They take care of younger children and are active in the community. Wemos believes that older women deserve more attention in development programmes and government policies. Those who provide care deserve to be well cared for themselves. Yet the fact that ageing is a development issue does not mean older women are simply dependents. The UN's Madrid assembly this year heard calls to end policies that equate ageing to dependence and illness and instead to recognise the huge contribution that older women can make informally caring for their families and friends. Aid programmes often contribute to the image of 'old age being a crisis' instead of looking at how old people become impoverished in the first place.

Many societies may also expect older women both to remain working and caring for their families while at the same time deny them a voice or social status. Meanwhile to have reached old age, women in developing countries may have endured a lifetime of disease, economic hardship, and social inequality, unimaginable in the developed world, which inevitably leaves its mark.

Their often-bleak socio-economic position may have an even greater bearing on their health than that of their sisters in the developed world. Income, education and even the most basic participation in political structures may barely exist in developing countries with its subsequent drain on their prospects for leading a healthy life.

The UN's 2nd World Assembly on Ageing met in Spain in 2002 to consider an International Strategy for Action on Ageing. Twenty years after the first assembly and action plan was adopted in Vienna the challenge is greater than ever. So too are the potential benefits to the real lives of countless older people. The UN calls for 'a change in attitude' among 'national and international policies' so 'the enormous potential of ageing in the 21st century is fulfilled'. It talks of ageing with 'security and dignity' and 'participation as citizens with full rights'. For the majority of the world's older citizens this remains an illusive ideal. Many governments and international agencies have been slow to react with realistic policies in spite of the predictability of global ageing. We can no longer afford this shameful neglect.

Wemos calls for an improvement in the position of older women throughout the world, particularly in the areas of care and welfare. It uses the slogan 'You're never too old to live'.

Women and the Environment

"Advancing gender equality, through reversing the various social and economic handicaps that make women voiceless and powerless, may also be one of the best ways of saving the environment, and countering the dangers of overcrowding and other adversities associated with population pressure. The voice of women is critically important for the world's future—not just for women's future."—Amartya Sen

The direct and critical relationship between women and natural resources draws its strength not from biology—that is, not because women are born female—but from gender, and the socially created roles and responsibilities that continue to fall to women in households, communities and ecosystems throughout the world.

Bangladeshi woman cooks with crop residue. Indoor air pollution kills more than 2.2 million people each year in developing countries.

Women have primary responsibility for rearing children, and for ensuring sufficient resources to meet children's needs for nutrition, health care and schooling. In the rural areas of developing countries, they are also the main managers of essential household resources like clean water, fuel for cooking and heating and fodder for domestic animals. Women grow vegetables, fruit and grain for home consumption and also for sale—often, as in much of Africa, producing most of the staple crops. In South-east Asia, women provide 90 per cent of the labour for rice cultivation.

Women are more than half (51 per cent) of the world's agricultural work force. As economic opportunities open up, women in developing countries are growing, processing and marketing non-food products made from natural resources, for consumption at home and, increasingly, overseas.

In Burkina Faso, for example, women are producing hundreds of tons of shea butter each year, selling much of it to European cosmetic markets. In Colombia, thousands of female workers are tending flowers for sale in the United States. But such livelihoods can also present new environmental and health risks: it is estimated that flower workers in Colombia are exposed to 127 different types of chemicals, many of which have been banned in the United States and the United Kingdom.

Many of these activities take place in the interstices of men's use of resources. Women occupy niches allowed by traditional gender structures or opened up by economic and social change. In coastal Mozambique, women are not allowed to come close to the boats men use for ocean fishing, or to do such fishing themselves, although they process and market the men's catch. Their aquatic space is close to the shore, where they harvest and sell shellfish, crabs and other small sea creatures—women's work that provides about 20 per cent of average monthly household income according to a recent study.

As poverty persists and, in many parts of the world, deepens, women's income from such activities becomes critical to family survival—reinforcing the importance of the environment in women's lives (and increasing the dangers posed by degraded environments). In the growing number of female-headed households, this work is essential, particularly for children; women already head almost a quarter of rural households in the world's poorest countries. Women's income can also create the conditions for expanded opportunities, choices and autonomy—all of which advance the larger goal of gender equity and equality.

Nature as Feminine Principle

Women have the responsibility for managing household resources, but they typically do not have managerial control. Given the variety of women's daily interactions with the environment, they are the most keenly affected by its degradation. For example:

Woman collects garbage in Mali dump. Women face a variety of health risks from toxic chemicals in the air, water and earth.

- Deforestation or contamination increases the time women must spend seeking fuelwood or safe, clean water, and increase women's risk of water-borne disease. In the state of Gujurat, India, women now spend four or five hours a day collecting fuelwood, where previously they would have done so once every four to five days.
- Soil erosion, water shortage and crop failures reduce harvest yields; soil exhausted from over-use reduces the productivity of household gardens.
- Toxic chemicals and pesticides in air, water and earth are responsible for a variety of women's health risks. They enter body tissues and breast milk, through which

they are passed on to infants. In a village in China's Gansu province, discharges from a state-run fertilizer factory have been linked to a high number of stillbirths and miscarriages. Water pollution in three Russian rivers is a factor in the doubling of bladder and kidney disorders in pregnant women, and in Sudan a link has been established between exposure to pesticides and perinatal mortality—with the risk higher among women farmers.

- In urban settings in particular, air and water pollution can be extreme, and sanitation and waste treatment poor or non-existent, presenting new threats to health, particularly for women, who have the highest levels of exposure. In the Indian cities of Delhi and Agra, for example, drinking water comes from rivers heavily polluted by DDT and other pesticides.

Degraded environments mean that women must spend more time and effort to find fuel or produce food, but their other responsibilities, for meeting household needs and ensuring family health, do not diminish. Gendered divisions of labour have so far resisted real change. In many countries, women already work 12 hours or more a day in and out of the home; in Africa and Asia, women work an average of 13 hours more each week than do men.

Powerlessness and its Impact

At the same time, women have little power over the conditions of their lives. Decision makers often overlook this reality, even though women's use and management of local environmental resources is fundamental to household and community well-being. Agricultural extension services are heavily biased towards men. Education and outreach efforts in support of sustainable farming and land management methods often pass them by.

National law or local customs often effectively deny women the right to secure title or inherit land, which means they have no collateral on which to raise credit. Poverty, precarious land tenure and lack of expert support discourage women from investing in newer technologies or long-term strategies such as crop rotation, fallow periods, sustainable levels of cultivation or reforestation. On the contrary, these factors encourage fast-growing cash crops such as cotton, which quickly exhaust the land, and woodland clearance for short-term income.

Such pressures on limited land resources deplete nutrients and degrade soils. Land degradation reduces yields, leading to a spiral of more intensive use, further degradation and still lower yields. Farmers may seek new land, but often find it only in frontier or marginal areas, especially if they are women and cannot close a sale or negotiate a loan.

In the worst-affected countries, HIV/AIDS has increased poverty and decreased choices, forcing people to fall back on natural resources to meet basic needs. In South Africa, large numbers of poor people, particularly women, are trying to produce food and fuel on marginal lands, increasing the pressure on fragile ecosystems.

Unsustainable land use can often be traced to denial of technical and financial resources. Given the opportunity, women may well have a predisposition to practice sustainable agriculture and maintain overall land quality—precisely because of their strong reliance on natural resources. A World Bank study in Ghana found that women's plots had a lower rate of decline in soil fertility than men's—even in the same household.

In India, women are leading rural movements to promote sustainable farming practices and resist large-scale agricultural operations that rely on intensive chemical fertilizers and pesticides. And in the United Kingdom, where farming is male-dominated, half of all organic farmers are women—10 times the proportion in the farming industry overall.

Women who lack rights to own and manage natural resources often lack rights in other aspects of their lives, reinforcing gender inequalities. Like millions of women throughout the world, women in the strongly patriarchal rural communities of south-east Madagascar have no access to the resources that bring status—property, cattle and farmland. As a result, they have little part in community or household decisions. This includes decisions about reproduction (fertility is high), marriage (early marriage is common) and education for themselves and their children (education rates for boys are low and for girls lower still).

In the past, large families were common in rural communities: children were important to agricultural productivity (especially on large land tracts), often joining their mothers (and at times fathers) in fields or household gardens, tending domestic animals and assisting with household resource needs—fetching water, and foraging for fuelwood and edible and medicinal plants. Rural women married young and had many pregnancies.

One legacy of high fertility, lower infant mortality and a limited supply of land is fragmentation. As they passed from one generation of sons to another, plots were divided again and again. Eventually the plots were simply not big enough to provide enough food for family or market. Pressures to increase yields have intensified, and men have left in search of non-farm employment. Without them, women's family burdens and responsibilities have increased, though urban relatives often send money to improve the remaining land, as well as for housing, education and health care.

Urbanization offers a series of risks and opportunities to women. Urban growth and poverty produces new environmental threats that increase health risks. Again, those most exposed are women and their children.

On the other hand, pregnancy and childbirth are generally safer in urban areas, where health care is more likely to be accessible. City life also offers women a broader range of choices for education, employment and marriage, but it also carries heightened risk of sexual violence, abuse and exploitation. For poor women, urbanization means less physical labour to find fuel, food and water, but they often lose direct control over quality or quantity. For the very poor, these basic resources are more expensive—in absolute as well as relative terms—than for better-off groups. In environmental terms, what urbanization offers the poor with one hand, it takes away with the other. The very poor in urban areas, for example those who live on and off garbage dumps, are arguably the most deprived on the planet, in human as well as economic terms. As women join the migration from rural to urban areas, they are vulnerable to economic and sexual exploitation—sweatshop labour, trafficking, abuse or violence; factory workers face possible exposure to chemicals, dust or other forms of pollution.

Along with the risks, however, go new economic opportunities. Freedom from the social and gender hierarchies of rural communities may also open up chances to go to school, college or university, to acquire marketable skills and to choose whether, when and whom to marry. Urban women are more likely to be able to decide when, if and how many children to bear, both because of changing gender relations and because they have easier access to reproductive health information and services. To be effective managers of household and other resources, both rural and urban women need a range of options: choices over family size and spacing; health care, including reproductive health; education; and partnership with men. There are many examples of programmes to empower women that reinforce both their management of resources and their reproductive health. Extension programmes can typically provide aspects of reproductive health care together with information and assistance for resources management.

Basic Needs in Rural and Urban Environments

Sustainable development demands recognition and value for the multitude of ways in which women's lives intertwine with environmental realities. Women's right to own and inherit land should be enforced; individual and communal security of land tenure should be guaranteed; women should have access to credit, and to agricultural extension and resource management services, and they should be included in decisions about the services' organization and content.

Proportion of Girls Entering and Completing Primary School, by Subregion

Women's involvement must extend to information, education and services for reproductive health and rights. Choice about fertility is a step towards equality: women thus empowered can intervene in other decisions in the household and the community, for example, education and health care for girl children; the use of common resources and the development of economic opportunities. Women's involvement in health and environmental decisions works to the benefit of individuals, society and the environment itself.

In fact, as a growing body of experience shows, reproductive health and environmental services can work very profitably together, if they are designed to meet communities' own priorities. Integration eliminates the need to duplicate outreach, and responds to women's interrelated needs. Trust is key in such efforts: in one Latin American project, a female staff member of an environmental organization who developed considerable rapport with local village residents was inundated with requests for reproductive health information and care. At the same time, a government health worker without similar rapport received few such requests. Not surprisingly, studies have also found that the most critical element of the success of integrated reproductive health and environmental services is the active engagement of women.

Shifting environmental conditions can begin new and more intense gender conflicts, but can also bring opportunities for women and men to negotiate gender equality.

For example, in Newfoundland, Canada, the collapse of North Atlantic fish stocks has brought mass unemployment to communities that once relied almost wholly on fish. Before the crisis, men did the fishing and women worked in fish processing plants. But with men and women both at home during the day, domestic conflict increased. Women wanted more help in the house, but also felt invaded; men often felt emasculated by their demands. Alcohol use and conflict with men outside the home also increased. Young women began to see husbands and boyfriends as undesirable, the number of female-headed households rose, and levels of migration for both women and men, especially those with more education, increased significantly.

A more positive response to a changed environment can be seen among salt miners in Bilma, Niger. For hundreds of years, large numbers of men crisscrossed the Sahara for months at a time, transporting and trading salt for fruit, grain and gold. In recent years, the value of salt has fallen and lorries have taken over much of the trade from camels, forcing most men into a more sedentary existence. In response, men and women have created new forms of partnership. Many women now work alongside their husbands scooping salt from pits—something not possible a generation ago. In those days, when a father died his daughters could not maintain his pits; boys or men were required. But today, when a woman marries she can join her new husband in the mine. Several couples also mine together, and the salt miners even include unmarried women.

Environmental change imposes new stresses and choices on women's and men's lives. Evolution in gender roles induced by environmental change can mean better communication and shared decision-making; but negotiating new roles and responsibilities can be a painful process. It is important to maximize social flexibility and the resources women and men can bring to negotiations with each other and with the natural world.

Forging New Relationships

Successful negotiation between women and men will be helped by having access to information and education, and to agricultural and reproductive health services. The support of laws and policies on women's rights and equality and on the sustainable use and protection of natural resources are also essential. With such support women and men can create a virtuous circle of sustainability and equity. Without it they are trapped in a vicious spiral of continuing environmental degradation, poverty, high fertility and limited opportunity, leading to environmental and social collapse.

Girl in Mali watches while the women cook. Support for women's rights can break the cycle of poverty, powerlessness and environmental degradation.

Women's groups are organizing to integrate women fully into the political process, so they can take their full part in making policy decisions affecting their lives, including policies on: the use of land and water resources for agriculture; power, drinking water and energy supply; health and education services; and economic opportunities. In many countries, they are succeeding.

A successful outcome will depend on forging new relationships between women and the environment, and between women and the world at large. Wangari Maathai is a Kenyan environmentalist and founder of the Green Belt Movement, which works with women in 20 countries to plant trees. As she suggests, such social and ecological transformations are well under way: "Implicit in the action of planting trees," she says, "is a civic education, a strategy to empower people and to give them a sense of taking their destiny into their own hands, removing their fear so they can stand up for their environmental rights. So that they [women] can control the direction of their own lives.

Women and Natural Resource Management

The international community has endorsed several plans of action for the full integration of women in all development activities. The Beijing Conference concluded that unless the contribution of women to environment and resource management is recognized and supported, sustainable development would remain elusive.

In Africa women are primary resource users and most of the responsibility for growing and collecting food, medicines, fuel, housing materials, providing cash income for schooling, health care and other family needs rests on their shoulders. As such, they do much of the work needed to maintain or restore the environment.

Because of the nature of their responsibilities and direct dependence on land-based resources, they are also the hardest hit by desertification, deforestation and misguided economic and development policies. Women may also be agents of environmental degradation by the nature of their activities and responsibilities. They can have an equally enormous impact on conservation because of their multiple roles. Their special knowledge of the environment is derived from growing food, collecting fodder, gathering firewood and water, caring for children, the sick and the elderly, tending domestic animals and gathering medicines. African women are also usually responsible for marketing agricultural produce. In Africa they do up to three-quarters of all agricultural work in addition to domestic responsibilities.

In Africa women produce up to 80 percent of the basic food commodities. In addition, their activities directly affect the environment, given that women have traditionally been responsible for bringing water and wood to the household. Women have the main responsibility for the health and nutrition of their families. They have multiple roles, and have to respond to family, economic and social expectations at the same time. They show imagination in doing so and are innovative and capable of developing a wide range of activities within the framework of the social economy (commercial and non-commercial). In Africa, the lives of women have not changed in a meaningful way. The women who spend eight hours a day gathering firewood are still doing that, women are still subjected to domestic violence, and employment of women remains limited to relatively few fields and relatively low jobs. Women and children are the ones who suffer most as a result of wars, political and ethnic conflicts.

African women are subjected to specific constraints due to gender inequalities, and these constraints shape the results they obtain. The constraints most frequently identified are: lack of access to credit and land, poverty, marginalisation, discriminatory and inadequate laws, lack of access to decision-making power, unjust and unfair cultural practices, women's heavy workload, lack of education and training and also the way in which women's activities are structured.

They are the key to the development of Africa and Africa's resources. Empowering women to ensure a better use, management and control of resources is vital for sustainable natural resource development. In order to be effective, women must gain more control of resources and of development planning and their needs and role must also be integrated into decision-making in general.

Women must be involved not only in the labour for forestry activities but also in decision-making and the control of resources. Key concerns for promoting women's participation in natural resource development activities should focus on their access to and control over resources. Activities that enhance women participation in sustainable development should emphasize the importance of two major types of resource: land, trees and other natural resources; and information and knowledge. Building on women's existing knowledge and environmental management skills is fundamental for their empowerment and their taking control of their lives.

Throughout Africa, women are actively involved in a wide range of forest-related activities, both those of a spontaneous nature and those fostered through development projects and programmes. In fact, with the exclusion of industrial timber and charcoal production, African women are the protagonists in activities related to the management and use of forest resources. Particularly important is the gathering of fuelwood, for domestic energy, as well as fruits, leaves, gums and medicinal and food products both for household use and sale in local markets. Women's participation in the production and dissemination of fuel-efficient cookstoves, in agroforestry, tree nurseries and horticulture are also well-documented. Tangible efforts are needed to train more women in forestry and natural resource activities in order to enhance their participation at all levels-from grassroots to international policy.

Women and Natural Resources

The linkage between women, natural resources and the domestic economies of poor rural households in India are fairly clear and they can be categorized into three patterns. First, natural resources are central to the livelihoods in India. Many studies have documented that poor households are dependent on free bio-mass goods and common property resources than better off households. Second, women are the primary gatherers and managers of biomass goods in poor rural households. As mentioned above, women perform key roles not only in the gathering but also in the processing, storing, utilization and marketing of free biomass goods. And third, women's roles and responsibilities are pivotal not only to the management of natural resources but also to the management of domestic economy. Studies have shown that women work longer hours, pool more of their income to the household budgets, manage the day today consumption and cash flow needs. Thus, natural resources provide both subsistence needs and cash incomes, particularly to poor rural households.

Effects of Degradation of Natural Resources on Women

- Decrease in quantity and quality of land, water resources and biomass resulting in decline of farm and animal husbandry activities.
- Change in access to natural resources due to increased competition.
- Migration of men to urban areas in search of alternate sources of income.
- Increased family responsibility on women.
- More time spent in collection of forest products, often leads to less time for other activities, such as agriculture, which results in lower levels of income or subsistence.
- Decline in the availability of the forest products, cutting down the women's primary source of income which used to come from the sale of products from cottage industries such as beedies, honey, bamboo-baskets, leaf plates, gum and brooms etc.
- Food insecurity – Basic needs of the family are not met.
- Stretched walking and working hours to fetch fuel wood, fodder and water causing drudgery and poor nutrition to women.
- Deprivation of basic social services such as education, particularly to girls, nutrition, sanitation, health which finally leads to severe poverty.

In fragile-eco regions the gradual degradation of natural resources will deplete the social resources of people such as nutrition, health (particularly of women and children), education, housing etc. With the migration of men to urban areas and increase in the responsibility and work load of women, the girl child of the family becomes victim of degradation. She has to discontinue her education in order to take care of her younger siblings and becomes their foster mother at a very young age of eleven or twelve, sometimes even at much lesser age. These girl children also attend to all domestic chores and feeds the animals while the mother is miles away in the jungles to collect fuel wood and forest produces or in the field attending to some farm activities. In many rural and tribal communities particularly among the resource poor some common social features/phenomena are observed such as 1) drop-out of girl from formal schools, 2) early child marriage, 3) early and frequent child births, 4) malnutrition and poor health, 5) maternal mortality, 6) infant morbidity and mortality, 7) large family size, 8) poor sanitation, 9) debts and 10) poverty. This social phenomenon is a clear picture of vulnerability of women to poverty.

The root cause of these problems is poverty caused due to the degradation of soil, water resources and the scarcity of biomass resources to meet daily needs. In addition to this ignorance of people also plays an important role in deteriorating the social conditions of the people leading to poor quality of life. The parents in resource poor families would like to shrug away with the responsibility of daughters by getting them married at a very young age with minimum expenses. But they are ignorant of the fact that early child marriage would not only spoil the future of their daughter but also becomes a fragile basis for future generations. What can be done to change this situation? Are there any measures to improve the quality of these social conditions and resources? Is there any way to save the future generation of girl children, women and the resource poor families from the vicious cycle of poverty caused due to the depletion and degeneration of the natural resources which in turn caused the depletion of social resources and poor quality of life.

Social regeneration is possible with regeneration of natural resources along with few other essential inputs from the service sectors/governments. But one can not think of successful social regeneration or social resource management in the absence of natural resource management. At this juncture it is worth remembering the historical "CHIPKO" movement in

Utttarakhand of Himalayas during early 70's to save the forest. This was a great movement lead by a few dynamic women leaders namely Gauri Devi, Gunga Devi, Hema Devi and Sarala Behan who could mobilize hundreds of women in the villages around 'Reni Gaon' which was the centre for "Save the Forest Movement". These women with the slogan of "CHIPKO" movement and collective action could make the Government change the policy regarding forests.

Last two decades various efforts are being made by both state and central governments, international donors and NGOs to conserve the natural resources by implementing various projects. To mention some of them, Drought Prone Area Development Programme (DPAP) focussed on non-arable lands, drainage lines for in-situ moisture conservation, agro-forestry, and pasture development and horticulture development. Integrated Wasteland Development Projects (IWDPs) concentrated on silvi pasture and soil and moisture conservation activities. Desert Development Programme (DDP) focussed on reforestation and the National Watershed Development Programme for Rainfed Areas (NWDPRA) combines the features of all these three programmes with additional dimension of improving arable lands through better crop management technologies. The Watershed Programme under the Ministry of Rural Areas and Employment aims to promote the economic development through optimum utilization of natural resources and to encourage restoration of ecological balance in the village through sustained community action and further development of natural resources in the watershed. It lays special emphasis on improving the economic and social conditions of the resource poor and the disadvantaged sections of the community namely assetless and women.

During the World Conference on Women conducted at Beijing in 1995, the specific commitments made by our country were –

- Formulation of a National Policy on Women
- Universalization of mother and child care programmes through ICDS and
- Setting up of Commissioner for women's rights.

In order to translate these commitments into action, a National Policy for Empowerment of Women has been finalized. The primary objective of Ninth Five Year Plan is Empowerment of Women and is committed to creation of an enabling environment where women can freely exercise their rights both within and outside home as equal partners along with men.

Gender Issues in Management and Sharing of Common Resources

Environmental degradation is not the only process that deprives women of natural resources. Ironically, afforestation can also have some of the same negative effects on women as deforestation has. In afforestation, often, the species are chosen primarily for men's enterprises and choice of species required by women either for subsistence needs or market oriented activities is always ignored. In addition to this, conversion of common lands into woodlots, monoculture plantations on private or common lands will restrict access and decrease the variety of available biomass goods to women.

Women have traditionally been responsible for subsistence and survival tasks like providing water and food, fuel and fodder collection. Thus their dependence on the environment is very crucial, being deeply linked with their survival. Degradation of the environment directly aggravates women's deprivation. Therefore it is important to re-establish the interdependence between women and natural resources and reverse the trend of existing developmental patterns which have a negative impact on it.

The debate on this link between gender issues, the environment and development policy has intensified during the last decade. Based on their own experiences, women have provided an entirely different perspective to the environmental debate, a contribution that has just begun to be acknowledged. Women have an important role to play in the development of sustainable and ecologically sound patterns of consumption and production as well as practical approaches to natural resource management. Women's experiences and contributions to maintaining an ecologically sound environment must therefore be central to the agenda for the twenty-first century.

In response, the government has begun to promote an active and visible policy of accepting women's role in all environmental policies and programmes. The lack of sufficient recognition and support for women's contributions to conservation and management of natural resources and safeguarding the environment is being addressed. This recognition may be one that has come only in the last decade. But women's participation in movements in different parts of the country, from the demands of women from West Bengal for land rights during the struggle for land reforms in 1979, to the historical Chipko Movement in the Garhwal Hills of Uttar Pradesh, has been very significant. Much of the environmental legislation which recognises the relationship of human beings with their environment have their roots in agitation and demands by women's groups.

Fuel and Fodder

To promote the regeneration, development and rehabilitation of the degraded forests with active involvement of the community, the mechanism of Forest Development Agencies (FDA) has been initiated at the Conservator's Division level in the country. It is proposed to universalize the FDAs in all the 775 divisions in a phased manner during the Tenth Plan. So far 270 FDAs have been constituted. This is both a financial mechanism as well as a coordinating body for promoting the development of Joint Forest Management in the Afforestation Programme. The major plank of the scheme is to promote micro planning for afforestation to ensure that the needs of the people for fuelwood and fodder are fully met. This will not only reduce the drudgery of the women but ensure the wage employment. This process will also have multiple impact on the quality of life of the people. The guidelines governing the constitution of the FDAs have also taken note of the gender issues. The following provisions have been made:

Vast majority of rural women still depend on the locally available non-conventional sources of energy such as fuel-wood, leaves, animal dung, crop-waste etc. The tribal and other women living in the vicinity of forest areas also depend on non-timber minor forest produce for their livelihood. Departmentalisation of forest management and commercialisation of extraction of forest resources directly impinge on the interests of these women. Tribal women's dependence on forest should not be taken as an encroachment on the forests. The complementarily of relationship between the women and the forest can be strengthened and institutionalised through the proper implementation of the mechanism of Joint Forest Management. Already there are instructions that 50 per cent of the members of the JFM should be women and that the 50 per cent of women members should be present for holding the General Body meeting. There are reports that these instructions are not being followed in many States.

Women are the most interested group for consumption of domestic fuel and therefore their involvement for the spread of non-conventional energy sources like bio-gas, non-smoke chullahs etc. are of critical importance for success of this programme. Air pollution arising out of conventional cooking system affects the health and the respiratory system of the women. The existing programme of smokeless chullahs and other non-conventional energy resources should be taken up on a massive scale for the benefit of women.

Care and Management of Natural Resources—Depletion of Natural Resources

United States burns 20.4 million barrels of oil per day. We are damaging our environment beyond repair by burning copious amounts of hydrocarbons into our atmosphere. According to Al Gore's "Inconvenient Truth", global warming is melting the ice shelf and global sea levels could rise by over 20 feet. Looking at the global temperature data and it's correlation to greenhouse gas emissions, I believe there is indisputable evidence that burning hydrocarbons is responsible for most of the global warming that is wreaking havoc on our weather systems.

Aside from the frightening global warming issue, I am also deeply concerned about our attitude with regard to consumption. Up until just last year, the US was the worlds largest consumer of natural resources. According to David Suzuki's "Sacred Balance" (I absolutely LOVED this book-everyone should read it), since 1940, Americans alone have used up as large a share of the Earth's mineral resources as all previous generations put together.

The real scary thing is, as of last year, consumption in China eclipsed that of the United States in all the worlds resources but oil, and China's 1.3 billion person economy is growing at a frightening 8% annually. Why is this concerning? There are around 6 billion people living on this rock today. Estimating future population growth at only 1% per year, the numbers are staggering. By 2015, experts estimate there will be 7 billion people on the planet. By 2050, there may be as many as 10 billion people living on Earth. Can mother Earth support this extended family? When will we reach the limit of our resources? We live in a culture where incentives exist to encourage doing more with more-not doing more with less. Doing more with less is called "efficiency", doing more with more is called "Gluttony". Bigger, faster, more powerful vehicles that consume more fuel at faster rates, larger meals wrapped in complex, land-fill bound packaging, disposable products filling store shelves-you get the picture. Take the new wave of hybrid cars for example. Hybrid technology that was intended to produce spectacular fuel economy, was flipped around by car makers to instead, produce more horsepower for their new hybrid SUV's! Less green, more mean.

Human Powered vehicles are all about trying to do more with less. How to go faster or farther with less energy. Technologies Incorporated into human powered vehicles like aerodynamics, wheel rolling resistance, mechanical efficiencies and size and weight optimization are directly applicable to the cars and boats and other vehicles that we rely upon in these modern times. Most importantly though, Interest in human power represents an essential shift in basic philosophy from one of 'feasting on earths resources' to a 'do more with less' ideal.

Sustainable Environment and Impact on Women

Sustainable development is a difficult concept to define; it is also continually evolving, which makes it doubly difficult to define. One of the original descriptions of sustainable development is credited to the Brundtland Commission: "Sustainable development is development that meets the needs of the present without compromising the ability of future generations to meet their own needs" (World Commission on Environment and Development, 1987, p 43). Sustainable development is generally thought to have three components: environment, society, and economy. The well-being of these three areas is intertwined, not separate. For example, a healthy, prosperous society relies on a healthy environment to provide food and resources, safe drinking water, and clean air for its citizens. The sustainability paradigm rejects the contention that casualties in the environmental and social realms are inevitable and acceptable consequences of economic development. Thus, the authors consider sustainability to be a paradigm for thinking about a future in which environmental, societal, and economic considerations are balanced in the pursuit of development and improved quality of life.

Principles of Sustainable Development

Many governments and individuals have pondered what sustainable development means beyond a simple one-sentence definition. The *Rio Declaration on Environment and Development* fleshes out the definition by listing 18 principles of sustainability.

- People are entitled to a healthy and productive life in harmony with nature.
- Development today must not undermine the development and environment needs of present and future generations.
- Nations have the sovereign right to exploit their own resources, but without causing environmental damage beyond their borders.
- Nations shall develop international laws to provide compensation for damage that activities under their control cause to areas beyond their borders.
- Nations shall use the precautionary approach to protect the environment. Where there are threats of serious or

irreversible damage, scientific uncertainty shall not be used to postpone cost-effective measures to prevent environmental degradation.

- In order to achieve sustainable development, environmental protection shall constitute an integral part of the development process, and cannot be considered in isolation from it. Eradicating poverty and reducing disparities in living standards in different parts of the world are essential to achieve sustainable development and meet the needs of the majority of people.
- Nations shall cooperate to conserve, protect and restore the health and integrity of the Earth's ecosystem. The developed countries acknowledge the responsibility that they bear in the international pursuit of sustainable development in view of the pressures their societies place on the global environment and of the technologies and financial resources they command.
- Nations should reduce and eliminate unsustainable patterns of production and consumption, and promote appropriate demographic policies.
- Environmental issues are best handled with the participation of all concerned citizens. Nations shall facilitate and encourage public awareness and participation by making environmental information widely available.
- Nations shall enact effective environmental laws, and develop national law regarding liability for the victims of pollution and other environmental damage. Where they have authority, nations shall assess the environmental impact of proposed activities that are likely to have a significant adverse impact.
- Nations should cooperate to promote an open international economic system that will lead to economic growth and sustainable development in all countries. Environmental policies should not be used as an unjustifiable means of restricting international trade.

- The polluter should, in principle, bear the cost of pollution.
- Nations shall warn one another of natural disasters or activities that may have harmful transboundary impacts.
- Sustainable development requires better scientific understanding of the problems. Nations should share knowledge and innovative technologies to achieve the goal of sustainability.
- The full participation of women is essential to achieve sustainable development. The creativity, ideals and courage of youth and the knowledge of indigenous people are needed too. Nations should recognize and support the identity, culture and interests of indigenous people.
- Warfare is inherently destructive of sustainable development, and Nations shall respect international laws protecting the environment in times of armed conflict, and shall cooperate in their further establishment.
- Peace, development and environmental protection are interdependent and indivisible.

The "Rio principles" give us parameters for envisioning locally relevant and culturally appropriate sustainable development for our own nations, regions, and communities. These principles help us to grasp the abstract concept of sustainable development and begin to implement it.

Sustainability

Here are some effective explanations of sustainable development created for different audiences.

Sustainable development has three components: environment, society, and economy. If you consider the three to be overlapping circles of the same size, the area of overlap in the center is human well-being. As the environment, society, and economy become more aligned, the area of overlap increases, and so does human well-being.

The National Town Meeting on Sustainability (May 1999) in Detroit, Michigan, established that the term "sustainable development," although frequently used, is not well understood. We believe that it means new technologies and new ways of doing business, which allow us to improve quality of life today in all economic, environmental, and social dimensions, without impairing the ability of future generations to enjoy quality of life and opportunity at least as good as ours.

The human rights community says that sustainability is attainable through and supported by peace, justice, and democracy.

The Great Law of the Hau de no sau nee (Six Nations Iroquois Confederation) says that in every deliberation we must consider the impact on the seventh generation.

Economics educators say sustainability is living on the interest rather than the principle.

UNIT-VII

Women and Society

Girl Child in Society

Perseverance and inspiration often leads to privilege but without hard work and dedication they'll be no success. The hardest profession to take in life is being a girl child. Discrimination and discrepancy are two most important factors that hamper the journey of every female from the earliest stage of life. Starting from her presence into her mother's womb to infancy, childhood and finally to adulthood, she is outnumbered by the male dominating society of the country.

India is a country where social disadvantage outweighs natural biological advantage of being a girl. A whole range of discriminatory practices including female foeticide, female infanticide, female genital mutilation, son idolization, early marriage and dowry have buried the future of the nation. In India, discriminatory practices have greatly influenced the health and well-being of a girl child, resulting in a higher mortality rate.

It is believed that every year 12 million girls are born in the country but unfortunately only 1/3 of those survive. Some are killed in the womb, some at the time of birth, some die due to ill health and some due to poor nutritional status. Only a few numbers of girls are able to survive till their 15th birthday.

Female feticide and infanticide are the most popular social evils prevailing in the country. This evil is the outcome of poverty, illiteracy and gender discrimination. The country fails to understand, how a mother can be so ruthless and vulnerable.

It is said that God created mothers because He could not be present everywhere. Its unbelievable to realize that a God's representative is continuously killing someone beautiful even before she can come out and see the beauty of nature.

It's painful to confess that the trend still exists in various parts of the country. States like Maharashtra, Haryana, Rajasthan, Tamil Nadu and Punjab are most popular for practicing female foeticide and infanticide.

Poverty, gender discrimination and son preference have also influenced the nutritional status of a girl child. There are almost 75 million malnourished children existing in the country. It is estimated that 75% of the total malnourished children are girls who show signs of chronic and acute malnutrition.

Girls who manage to cross this hard phase of life, gets trapped by the evil society during adolescence and teenage. These are the stages where more nutrition is required for normal growth and development. Unfortunately, nutritional needs are neglected for girls and they are often kept locked within the four walls.

Exacerbate discrimination against female for nutrition and education has led to an increase in child marriage, reduction in fertility rates and population growth, potentially, women's participation in nurturing the future of every nation.

Improper nutrition during adolescence results in various reproductive health disorders. The effects of these disorders further exacerbates by early marriage, closely spaced pregnancies, poor access to information about family planning, traditional practices, etc.

Girl child is the future of every nation and India is no exception. A little amount of care, a handful of warmth and a heart full of love for a girl child can make a big difference. Close your eyes, free your thoughts and hear the voice of God, He is saying something to all of us, "Save Me".

Child Labourers

Child labour, or child labour, refers to the employment of children at regular and sustained labour. This practice is considered exploitative by many international organizations and is illegal in many countries. Child labour was utilized to varying extents through most of history, but entered public dispute with the beginning of universal schooling, with changes in working conditions during industrialization, and with the emergence of the concepts of workers' and children's rights.

Child labour is common in some parts of the world, and can be factory work, mining, prostitution, quarrying, agriculture, helping in the parents' business, having one's own small business (for example selling food), or doing odd jobs. Some children work as guides for tourists, sometimes combined with bringing in business for shops and restaurants (where they may also work as waiters). Other children are forced to do tedious and repetitive jobs such as: assembling boxes, polishing shoes, stocking a store's products, or cleaning. However, rather than in factories and sweatshops, most child labour occurs in the informal sector, "selling many things on the streets, at work in agriculture or hidden away in houses—far from the reach of official labour inspectors and from media scrutiny." And all the work that they did was done in all types of weather; and was also done for minimal pay. As long as there is family poverty there will be child labour.

According to UNICEF, there are an estimated 158 million children aged 5 to 14 in child labour worldwide, excluding child domestic labour.

Changing Role of Women

In nineteenth century Britain, families were usually large and, in most households, men, women, and children all contributed towards the family wage. Although they were economically very important, women in Britain had fewer rights in law than men. Until 1857, a married woman had no right to divorce her husband, and until 1882 a woman's earnings, along with any property or money she brought to the marriage, automatically belonged to her husband.

In the late nineteenth and early twentieth centuries, an increasing number of women campaigned and demonstrated for greater rights and, in particular, the right to vote. However, the protests and demonstrations were halted during the First World War, as women joined in the war effort and took on a much greater variety of work than they had done before. Women (over the age of 30) were finally given the right to vote and to stand for election for Parliament after the War had ended in 1918. It wasn't until 1928 that women in Britain received voting rights at the same age as men.

Despite these improvements, women still faced discrimination in the workplace. When a woman married, it was quite common for her to be asked to leave work by her employer. Many jobs were closed to women, and women found it very difficult to enter university. The 1960s and 70s saw increasing pressure from women for equal rights and, during this period, laws were passed giving women the right to equal pay and prohibiting employers from discriminating against women because of their sex.

Marriage

Women were expected to marry and have children. This is what their lot in life was. If a woman didn't marry, there were few reasons. One, her family must have needed her at home to help them with their other children or to make tribute cloth. It was also possible that she would join the priesthood and live in the church. She could also live as a prostitute but we will talk about that later.

Marriage was a step though that most women in Aztec society made. They had a strict marriage plan that was followed by all Aztec societies. The courtship was initiated by the boys family in most all cases. They would send a matrimonial agent to the house of the girl and make their plea. In Aztec culture, it was made that the first attempt be denied by the girls family, they usually claiming their daughter to be too young. But this was not to be taken seriously, it was simply their way of one wooing the other and it lasted for many days.

Once the offer was accepted by the parents of the girl, she was lectured most repetitively by her family about what she was to do as a new bride. She of course, was not allowed to offer an opinion and so listened respectfully as she was told she was no longer a child but a woman and to behave as so. It is unsure in Aztec society, even with Sahagun's readings, if the girl was to give a dowry or if the boy offered gifts to her family. It is known that in Mayan society, a young man must work in the house of his in-laws for at least four years.

Once the wedding was announced, the relatives and friends of both families were invited to celebrate and the priests were ordered to pick the date for the wedding. They would pick a "good" day for the wedding to be held so that the new bride and groom would be prosperous. On the day of the wedding, the bride was washed, hair was cleaned, face was made up with ochre and powdered with sulfur purites, so to give the appearance of shining. Feathers of exotic birds were put on her arms and legs and she was dressed in the finest embroidered garments the family owned.

At sunset, the groom's family came to her house and would give their thanks and apologies to the family of the bride. Then the bride would kneel on a black cloth and an older woman would pick her up and carry her on her back to the house of the groom. The female relatives would follow in line behind. Once at the house of the groom, the bride would be set upon the hearth and the groom would sit next to her on her right. The matrimonial agent would tie the ends of the man's shirt to the brides garment and then feed each of them four bites of maize cake. This signified the marriage ceremony and they were now husband and wife.

After this, priestesses would come and lead the new couple to a room where they were to be left alone, with only priestesses outside to stand guard. The rest of the family would have festivities for the next four days. *Marriage signified the bondage of a woman transferring from their father to their husband.*

Single Parent

A single parent (also lone parent and sole parent) is a parent who cares for one or more children without the assistance of another parent in the home. "Single parenthood" may vary according to the local laws of different nations or regions.

Single parenthood may occur for a variety of reasons. It could be opted for by the parent (as in divorce, adoption, artificial insemination, surrogate motherhood, or extramarital pregnancy), or be the result of an unforeseeable occurrence (such as death or abandonment by one parent).

The living and parenting arrangements of single parents are diverse. A number live in households with family or other adults. When parents separate, one party usually parents for the majority of the time but most continue to share parenting to some extent with the other parent.

Single parenthood is a stage of life rather than a lifelong family form. Many re-partner and form a stepfamily.

Widows

A widow is a woman whose husband has died. A man whose wife has died is a widower. The state of having lost one's spouse to death is termed widowhood or (occasionally) viduity. The adjective is widowed.

Economic Position of Widows

The economic position of widows has been an important social issue in many societies. In societies in which the husband was typically the sole provider, his death could plunge his family into poverty. This was aggravated by women's longer life spans, and that men generally marry women younger than themselves. Many charities existed to help widows and orphans (often, not children without parents, but children without a contributing father) in need.

However, even in some patriarchal societies, widows could maintain economic independence. A widow could carry on her late husband's business and consequently be accorded certain rights, such as the right to enter guilds. More recently, widows of elected officials have been among the first women elected to office in many countries (e.g. Corazon Aquino).

There were implications for sexual freedom as well; although some wills contained *dum casta* provisions (requiring widows to remain unmarried in order to receive inheritance), in societies preventing divorce, widowhood permitted women to remarry and have a greater range of sexual experiences.

In some other cultures, widows are treated differently. For instance, in India there is often an elaborate ceremony during the funeral of a widow's husband, including smashing the bangles, removing the bindi as well as any colorful attire, and requiring the woman to wear white clothes, the colour of mourning. Earlier it was compulsory to wear all white after the husband was dead, and even Widow burning (sati or suttee) was practiced sometimes.

However in modern-day culture this has gradually given way to wearing colored clothing. Sati practice has been banned in India for more than a century. The ban began under British rule of India owing to the persistence of social reformer RajaRam Mohan Roy.

In other cultures, widows are *required* to remarry within the family of their late husband; see widow inheritance. This started as a custom to ensure that no widow could be kicked out of her home and face a life without financial provision, but it can also be used to keep money within the family. In addition, it is an important factor in the transmission of HIV within certain communities, e.g. the Luo, and is being challenged on human rights grounds.

Cultural References to Widows

- The Wife of Bath in Geoffrey Chaucer's *Canterbury Tales* refers to having been widowed five times, permitting her greater sexual experience.
- Water (2005 film) a film directed and written by Deepa Mehta, explores the lives of widows at an ashram in Varanasi, India.
- Baabul (2006 film), is an Indian film about a widow's remarriage.
- The plot of the Disney film Up was centered around a widower determined to fufill his deceased spouse's dream and avoid house eviction by lifting his residence off the ground with balloons.

Women and Development (WAD) and Gender and Development (GAD)

Internationally, the women's movement has given birth to a number of nongovernmental organizations (NGOs) and groups that continue to challenge many of the implied and stated assumptions of the traditional feminist movement. These NGOs and groups offer indigenous approaches to solving women's problems in their particular environments. The focus of many NGOs is action, developing programmes and institutions to improve the daily lives of women in their communities.

As we have seen, the general belief among women's NGOs and other development institutions is that the concepts of modernization and development have often led the primary international agencies to effectively ignore the plight of women in the societies they target and, in many instances, make the women worse off. The failure of their programmes has forced indigenous NGOs and other entities to develop their own solutions.

Initiatives to improve women's economic situations demonstrate the need for indigenous solutions to women's problems. Nancy Barry, President of Women's World Banking, remarked, "What has become very clear is that what women need is access, not subsidies. They need opportunities, not paternalism" (Howells 1993).

Research and Action

Research should inform both theorizing and policy-making, to make these credible. The women's movement and the various national and international institutions involved in development have recognized the importance of research and data, as illustrated in the foreword to the United Nations document *The World's Women 1970–1990*:

> *For many years, women's advocates have challenged stereotypes depicting women as passive, dependent and inferior to men. But efforts to reinforce their challenges with hard evidence have been undercut by serious limitations in available statistics and analysis, including a male bias in the definition and collection of many*

statistics and indicators. ... Putting this kind of numerical and analytical spotlight on the needs, the efforts and the contributions of women is one of the best ways to speed the process of moving from agenda to policy to practice to a world of peace, equality and sustained development. — United Nations (1991)

The creation of Development Alternatives with Women for a New Era (DAWN) and DAWN's stated objectives are evidence that NGOs emphasize research. Discussed below are some currently active women's NGOs. Research is a critical activity of each of them. The exercises in each section use the following abbreviations for development approaches: WID, women in development; WAD, women and development; and GAD, gender and development.

Women's World Banking

Women's World Banking (WWB) is a nonprofit financial institution created in 1979 to give poor female entrepreneurs access to financing, market information, and training. It grew out of the 1975 United Nations World Conference on Women, held in Mexico City, to address the need for global structures to fund women in microenterprises. WWB currently operates in more than 50 countries and has provided assistance to more than 1 million clients internationally. WWB's goal is to help poor women create wealth.

Four basic principles inform WWB's policy formulation and operations:

"Local-global" should replace "North-South" as the prevailing paradigm, to reflect the belief in local initiative and local institutions;

Women have the power to transform the Earth through their local institutions (Nancy Barry, cited in Howells 1993);

Women are dynamic economic agents, not passive beneficiaries of social services; and

"Lateral learning," a training methodology through which women share their business knowledge with each other and thus learn from their peers, is important.

Self-employed Women's Association

The Self-Employed Women's Association (SEWA) is a union of 40 000 of India's poorest women. It is an example of a new development model relevant to low-income earners. The membership covers the range of self-employed women typically working in the informal sector and effectively marginalized by mainstream development strategies:

SEWA successfully integrates a complex myriad of lives, occupations and issues into one union. Under SEWA, women have forged a new model of what a trade union can be — a Third world model, which defies conventional conceptions about who unions organize and what they do for their members. Most unions in the world organize workers in one kind of industry, who share one fixed workplace, and concern themselves with problems which revolve only around the work issues of their members. Some unions do take up issues related to women workers, or include a women's wing in the larger body of the union, but there are very few unions in the world which are devoted entirely to a female membership, as SEWA is.

SEWA organizes women who work in their homes, in the streets of cities, in the fields and villages of rural India, with no fixed employer, carving their small niches in the economy, day by day, with only their wits to guide them against incredible odds of vulnerability, invisibility, and poverty.These then are the common denominators around which SEWA has gathered 30,000 members into its fold since its inception in 1972: they are women, they are "self-employed," and they are poor. From these common bases, diverse individuality in trades, religious and ethnic backgrounds, and living environments are brought together.

Where these women are individually extremely vulnerable to the forces of their day-to-day poverty which are compounded by financial exploitation, physical abuse, and general social harassment, they have found that collectively they are able to struggle against these forces and odds to effect change in their lives and work. SEWA's choice of the term "self-employed" to define this large sector of workers was consciously made to give positive status to people who are often described negatively as informal, unorganised, marginal, or peripheral. — Rose (1992, pp. 16–17)

The WAD approach has been criticized for failing to challenge male-dominated power structures and for failing, as a result, to transform existing social structures. SEWA appears to fall into this category. However, further examination of SEWA's approach to organizing women demonstrates that the institution recognizes the importance of confronting existing power structures:

There is not just one goal which is fought for. Women understand that change is a process of struggles. Their experience has equipped them for this — they have struggled all their lives. ...

Whether small or large in nature, the changes this convergence has generated continue to influence increasingly broader spheres. The day-to-day, grassroots changes centre around trying to improve women's working situations. The tactics vary with each individual trade, but usually begin with confronting the direct exploiter and presenting him with demands for change. For women engaged in piece-rate work, this means asking the contractor for higher wages. For vendors, it means confronting the police officers who beat the women and extract bribes from them on charges of "encroachment." For women providing services, it means ensuring fair wages and steady work.

From the beginning of SEWA's work, however, it has been apparent that this direct confrontation could never accomplish all the long-term, structural and social changes needed to seriously change women's lives. Women who earn just enough each day to keep their families going are vulnerable. Missing one day's work can mean a crisis in the family. ...

Yet SEWA has found that the only way to bring change is to "organise, organise, and organise some more." In numbers they have found voice and strength. When they stand in sufficient numbers, their voices do shake the balance and change things in their favour — from the tactics of their neighbourhood trader or local landowner, up to the national and international policies. Once they have policy backing, the ground is firmer from which to organise more women and push their demands into broader spheres. —Rose (1992)

Gender Equality and Development

- Gender Equality Guidelines
- Australia's approach to eliminating violence against women
- Integrating gender equality in the Solomon Islands programme
- Publications & research
- Workshop: Gender, Youth and Economic Empowerment in the Pacific

Gender equality means women and men have equal opportunities to realise their individual potential, to contribute to their country's economic and social development and to benefit equally from their participation in society.

Gender inequality restricts a country's economic growth. Removing inequalities gives societies a better chance to develop. When women and men have relative equality, economies grow faster, children's health improves and there is less corruption. Gender equality is an important human right.

While gains have been made, gender inequalities in health and education are still striking given that:

- Two-thirds of the 800 million people in the world who lack basic literacy skills are female
- Women hold an average of three per cent of seats in national parliaments in Pacific island countries, and an average of 19 per cent of seats in East Asia and
- half a million women die each year from complications during pregnancy-99 per cent of them in developing countries.

Investments in women's and girls' education and health yield some of the highest returns of all development investments, including reduced rates of maternal mortality, better educated and healthier children and increased household incomes.

Achieving gender equality extends beyond improving female health and education. It means access to economic resources, participation and leadership in decision making, respect for the human rights of women, and an increased capacity to tackle gender inequalities. These are the four interrelated factors that development investments need to address to advance gender equality. Strategies and targets need to engage women and girls more effectively, and the effectiveness of these strategies needs to be monitored.

Development results cannot be maximised without attending to the different needs, interests, priorities and roles of women, men, boys and girls, and the relations between them. Development programmes cannot succeed without the participation and cooperation of all members of the community.

Gender and Australia's Aid Programme

Gender equality is a guiding principle of the Australian aid programme and is integral to all Australian Government aid policies, programmes and initiatives.

Australia's commitment means that women's and girls' views, needs, interests and rights shape the development agenda as much as men's and boys'. Women and men will participate in and benefit equally from the aid programme, and development will support progress towards equality between women and men, boys and girls.

Policy Framework

The publication Gender Equality in Australia's Aid Programme-Why and How, sets out what Australia aims to achieve through the aid programme.

The goal of the policy is to reduce poverty by advancing gender equality and empowering women. Australia aims to:

- Improve the economic status of women
- Promote equal participation of women in decision making and leadership, including in fragile states and conflict situations
- Improve equitable health and education outcomes for women, men, girls and boys

- Ensure gender equality is advanced in regional cooperation efforts.

Progress towards gender equality depends upon strategic and well targeted interventions. The policy provides direction for setting priorities. An important priority is to ensure that all country and regional strategies and their performance frameworks integrate gender equality objectives and indicators and identify actions for tackling inequality.

In addition, each country programme will develop integrated gender equality strategies at the initiative level in priority areas. Within selected country programmes we will also scale-up specific initiatives to advance gender equality and empower women.

Australia and the international community have learned important lessons about the operating principles that must underpin efforts to promote gender equality through aid. Australia will work to:

- Strengthen partner ownership and support country-driven priorities on advancing gender equality
- Engage with both men and women to advance gender equality
- Strengthen accountability mechanisms to increase effectiveness
- Collect and analyse information to improve gender equality results.

Working with partner countries to strengthen their capacity to implement and monitor gender equality measures continues to be a fundamental requirement. Getting results requires partner government commitment to implement their priorities for gender equality. Australian assistance will align to the individual country's priorities and policy frameworks, and address their particular capacity constraints.

Monitoring and evaluation is critical to achieving gender equality results and for gathering evidence on the contribution that gender equality makes to poverty reduction and sustainable development.

Monitoring of gender equality results in country and regional programmes through their annual performance updates will strengthen accountability, and help to identify areas where gender capacity building is needed.

Women, Gender and Development Directorate

Description and overview of the Directorate:

- *The Operational Framework:* The new AU dispensation vis-à-vis promotion of gender equality heralds a new era in the way gender issues are thenceforth to be managed on the continent, and goes a long way towards valorizing efforts and initiatives in this regard. Article 4(1) of the Constitutive Ac mandates the Union to function in accordance with the principle of "promotion of gender equality", and, according to Article 8 of the Statutes of the Commission of the Union, ultimate responsibility for gender mainstreaming within the Commission lies with the Chairperson. To facilitate execution of this mandate, Article 12(3) of the Statues provides that a mechanism "shall be established in the Office of the Chairperson to coordinate all activities and programmes of the Commission related to gender issues". The Women, Gender and Development Directorate, (Gender Directorate) is that mechanism-it is the vehicle via which the Commission advances the principle of gender equality through gender mainstreaming.
- *Rationale and General Objective:* To date the women of Africa, like women elsewhere, have not been included as full, equal and effective stakeholders in processes that determine their lives. For example, women continue to have less access to education than men; they continue to have less employment and advancement opportunities; their role and contribution to national and continental development processes are neither recognized nor rewarded; they continue to be absent from decision-making; and, although they bear the brunt of conflicts, women are generally not included in peace negotiations or other initiatives in this regard.

The general objective of the gender programme of the AU is to redress the inequities inherent in such a situation, and thereby ensure that women and men have equal access to factors needed for their equal and unhindered participation in development and other processes that shape and define their conditions of life and work.

- *Programmatic Thrust and Activities:* The AU gender programme involves both stand-alone women's empowerment programmes, as well as programmes to incorporate gender into all the activities of the Commission. In this regard, the Gender Directorate has a two-fold approach to its work. First, a women-targeted women-in-development approach which recognizes that women are starting from a more disadvantaged position than men, and, therefore, seeks to remove the obstacles that women suffer. This is in order to empower women so as to enable them to compete on a level of equality with men. The second is a more holistic, all-encompassing gender-and-development approach, which seeks to ensure that women are part of mainstream activities as equal stakeholders with men.

  The first approach involves activities that include specialist women's empowerment programmes such as women and education; women and health; women and poverty eradication; women in agriculture; women, trade and the economy; women in the peace process; women in politics and decision-making; the gender dimensions of ageing, and women within the NEPAD process, among others.

  The second approach involves activities directed at ensuring that the Commission takes gender into consideration in all its work, so that the needs of both women and men are taken into consideration across the whole spectrum of AU activities, so as to enable both men and women to benefit equally.

  In other words, both the women-in-development and the gender-and-development approaches being adopted by the Gender Directorate are informed by and drew from the African and Beijing Platforms for Action.

- *Core Functions:* In line with the preferred approach of the gender programme of the Commission, the core functions of the Gender Directorate are: gender mainstreaming; coordination; advocacy; policy; performance tracking, monitoring and evaluation; gender training and capacity building; research; communication, networking and liaison.

This is in addition to the specialist programmes that are undertaken within the women's empowerment framework in line with the need to even out the playing field that is currently disproportionately skewed in favour of men, as already indicated above.

In undertaking its work, the Gender Directorate continues to follow-up on, and consolidate, activities that have been successfully pursued by the OAU in the past. These include, among others, the AU Policy Framework and Plan of Action on Ageing; the Draft Protocol to the African Charter on Human and Peoples' Rights on the Rights of Women in Africa; the Addis Ababa Declaration on the Eradication of Harmful Traditional Practices; the African Women Committee on Peace and Development; the Plan of Action on Enhancing the Participation of Refugee, Returnee and Internally Displaced Women and Children in Post-Conflict Reintegration, Rehabilitation, Reconstruction and Peace Building; and the Kampala Declaration and Plan of Action on the Empowerment of Women Through Functional Literacy and Education of the Girl-Child.

In undertaking its work, the Gender Directorate also continues to place emphasis on partnership, both internally within the Commission, and externally with the other stakeholders. Externally, this involves outreach activities directed at bringing in more actors to buy into and push the continental gender agenda forward, thereby making the gender programme of the Commission both more grounded and more relevant to the actual needs of its constituency. Internally, such an approach entails ensuring that whatever programmes the Commission offers to its Member States and other stakeholders are already engendered by the time they leave the Commission, so that the Commission leads by example, as it should.

State Policy and Programmes Women Development Approaches in Indian five year Plans

The National policy for the empowerment of women (2001) in its action plan numbered 12.2 says *"The strategy of Women's Component Plan adopted in the Ninth Plan of ensuring that not less than 30% of benefits/funds flow to women from all Ministries and Departments will be implemented effectively so that the needs and interests of women and girls are addressed by all concerned sectors. The Department of Women and Child Development being the nodal Ministry will monitor and review the progress of the implementation of the Component Plan from time to time, in terms of both quality and quantity in collaboration with the Planning Commission*". The shift in thinking and development approach on women is reflected in concrete measures in the decentralized planning process which was initiated in Kerala and it led to certain changes in the position and status of women in the state of Kerala.

The gradual evolution of the Women Component Plan (WCP) in the decentralized planning process in Kerala and the role of the women as perceived in the WCP can only be understood by looking at how the concept of 'development' emerged and changed over the years at the International and national level, how this further had an impact on the developmental plans at various levels and on the understanding regarding the role of women in these plans.

In the first part of this paper, we will be dealing with the evolution of the concept of development at the International and national levels and the factors which influenced such a change. In the second part, the background of Kerala, the status of women and the approaches of the decentralization initiative are discussed.

The concept of women in development emerged in the 70's within the broader institutionalized field of modernization and development and the feminist movement in the west. The will to realize a programme of 'development' to address poverty in the third world was announced by the US President Truman in 1949. It was his intention that the old imperialism of exploitation for foreign profit was to be replaced with a democratic development programme of 'fair dealing'. The target of this programme was the poverty and misery of 'under development' which was viewed as threatening to the security of the Third world and the first world(the developed world called themselves the first world in juxtaposition with the socialist second world). It was an entirely western project to 'modernize' the post colonial societies with a precise mission to curb the attraction towards 'communism'. Modernization meant shattering the existing traditional ties and feudal mode of production, imposing the logic of modern science as the basis for developing the productive forces and transforming the society which they called 'living at subsistence' and therefore poor, into growth oriented and richer societies

An array of institutions-the International bank for Reconstruction and Development (the World Bank), the International Monetary Fund (IMF), a number of UN agencies and programmes, major multilateral and bilateral agencies and educational and research centers-grew rapidly into a powerful development apparatus. The ideology of this apparatus was predicated on a faith in the value of a planned, managerial and interventionist approach to growth and national development.

After the 1st development decade, which focused on *the growth model*, there was increasing dissatisfaction and disillusionment. It was this dissatisfaction, which led to the reformulation of development goals to take greater account of poverty, distribution and the meeting of basic needs. In the 70's, the UN development strategy declared that the "Ultimate objective of development must be to bring about sustained improvement in the well being of the individual and bestow benefits on all. If undue privileges, extremes of wealth and social injustice persist, then development fails in its essential purpose".

There was new sensitivity to the links between economic and social justice. These changes in the ideological development also resulted in greater attention being paid to women's issues especially in areas of *food and population*. With this, greater importance was given to women, her role in the family, the food chain and population control. There was a growing trend emphasizing that a "dollar spent on preventing births added one hundred times more to income per head in the developing world than it would in other forms of aid". (Enke, 1969). Women were therefore brought into the policy process on *very sex specific terms* – as housewives, mothers, and 'at-risk' reproducers. So while mainstream development efforts targeted only men, *women were relegated to welfare through investments in nutrition education, home economics, family planning* etc. Emphasizing the 'reproductive' role of women *made invisible the actual labour of women in the household.*

The publication of Esther Bosrup's book "Women's role in economic development" focused women in new perspective. She challenged the stereotyped assumptions of female domesticity and argued that 'various colonial and post colonial governments had systematically bypassed women in diffusion of new technologies, extension services and other productive inputs because of their misconceptions of what women did'. Women were recognized as economic actors and contributing to development process. She challenged the assumption that the benefits of development would automatically trickle down to the poor; she pointed out that women's declining status is a clear indication of the contrary and that the few opportunities available to women in modern sector meant that they were bound to large extent to the subsistence and informal sectors

The basic problem of development for women prior to 1975 was that policy makers did not 'see' women. There fore the 1st wave of official feminism within the international development agencies was to make women 'visible' as a category in development research and policy. This has come to be characterized as the WID (Women In Development approach). The declaration by UN of the international year in 1975 and later the decade for women with the official themes of *equality, peace and development* signified the new visibility of WID in international forums.

In the 70's and 80's insights from the women's movement were fed into the thinking and practice of development aid, resulting first in the Women and Development (WID) and later into Gender and Development (GAD) approaches The WID approaches targeted women for development, co operation and integrating them in to the general activities of such practices. According to Carolyn Hannan, the integration strategy is about "women's involvement-participation, representation, parity, and numbers-usually in a development agenda decided upon by others". WID made women a constituency in the development discourse and practice. However women were viewed in isolation, not in relations and as a homogenous group free from conflicts of interests. Even though much of the strategy was one of integration into development projects and institutions, the silence of *addressing the structural constraints and the way institutions are gendered,* led to an isolation, where much of the efforts stopped at "*adding on*" women to mainstream development. Mainstream development itself was critiqued by feminists as one, which followed the market mechanism and where women's contributions were invisible, and without value. The inter linkages between class structures and other power structures like caste, ethnicity and race were also missed out in this approach.

Buvinic (1983) has suggested that approaches to WID can be classified as '*Welfare, Anti-poverty and Equity*. Moser (1989) added two further classifications: *Efficiency and Empowerment*. Each of these policy approaches represents a different set of imperatives, but they should not be regarded as either chronologically or mutually exclusive'. For analytical purposes, however, welfare and efficiency has been constituted as the two dominant and opposing approaches, located as it were at the either end of the policy spectrum.

Since the 1950's, women have been perceived in development theory and practice only as 'mothers' and passive receivers of 'welfare' with the narrow aim of making women better mothers for their children. Equity argument expected of women to have the possibility to take part in public spheres, instead of being confined within domestic sphere as in the welfare approach.

In the Anti-poverty approach, the new visibility of women's poor positions around the world was connected to under development but not to subordination. The basic needs of the family were in focus rather than the unequal access to resources which lead to, for example lack of clean water being seen as a "women's problem".

The approach that really made an impact on moving WID into a higher politics was "Efficiency". Women were instruments, agents who could manage most of the 80's economic and environmental crisis only by a small amount of investment. For example micro-credit programmes, which could create a positive outcome in the cost-benefit analysis was widely adopted world over. The *Equity* approach was too radical to be incorporated in to the official programmes. We will talk about the *Empowerment* approach later.

The first world plan of action that emerged out of the first International Conference of women(1975)in Mexico contained a 'bold women's agenda' which called for the achievement of equality between sexes within the context of changed relations between north and south. It also called for the re assessment of the family and societal roles assigned to different sexes. However, when time came for implementation, this early call for radical change soon evaporated.

Collectivity and Group Dynamics-Self Help Groups Women and Leadership

In the early decades of planning problems of women were looked upon as problems of social welfare, rather than of development. The drawback of the welfare approach was that it did nothing to eliminate the social discrimination against and subordination of women. In almost all plans for poverty alleviation and social change, disadvantaged women became a 'target' in developmental activities rather than a group to be co-opted as active participants (Beijing Conference, 1996). Since 1970, policy makers and academicians started thinking as to how development programmes could be linked to poor women.

Women issues are development issues and by-passing them in development programmes means leaving almost half of human resources outside development intervention (CIRDAP Development Digest, 1998). Issues of poverty among women are quite distinct and complicated. Their general poverty conditions, morbidity, lack of food, drinking water, and sanitation facilities are some of the major issues that need attention. Female members of a poor household are often worse off than its male members because of gender discrimination in the distribution of food and other entitlements within the household. 'Increasingly poverty has a woman's face' (Human Development Report, 1995). The Human Development Reports of UNDP from 1990 onwards attest to the fact of growing feminisation of poverty.

Review of Policy Approaches to Women

"Nothing, arguably, is as important today in the political economy of development as an adequate recognition of political, economic, and social participation and leadership of women" (Amartya Sen, 1999). While a large part of the world continues to look at women's issues in terms of paternalism and well-being, the concept of women's empowerment in the social, political, and economic order as a pre-requisite of human development is hardly given the priority that it deserves. Throughout the Third World, particularly in the past 15 years, there has been a proliferation of policies, programmes, and projects designed to assist lowincome women. This concern for low-income women's needs has coincided historically with recognition of their important role in development. Since the 1950's, many different intervention strategies have been formulated to address women's needs which reflect changes in macro-level economic and social policy approaches to Third World Development, as well as in state policy towards women.

The Concept of Self-help Group

Experience in many countries demonstrates that poor women make investments wisely and earn returns (Human Resource Development, 1995). However, the flow of financial assistance to them was too marginal, if at all, to enable them to cross the poverty line.The need to create a grassroots organisational base to enable women to come together, to analyse their issues and problems themselves, and to fulfil their needs was strongly advocated.

In fact, experience shows that some of the successful 'group-based participatory programmes' have made significant improvement in the conditions of living poor women. The concept of self-help groups gained significance, especially after 1976 when Prof. Mohammed Yunus of Bangladesh began experimenting with micro-credit and women SHGs.

The strategy made a quiet revolution in Bangladesh in poverty eradication 'by empowering the poor women'.

SHGs are small informal associations created for the purpose of enabling members to reap economic benefit out of mutual help, solidarity, and joint responsibility. The benefits include mobilisation of savings and credit facilities and pursuit of group enterprise activities. The group-based approach not only enables the poor to accumulate capital by way of small savings but also helps them to get access to formal credit facilities (Shylendra, 1998). These groups by way of joint liability enable the poor to overcome the problem of collateral security and thus free them from the clutches of moneylenders.

The joint liability not only improves group members' accessibility to credit, but also creates mechanisms like peer monitoring leading to better loan recoveries (Stiglitz, 1993). Besides, some of the basic characteristics of SHGs like small size of membership and homogeneity of composition, bring about cohesiveness and effective participation of members in the functioning of the group (Fernandez, 1994). In general, SHGs created on the above lines of functioning have been able to reach the poor effectively, especially women and help them obtain easy access to facilities like savings and credit and empower them (National Bank, 1995).

Studies reveal that certain elements become crucial or critical for the successful formation and functioning of the groups. These include voluntary nature of the group, small size and homogeneity of membership, transparent and participative decision-making, and brisk use of funds for micro-enterprise creation. (Fernadez, 1994). Regular meeting of the members fosters meaningful relationship among them and issues other than thrift and credit, issues on gender and social problems also get a platform for discussion.

Micro-financing: Shift from the Traditional Banking System

Micro-financing has turned out to be an effective strategy for formal financing agencies.

Group lending minimises transaction cost and at the same time the members of a group can avail small loans through that group. The chances of misutilisation are minimal and there is assured repayment because of peer monitoring by the group. The group concept has enabled the rural poor to develop the savings habit and minimise extravagance.

For the SHG members, the system has been found beneficial because of minimal procedural formalities, access to institutional credit without collateral offering, full autonomy in the selection of activity, and the availability of thrift for meeting urgent needs. The skill needed for filling the application forms and the absence of procedural formalities have made the programme customer-friendly. Besides, the flexible repayment schedule enables them to repay as and when it is convenient. The group will see to it that prompt repayment is made, as they are likely to get repeat loans. The micro-sized, supplementary income-generating activities pursued by the members defy the conventional standards of unit cost and unit size prescribed by banks and government departments. The smaller unit size allows women to pursue the activities in their spare time and contribute to the family's income.

Panchayati Raj

The Panchayat is a South Asian political system mainly in India, Pakistan, and Nepal. "Panchayat" literally means assembly (*yat*) of five (*panch*) wise and respected elders chosen and accepted by the village community. Traditionally, these assemblies settled disputes between individuals and villages.

Modern Indian government has decentralised several administrative functions to the village level, empowering elected gram panchayats. Gram panchayats are not to be confused with the unelected khap panchayats (or caste panchayats) found in some parts of India.

The term 'panchayat raj' is relatively new, having originated during the British administration. 'Raj' literally means governance or government. Mahatma Gandhi advocated *Panchayati Raj*, a decentralized form of Government where each village is responsible for its own affairs, as the foundation of India's political system. His term for such a vision was "Gram Swaraj" (Village Self-governance).

It was adopted by state governments during the 1950s and 60s as laws were passed to establish Panchayats in various states. It also found backing in the Indian Constitution, with the 73rd amendment in 1992 to accommodate the idea. The Amendment Act of 1992 contains provision for devolution of powers and responsibilities to the panchayats to both for preparation of plans for economic development and social justice and for implementation in relation to twenty-nine subjects listed in the eleventh schedule of the constitution.

Political Role and Participation

A key part of Womankind's work is to promote women's civil and political participation.

Throughout the world, the power relations that shape social, political, economic and cultural life prevent women from participating fully in all areas of their lives, whether it's in the home, or in the public arena. While women's dedicated efforts to challenge the status quo have allowed more women to reach positions of power in recent years, women:

- continue to be under-represented in all areas of decision-making, such as religion, the media, culture and the law
- still face significant barriers to their full and equal participation in the structures and institutions which govern their lives.

Womankind seeks to empower and enable women to overcome the obstacles which prevent them from participating on an equal footing with men, through a combination of education, training, networking and lobbying.

What do we mean by women's civil and political participation?

Women's civil and political participation refers to women's ability to participate equally with men, at all levels, and in all aspects of public and political life and decision-making. It extends to other arenas, such as family life, cultural and social affairs and the economy.

So, whether it's deciding how the household income is spent or determining how the country is run, WOMANKIND believes that women have the right to an equal say in all matters that have an impact on their lives. This right is enshrined in a number of human rights instruments, as well as in national constitutions and laws.

Several human rights mechanisms, including the International Convention on Civil and Political Rights and the International Convention for the Elimination of All Forms of Discrimination Against Women, elaborate the nature of women's civil and political rights and the steps required to promote greater equality between women and men in this area. The Beijing Platform for Action, the principal international action plan on women's rights, contains a section on women in power and decision-making, which states that the empowerment and autonomy of women and the improvement of women's social, economic and political status is essential for the achievement of both transparent and accountable government and administration and sustainable development in all areas of life.

Women's participation in public life and decision-making depends on several factors, including:

- an awareness of their rights and how to claim them
- access to information about laws, policies and the institutions and structures which govern their lives
- confidence, self-esteem and the skills to challenge and confront existing power structures

- support networks and positive role models
- an enabling environment, meaning a political, legal, economic and cultural climate that allows women to engage in decision-making processes in a sustainable and effective way

What are the obstacles to women's civil and political participation?

There are a number of factors which constrain women's participation in public life and decision-making, including:

- economic dependency and a lack of adequate financial resources
- illiteracy and limited access to education and the same work opportunities as men
- discriminatory cultural and social attitudes and negative stereotypes perpetuated in the family and in public life
- burden of responsibilities in the home
- intimidation, harassment and violence
- lack of access to information

What is Womankind doing to tackle these barriers and to promote women's civil and political participation?

Women around the world have demonstrated the huge contribution they can make when given the opportunity to sit in public office or to participate in or lead the work of community and informal organisations. WOMANKIND supports the efforts of women, including the most marginalised, such as indigenous women, to challenge their unequal status with men and to bring the issues of concern to them to the decision-making table.

In Albania we support training for existing and potential women leaders in local and national elections. We work with a range of actors, including journalists and politicians, to change negative attitudes and to create an enabling environment for women's participation.

In Afghanistan we provide training in basic health and literacy skills and human rights education to give women the practical skills they need to move out of poverty and to take part in the development of their communities and countries. We also support the lobbying of decision-makers to increase women's representation at all levels of government.

In India Womankind has supported education and training for women from the poorest and most marginalized dalit and tribal communities in Tamil Nadu state to give them the confidence and skills to speak out about the issues that concern them, such as electricity and water for their communities. Some of the women have gone on to stand for local council elections.

- In September 2004, Womankind brought together partners from Albania, South Africa and Zimbabwe, for a learning exchange to share ideas and strategies for strengthening women's participation in politics at local and national level.
- In March 2005, Womankind hosted a panel discussion on the theme of 'women and governance in times of conflict' at the annual Commission on the Status of Women. Partners from Somalia, Afghanistan, Israel, Zimbabwe and South Africa were invited to share their experiences of working to increase women's participation in conflict-resolution and peace-building with an audience of activists, including the Nobel Peace Prize Laureate, Wangari Maathai, and policy-makers.

How Does This Fit with Womankind's Work to Reduce Violence Against Women?

The issues of violence against women and women's participation in political and civil life are closely linked. Violence against women acts as a barrier to women's participation in decision-making, whether it's in the home or in the community. For example, domestic violence may affect the mental health of women and cause low self-esteem, anxiety and fear, which hampers their ability to travel outside the home and to get involved in public life. Conversely, women's isolation from public and community life is known to contribute to increased violence, whereas increasing their participation in community groups and social networks has been shown to decrease their vulnerability to violence by helping them find support and solutions to the problem, such as legal protection, counselling and advice. Womankind's work to promote civil and political participation therefore seeks to complement the work that we do to reduce violence against women so as to maximise the impact and longer-term benefits for women.

Political Participation of Women in Kerala

In Kerala, a State known for its socioeconomic,demographic and developmental features, a good proportion of women willingly exercise their franchise in elections. The State, in fact, has the highest percentage of women voting. The proportion of votes cast by women in the elections held in Kerala was around 50 per cent.

This enthusiasm is however, absent when it comes to political participation. It is evident from the low proportion of women in the State Legislative Assembly and women representatives of Kerala in the Lok Sabha, Rajya Sabha and local bodies. In 1957, for instance, the number of women in the State Assembly was only six out of the total 121 members. In 1991, the number was eight in the house of 141. In the present Assembly, there are 13 women legislators (table 1). There is only a single woman among the twenty Members of Parliament (MP) elected in the recent 1998 Lok Sabha election.

Kerala has a total of 2,001 women panchayat members. In the municipalities and corporations of Kerala, the elected women form 34.58 per cent ie., hardly 1.25 per cent excess of the mandatory 33.33 per cent. However, to find adequate number of women to contest the elections was a difficult task for almost all the major political parties.

This is clear from the total number of men and women candidates in the fray. The figures indicate that women candidates in the fray (grama panchayat, block panchayat, district panchayat, municipalities and municipal corporations combined) were proportionately low. There were only 17,869 women against 40,220 men to contest the elections which is, hardly 31 per cent of the total number of the contestants.

NGOs and Women Development

The Tamil Nadu Women's Development Project (TNWDP) has considerable achievements. It has almost reached the quantitative targets of loans disbursed and has overachieved by 40% the number of groups to be formed specified in the Appraisal Report. Its strongest positive points are the following:

i) Women's groups have been formed and group members have been helped to develop the habit of systematic savings.

ii) It has made it possible for unregistered self-help women's groups to open savings bank accounts, an important achievement in itself.

iii) When the Non-Governmental Organisations (NGOs) involved in the project, and the bank's branches allowed groups to rotate their savings as small, flexible, internal loans for a minimum of one year, group members were able to develop a "repayment culture".

iv) The recovery rate of bank loans is excellent due to the extensive support system developed by the project. This has demonstrated that banks can give loans to women's self-help groups and enjoy high repayment rates. As a result of this positive experience, the Indian Bank is now in the process of experimenting with a scheme that will further decrease transaction costs through investment group lending.

v) Despite initial difficulties, good coordination has been established between the Government, the Tamil Nadu Women's Development Corporation and officers from line departments, the Bank and the NGOs.

vi) There is evidence of considerable social impact of the project on women, especially in well functioning, homogeneous groups of very poor women, in which women report a greater degree of self-confidence, greater mobility, and greater ease to visit banks and to converse with different officials visiting the village, compared to what was the case before group formation.

Limitations

The project has placed very heavy emphasis on loan disbursement and recovery, almost to the neglect of beneficiary training. A key reason for this to happen has been that NGOs are paid on the basis of the number of beneficiaries that get loans from the bank. Furthermore, the overemphasis on land-based activities has limited the inclusion of some of the poorest women.

Recommendations

In view of the fact that up to December 1994, on the basis of claims filed the project has utilised only 34.63% of available project funds, and given that the perception that "the project is coming to a close" is creating uncertainty among the project staff, some of which are looking for other opportunities (the same being also the case with the concerned NGOs), the Mission recommends the extension of the project for another two to three years, without additional funds but with the condition that the following changes in the overall strategy of the project will be immediately implemented:

i) Additional targets are set referring to the number of well functioning groups with high member solidarity and cohesion and an active participatory process and to the training of beneficiaries in group dynamics and participation skills as well as in practical, technical skills.

ii) The emphasis is no longer placed on creating new groups but on the consolidation of existing groups and on the improvement of those groups to be classified in the second and third best category (according to the criteria proposed in Annex 1 of this report). The Mission recommends that no more than 600 new groups are created from 1 April 1995 to 31 March 1996 and that those groups are limited within the villages already reached by the project. After 1 April 1996, it is recommended that no new groups are created because it is important, from the point of view of sustainability, to give to new groups the full benefit of all project services and resources. Half of these groups should be entirely made up of landless women and the other half should be representative of the different types of truly poor women.

iii) The needed adjustments to group size should be made in the following fashion: (a) groups with up to 20 members are left as they are; (b) groups with over 20 members should be allowed to divide themselves into groups of no more than 20 members, in such a way that group homogeneity is increased.

iv) There is a need to diversify the profitable productive activities for which loans are available to women in order to increase women's awareness and empowerment. Poor, illiterate village women have a very limited exposure to productive activities beyond milk cows, sheep and goats. This diversification, however, needs to be based on the results of good market research undertaken in the different localities of project concentration. The project is advised to avail itself of market research capability on a contractual basis.

v) Banks should allow the groups to withdraw their savings, after completion of three months for the purpose of extending small, internal loans. Also applications for bank loans should not be accepted before a minimum of one year of high loan-savings ratio through the rotation of small, internal loans to a large number of group members.

vi) The Capital Development Fund (CDF) of Rs.7500 should be handled as a grant to the group.

vii) All attempts to create some kind of group federation should not be undertaken until the groups have attained a mature level of functioning, appreciate themselves the importance of such federation, and are in a position to control it. The present experience indicates that such federations should limit themselves to a social and information sharing role, refraining from playing any kind of financial role. The mission, therefore, recommends that all financial contributions already made by the groups to any type of federation or cluster be returned to the groups (as well as interest payments made for the CDF).

viii) The Mission recommends that the basis for payment for NGO services needs to be changed. From now on, they should be paid exclusively on the basis of number of beneficiaries trained in group dynamics and/or in technical skills.

ix) Taking into consideration the pattern already set during the fourth year, starting from the fifth year the type and size of payment extended to animators should be up to the individual group and on the nature of services rendered.

x) The bank loan should be adequate to purchase the asset financed without the beneficiary having to supplement it from other sources and banking plans should be implemented on a flexible basis.

xi) The admissible subsidy should be given as "bonus" on completion of full repayment of the loan. Groups should also be given the option to maintain the funds in the bank as a risk coverage for future loans.

xii) Through appropriate amendments to its rules, Indian Bank should begin to give the loans under the project to the best groups thus treating them as financial intermediaries.

xiii) Simplified procedures for keeping accounts by the groups need to be immediately developed through a short-term consultancy. On the other hand, passbooks regarding small, internal loans need to be issued that will allow both Project Implementation Units (PIUs) and Project Management Unit (PMU) to collect detailed data and to follow-up this issue.

xiv) The groups should be able to charge a small service charge for loans received by beneficiaries. While the groups should decide themselves, a guideline of 1% to 2% (on the total amount of the loan) could be suggested.

xv) In mature, well functioning groups, a system of individual deposits should be introduced on a pilot basis.

xvi) The project should provide funds for computerisation of ten Indian Bank branches serving more than 50 groups in order to speed up loan sanction and to diminish lender and borrower transaction cost.

xvii) Intensive efforts need to be made by the project so that different types of training, including training in groups dynamics, group management and participation as well as technical/skills training are provided to all women group members.

xviii) Depending on available training capacity on the part of line ministries and NGOs, the technical training may be offered by technical people attached to the NGO, by members of line ministries or by technical trainers retained on a contractual basis by the project.

xix) In all cases, in order to accommodate women's work overload and multiple responsibilities, their training should be offered at the village level and should be practical, on-the-job training, well adjusted to women's reality.

xx) Training in poverty and gender issues should be extended to all project officers, deputized members of line ministries and bank officers at district and branch levels as well as to NGOs.

xxi) An appropriate consultant should be commissioned by the project to identify training needs (group dynamics, group management, gender and poverty issues and credit related subjects including microenterprises) of collaborating NGOs and arrange for such training to be provided by specially trained trainers.

xxii) A short training in participation should be given to animators in order to enable them to modify their own often dominating behaviour and to create a participatory environment for all women members.

xxiii) An important training aid to be developed is a video of the behaviours and interactions between women members in a well functioning group, illustrating successful group dynamics, active participation and democratic decision making. The video could also include a contrast with a group that is not functioning well. Specific funds should be allocated for these and other communication activities.

xxiv) All training activities and particularly the quality of training offered to all target groups and especially to beneficiaries needs to be carefully monitored by the project, mainly by the Training Coordinator, and in his absence by contracted training specialists.

xxv) Data concerning all types of training of beneficiaries as well as data regarding the classification of the groups with regard to the degree of consolidation (according to the proposed criteria) should be disaggregated by branch and by collaborating NGO in order to allow for corrections and changes in direction.

xxvi) Animators and supervisors should be trained in recording the number of trained beneficiaries, the type of training provided, and the number of visits by the technical staff (e.g. veterinarians) to the group.

Lessons Learned

The TNWDP provides a number of important lessons that can benefit the planned National Women's Project in India. Four outstanding lessons are the following:

(a) There is a striking diversity of results not only among districts but even within districts of a same state. This should lead to great caution in replicating experiences such as those of the Tamil Nadu Development Project. Crucial success factors are the presence of motivated and competent NGOs, committed financial institutions and adequate procedures (particularly with respect to the mode of payment to NGOs).

(b) The poorest women included in groups and provided with appropriate support services performed as well as less poor women with respect to savings, loan repayment and ability to productively utilize loans.

(c) Direct subsidies provided to the beneficiaries as a bonus after loan repayment do not constitute a significant motive for members of well functioning groups. On the contrary, they may be creating expectations for future subsidies that cannot be fulfilled; and

(d) A key indicator of the dynamism and cohesion of a group is the degree of rotation to all members of small, internal loans based on their savings prior to applying for bank loans.

National and International Funding Agencies

Various national and international agencies have identified priority areas for funding of collaborative research. The proposals submitted to the funding agencies need to be original and address the research areas prioritized by an agency. There are certain important considerations which need to be followed by a researcher for successful international collaboration viz. presentation of the proposal, justification for foreign collaboration, technology transfer, capacity building, ethical and IPR issues, transfer of human biological material, etc. As a condition of grant support, institutions in receipt of funds are responsible for ensuring that the investigator fully complies with the requirements for the storage, use and transfer of biological materials and any additional provisions to safeguard security that are specified in regulations. Parent institutions of the investigators are also required to accept responsibility for the management, monitoring and control of research work funded by international grants and for ensuring that permanent/temporary staff and students employed to undertake such work receive appropriate training.

UNIT-VIII

Justice for Women

Indian Constitution and Provisions Relating to Women Personal Laws

The India polity more or less has a always tried to cope with the contemporary need – based development of laws for the specified purposes. It may be in the field of Human Rights, Politics, Civil Rights, Constitutional Rights or Social Transfer. Still the judicially always inspires directly or indirectly to meet the challenges as per need, either by precedents, directions or suggestions etc. The Supreme Court in a case1 observed that "it is well accepted by thinkers, philosophers and academicians that if JUSTICS, LIBERTY, EQUALITY and FRATERNITY, including social, economic and political justice, the golden goals set out by the Preamble of the Constitution, are to be achieved, the Indian polity has to be educated and educated with excellence.

This is because the Constitution is not to be construed as a mere law, but as the machinery by which laws are made. The Constitution is a living and organic thing which, of all instruments has the greatest claim to be constructed broadly and liberally.

Article 14 and 16 (A) of the Constitution intend to remove social and economic inequality to make equal opportunities available. In reality the right to social and economic justice envisaged in the Preamble and elongated in the Fundamental Rights and Directive Principles of the Constitution, in particular Articles 14, 15, 16, 21, 38, 39 and 46 are envisaged to make the equality of the life of the poor, disadvantaged and disabled citizens of the society, meaningful.

Further the Preamble which is invoked to determine the abmit of both fundamental rights and Directive Principles as observed by the Supreme Court in Various cases embraces all the new laws after make Constitution.

This reasons, why the Government organs owe origin to the Constitution and derive their authority from and discharge their responsibilities within the framework of the Constitution.

The Supreme Court in some cases held that the social justice enables the courts to uphold legislations to remove economic inequalities, to remove economic inequalities, to provide a decent standard of living to the working people and to protect the interests of the weaker sections of the society.

The democratic socialism aims to end poverty, ignorance, disease, and inequality of opportunity. This socialistic concept ought to be implemented in the true spirit of the Constitution. Article 14 is to be understood in the light of directive principles. Articles 14 guarantees equal treatment to persons who are equally situated.

Besides clause (3) of Articles 15, which permits special provision for women and children, has been widely resorted to and the courts have upheld the validity of special measures in legislation or executive orders favouring women. In particular, provisions in the criminal law, in favour of women, or in the procedural law discriminating in favour of women have been upheld.

Article 21 spells that no person shall be deprived of his life or personal liberty except according to procedure established by law. This Article if read literally is a colorless Article and would be satisfie, at the moment, it is established by the State that there is a law which provides a procedure which has been followed by the impugned action. But the expression "procedure established by law" in Article has been judicially constructed as meaning a procedure which is reasonable, fair and just.

The right to life and the right to personal liberty in India have been guaranteed by a constitutional provision, which has received the widest possible interpretation. Under the canopy of Article 21 of the Constitution, so many rights have found shelter, growth and nourishment. An intelligent citizen would like to be aware of the development in this regard as they have evolved from precedents of courts.

This Article lays down that no person shall be deprived of life or personal liberty, except according to procedure established by law.

This Ariticle, hence gives a positive effect by judicial interpretation. This right is a fundamental right, enforceable against the State, and Judicial decisions have imposed, on the State, several positive obligation.

A question arises while going through the constitutional provisions that why a constitutional provision arises on various subjects. Is the ordinary law not enough? To the answer it is true that Indian Penal Code contains adequate provision to punish a person who takes away or attempts to take away the life of another. But the impact of constitutional provision to take away the life of another. But the impact of constitutional provision lies in this respect, that by being elevated to the pedestal of a fundamental right, the right is placed beyond the reach of ordinary legislation inspired by political motives. Hence it can be said that the enumerative rights can derive from Article 21.

Article 39 (a) among other things provides that the State shall in particular, direct its policy towards securing that al citizens, men and women equally have the right to an adequate means of livelihood. This Article has been described as having the object of securing a welfare state may be utilized for construing provisions as to fundamental rights.

Further Article 51 A (e) imposes that duty of every citizen in India to renounce practices derogatory to the dignity of women.

Section 14 of the Hindu Succession Act, 1956 should be construed harmoniously with the constitutional goals of removing gender based discrimination and effectuating economic empowerment of Hindu women.

The right to elimination of gender based discrimination so as to attain economic empowerment, forms pat of Universal Human Rights. Article 2 (f) of CEDAW States are obliged to take all appropriate measures; including legislation, to abolish or modify gender based discrimination in the existing laws, regulation, customs and practices that constitute discrimination against women. Article 15(3) of the Constitution of India positively protects such acts or actions.

Moreover the Constitution of India is a basic document which provides for women empowerment within the framework of the plenary provision of Articles 14, 15 (3), 21, 39 (a), 51A (e) and Preamble. The courts always try to interpret the cases which are detriment to women within the area of social justice with these Articles.

Labour Laws

The law relating to labour and employment in India is primarily known under the broad category of "Industrial Law". Industrial law in this country is of recent vintage and has developed in respect to the vastly increased awakening of the workers of their rights, particularly after the advent of Independence. Industrial relations embrace a complex of relationships between the workers, employers and government, basically concerned with the determination of the terms of employment and conditions of labour of the workers. Escalating expectations of the workers, the hopes extended by Welfare State, uncertainties caused by tremendous structural developments in industry, the decline of authority, the waning attraction of the work ethics and political activism in the industrial field, all seem to have played some role.

Historical Background

The history of labour legislation in India is naturally interwoven with the history of British colonialism. The industrial/labour legislations enacted by the British were primarily intended to protect the interests of the British employers. Considerations of British political economy were naturally paramount in shaping some of these early laws. The earliest Indian statute to regulate the relationship between employer and his workmen was the Trade Dispute Act, 1929 (Act 7 of 1929). Provisions were made in this Act for restraining the rights of strike and lock out but no machinery was provided to take care of disputes.

The original colonial legislation underwent substantial modifications in the post-colonial era because independent India called for a clear partnership between labour and capital. The content of this partnership was unanimously approved in a tripartite conference in December 1947 in which it was agreed that labour would be given a fair wage and fair working conditions and in return capital would receive the fullest co-operation of labour for uninterrupted production and higher productivity as part of the strategy for national economic development and that all concerned would observe a truce period of three years free from strikes and lockouts. Ultimately the Industrial Disputes Act (the Act) brought into force on 01.04.1947 repealing the Trade Disputes Act 1929 has since remained on statute book.

Object of the Act

The Industrial Disputes Act, 1947, is, therefore, the matrix, the charter, as it were, to the industrial law. The Act and other analogous State statutes provide the machinery for regulating the rights of the employers and employees for investigation and settlement of industrial disputes in peaceful and harmonious atmosphere by providing scope for collective bargaining by negotiations and mediation and, failing that, by voluntary arbitration or compulsory adjudication by the authorities created under these statutes with the active participation of the trade unions. With the aid of this machinery, industrial law covers a comprehensive canvas of state intervention of social control through law to protect directly the claims of workers to wages, bonus, retiral benefits such as gratuity, provident fund and pension, claims, social security measures such as workmen's compensation, insurance, maternity benefits, safety welfare and protection of minimum of economic well-being. Job security has been particularly protected by providing industrial adjudication of unfair discharges and dismissals and ensuring reinstatement of illegally discharged or dismissed workmen.

Protection has gone still further by laying down conditions of service in specified industries and establishments and limiting the hours of work. By and large, all these subjects are "connected with employment or non-employment or terms of employment or with the conditions of labour" of industrial employees. In other words, these matters are the subject matter of industrial disputes, which can be investigated and settled with the aid of the machinery provided under the Act or analogous State statutes.

Mechanism of Disputes Settlement

The principal techniques of dispute settlement provided in the I.D. Act are collective bargaining, mediation and conciliation, investigation, arbitration, adjudication and other purposes.

Collective Bargaining

Collective bargaining is a technique by which disputes of employment are resolved amicably, peacefully and voluntarily by settlement between labour unions and managements. The method of collective bargaining in resolving the Industrial dispute, while maintaining industrial peace has been recognized as the bed rock of the Act. Under the provision of the Act, the settlement arrived at by process of collective bargaining with the employer has been given a statutory recognition under Section 18 of the Act. Under the Act two types of settlement have been recognised:

1. Settlement arrived in the course of conciliation proceeding before the authority. Such settlements not only bind the member of the signatory union but also non-members as well as all the present and future employees of the management.
2. Settlement not arrived in the course of conciliation proceedings but signed independently by the parties to the settlement binds only such members who are signatory or party to the settlement.

Section 19 of the Act prescribes the period of operation inter alia of such a settlement and envisage the continuation of the validity of such a settlement unless the same is not replaced by another set of settlement, while Section 29 prescribes the penalty for the breach of such a settlement.

Mediation and Conciliation

Under the Act, an effective conciliation machinery has been provided which can take cognizance of the existing as well as apprehended dispute, either on its own or on being approached by either of the parties to the dispute. The Act further makes conciliation compulsory in majority of disputes.

Investigation

Section 6 of the Act empowers the government to constitute a court of inquiry, for inquiring into any matter pertaining to an Industrial Dispute. The procedure of the court of inquiry has also been prescribed by Section 11. While the report of the court is not binding on the parties, many time it paves the way for an agreement.

Arbitration

Voluntary arbitration is a part of the infrastructure of resolving the Industrial Dispute in the Industrial adjudication. Section 10 of the Act provides for the provision for resolving the Industrial Dispute by way of arbitration, which leads to a final and binding award. However, in India arbitration is not a preferred way of resolving Industrial Disputes.

Adjudication

Adjudication means a mandatory settlement of Industrial Disputes by labour courts, Industrial Tribunals or National Tribunals under the Act or by any other corresponding authorities under the analogous state statutes. By and large, the ultimate remedy of unsettled dispute is by way of reference by the appropriate government to the adjudicatory machinery for adjudication. The adjudicatory authority resolves the Industrial Dispute referred to it by passing an award, which is binding on the parties to such reference. There is no provision for appeal against such awards and the same can only be challenged by way of writ under Articles 226 and 227 of the Constitution of India before the concerned High Court or before the Supreme Court by way of appeal under special leave under Article 136 of the Constitution of India.

However before the provisions of the Act, 1947 may become applicable certain pre-requisite conditions must exist.

1. The dispute must relate to an 'Industry';
2. Section 2(j) of the Industrial Dispute Act gives a comprehensive definition of 'industry'. The definition of industry in this clause is both exhaustive and inclusive and is quite comprehensive in its scope. It is in two parts, the first part says that 'it means any business, trade, undertaking, manufacture or calling of employees and then goes on to say that it, includes any calling, services employment, handicraft or industrial occupation or avocation or workmen. Thus one part of the definition defines it from the standpoint of the employer; the other from the standpoint of the employees.

   This definition has undergone variegated judicial interpretation. In case of Bangalore Water Supply and Sewage Board Vs. A. Rajagappa [(1978) 1 LLJ 349] a 7 judges bench of the Supreme Court has given the widest possible meaning of the term 'industry' which virtually covers almost all organized activities under the ambit of the term 'industry'. After the decision of the Supreme Court in Bangalore Water Supply and Sewage Board case the question to be asked is not what is an industry, but what is not an industry. Further, even after the Bangalore Water Supply and Sewage Board decision there is much left to be desired with the interpretation of industry and the need for legislative reforms has been accentuated by all concerned. A very sensible and pragmatic definition of the term 'industry' has been attempted in the Industrial Relations Bill of 1978. With the dissolution of the Parliament in 1979 the Bill lapsed.

   The definition has been amended by the Parliament in the Industrial Disputes (Amendment) Act, 1982 with new definition of industry in Section 2(j). However the amendment has yet to be brought into force. There is an urgent need for a comprehensive and practical definition of the 'industry'.

3. Under this Act an Industrial Dispute can be raised only by 'workman' employed in an 'industry'. Section 2(s) of the Act defines 'workman', which means any person employed including an apprentice, in any industry to do any skilled, unskilled, manual, clerical, supervisory or technical work for hire or reward, whether the terms of employment be expressed or implied. The definition of workman under the Act also includes any person who has been dismissed, discharged or retrenched in connection with or as a consequence of any dispute. However, it excludes inter alia any person who has been employed mostly in managerial or administrative capacity or in supervisory capacity drawing wages exceeding 1600/-per month or exercises either by the nature of the duty attached to the office or by reason of the powers vested in him, functions mainly of a managerial nature. However, in this regard it is not the nomenclature or designation of the employee but the actual nature of duties performed by him/her that will determine the status of such employees. Furthermore, before an Industrial Dispute can be referred for adjudication, it is necessary that their exists a relationship of employer and employee between the workman and the management.

One of the short-comings of the present definition of the workman, as the experience has shown is its over emphasis on the criteria of nature of duties performed by an employee irrespective of the status, position and wage of such an employee in the hierarchy of the management in determining whether such employee will come under the category of workman. For example, in India even the Pilots and Engineers of aircraft have been covered under the definition of workman although in terms of their salary and wages and authority they exercise, by no stretch of imagination, they can be equated with labour and working force of the industry. In some cases, even doctors have been recognized as workman as they perform technical or skilled job. This area of the definition of workman requires an urgent legislative modification. Stressing the need for recasting the definition of workman, the Second National Labour Commission recommended as follows:

> *"Relatively better off section of employees categorized as workmen like Airlines Pilots, etc, do not merely carry out instructions from superior authority but are also required and empowered to take various kinds of on the spot decisions in various situations and particularly in exigencies. Their functions therefore, cannot merely be categorized as those of ordinary workmen. We, therefore, recommend that Government may lay down a list of such highly paid jobs who are presently deemed as workmen category as being outside the purview of the laws relating to workmen and included in the proposed law for the protection of non workmen. Another alternative is that the Government fix a cut off limit of remuneration, which is substantially high enough, in the present context, such as Rs. 25,000/-p.m. beyond which employees will not be treated as ordinary 'workman'."*

4. The dispute must be an 'Industrial Dispute'. Section 2(k) of the Act defines 'Industrial Dispute' and only disputes covered under the definition can be referred for conciliation or adjudication under the Act. The definition of 'Industrial Dispute' in section 2(k), can be divided into two parts viz :

1. Dispute or difference
   - i. between employer and employers
   - ii. Between Employer and workman
   - iii. Between Workman and workman
2. Subject matter of dispute.
   - i. Connected with the employment or non-employment
   - ii. The terms of employment
   - iii. With the condition of labour.

Space does not allow a detailed discussion of all the provisions of the Act, but provisions that deal with job losses must be noted. Under the present law any Industrial Establishment employing more than 100 workers must make an application to the Government seeking permission before resorting to lay-off, retrenchment, or closure of undertaking. Employers resorting to any of the said forms of creating job losses without seeking prior permission as aforesaid act illegally and workers are entitled to receive wages for the period of illegality. However, an Industrial Establishment employing less than 100 workers can retrench its surplus employees in accordance with the provisions provided under Section 25F, 25G & 25H of the Act without seeking the permission of the appropriate government. Under Section 25 F of the Act the retrenchment compensation to be offered to a retrenched workman has to be 15 days salary for every completed year of service and an amount equivalent to one month salary. However, it has been felt that the present retrenchment compensation provided under the Act is wholly inadequate and there is an urgent need for enhancing the compensation to a realistic standard.

However, the service of an employee can be terminated by an order of discharge simplicitor without complying with the provisions contained in Section 25 F of the Act if such an employee has been appointed for a fixed period under the contract of fixed term appointment and his/her services is terminated either on the ground of expiry of the fixed period or in stipulation of the provision contained therein.

The Reserve Bank of India commissioned a study into the causes of sickness in Indian industry and they reported cryptically, 'Sickness in India is a profitable business'. This chapter (V-B) in the Act, which has been identified as offering high rigidity in the area of labour redundancy, has been targeted for change under globalisation and liberalisation.

A feature of the Act is the stipulation that existing service conditions cannot be unilaterally altered without giving a notice of 21 days to the workers and the trade union. Similarly if an industrial dispute is pending before an authority under the

Act, then the previous service conditions in respect of that dispute cannot be altered to the disadvantage of the workers without prior permission of the authority concerned. This has been identified as a form of rigidity that hampers competition in the era of the World Trade Organisation.

A permanent worker can be removed from service only for proven misconduct or for habitual absence or due to ill health or on attaining retirement age. In other words the doctrine of 'hire and fire' is not approved within the existing legal framework. In cases of misconduct the worker is entitled to the protection of Standing Orders to be framed by a certifying officer of the labour department after hearing management and labour, through the trade union. Employers must follow principles of 'natural justice', which again is an area that is governed by judge-made law. An order of dismissal can be challenged in the labour court and if it is found to be flawed, the court has the power to order reinstatement with continuity of service, back wages, and consequential benefits. This again is identified as an area where greater flexibility is considered desirable for being competitive.

Strikes and Lockouts

Workers have the right to strike, even without notice unless it involves a public utility service; employers have the right to declare lockout, subject to the same conditions as a strike. The parties may sort out their differences either bilaterally, or through a conciliation officer who can facilitate but not compel a settlement, which is legally binding on the parties, even when a strike or a lockout is in progress. But if these methods do not resolve a dispute, the government may refer the dispute to compulsory adjudication and ban the strike or lockout. However in recent times the Higher Courts have deprecated the tendency to go on strike quite frequently. Furthermore, the Supreme Court of India has also held that government employees have no fundamental right to go on strike.

The Regulation of Contract Labour

The most distinct visible change in the time of globalisation and privatization is the increased tendency for outsourcing, offloading or subcontracting. The rationale is that the establishment could focus on more productivity in the core or predominant activity so as to remain competitive while outsourcing the incidental or ancilliary activities.

The Contract Labour (Prohibition and Regulation) Act 1970 provides a mechanism for regulating engaging of contractor and contract labour. The Act provides for registration of contractors (if more than twenty workers are engaged) and for the appointment of a Tripartite Advisory Board that investigates particular forms of contract labour, which if found to be engaged in areas requiring perennial work connected with the production process, then the Board could recommend its abolition under Section 10 of the Act. A tricky legal question has arisen as to whether the contract workers should be automatically absorbed or not, after the contract labour system is abolished. Recently a Constitutional Bench of the Supreme Court has held that there need not be such automatic absorption.

Employment Injury, Health, and Maternity Benefit

The Workmen's Compensation Act 1923 is one of the earliest pieces of labour legislation. It covers all cases of 'accident arising out of and in the course of employment' and the rate of compensation to be paid in a lump sum, is determined by a schedule proportionate to the extent of injury and the loss of earning capacity. The younger the worker and the higher the wage, the greater is the compensation subject to a limit. The injured person, or in case of death the dependent, can claim the compensation. This law applies to the unorganised sectors and to those in the organised sectors who are not covered by the Employees State Insurance Scheme, which is conceptually considered to be superior to the Workmen's Compensation Act.

The Employees' State Insurance Act, 1948 provides a scheme under which the employer and the employee must contribute a certain percentage of the monthly wage to the Insurance Corporation that runs dispensaries and hospitals in working class localities. It facilitates both outpatient and in-patient care and freely dispenses medicines and covers hospitalization needs and costs. Leave certificates for health reasons are forwarded to the employer who is obliged to honour them. Employment injury, including occupational disease is compensated according to a schedule of rates proportionate to the extent of injury and loss of earning capacity. Payment, unlike in the Workmen's Compensation Act, is monthly. Despite the existence of tripartite bodies to supervise the running of the scheme, the entire project has fallen into disrepute due to corruption and inefficiency. Workers in need of genuine medical attention rarely approach this facility though they use it quite liberally to obtain medical leave. There are interesting cases where workers have gone to court seeking exemption from the scheme in order to avail of better facilities available through collective bargaining.

The Maternity Benefit Act is applicable to notified establishments. Its coverage can therefore extend to the unorganised sector also, though in practice it is rare. A woman employee is entitled to 90 days of paid leave on delivery or on miscarriage. Similar benefits, including hospitalisation facilities are available under the law described in the paragraph above.

Retirement Benefit

There are two types of retirement benefits generally available to workers. One is under the Payment of Gratuity Act,1972 and the other is under the Employees Provident Fund Act. In the first case a worker who has put in not less than five years of work is entitled to a lump sum payment equal to 15 days' wages for every completed year of service. Every month the employer is expected to contribute the required money into a separate fund to enable this payment on retirement or termination of employment. In the latter scheme both the employee and the employer make an equal contribution into a national fund. The current rate of contribution is 12 percent of the wage including a small percentage towards family pension. This contribution also attracts an interest, currently 9.5 percent per annum, and the accumulated amount is paid on retirement to the employee along with the interest that has accrued. The employee is allowed to draw many types of loan from the fund such as for house construction, marriage of children, and education etc. This is also a benefit, which is steadily being extended to sections of the unorganised sector, especially where the employer is clearly identifiable.

Indian labour laws divide industry into two broad categories:

1. *Factory:* Factories are regulated by the provisions of the Factories Act, 1948 (the saidAct). All industrial establishments employing 10 or more persons and carrying manufacturing activities with the aid of power come within the definition of Factory. The said Act makes provisions for the health, safety, welfare, working hours and leave of workers in factories. The said Act is enforced by the State Government through their 'Factory' inspectorates. The said Act empowers the State Governments to frame rules, so that the local conditions prevailing in the State are appropriately reflected in the enforcement. The said Act puts special emphasis on welfare, health and safety of workers. The said Act is instrumental in strengthening the provisions relating to safety and health at work, providing for statutory health surveys, requiring appointment of safety officers, establishment of canteen, crèches, and welfare committees etc. in large factories.

   The said Act also provides specific safe guards against use and handling of hazardous substance by occupiers of factories and laying down of emergency standards and measures.

2. *Shops and Commercial Establishments:* 'Shops and Commercial Establishments' are regulated by Shops and Commercial Establishments Act which are state statutes and respective states have their respective Shops and Commercial Acts which generally provide for opening and closing hour, leave, weekly off, time and mode of payment of wages, issuance of appointment letter etc.

Statutory Regulation of Condition of Service in Certain Establishments

There is statutory provision for regulating and codifying conditions of service for an industrial establishment employing more than 100 workmen under the provisions of Industrial Employment (Standing Orders) Act, 1946 (this Act). Under the provisions of this Act every employer of an Industrial Establishment employing 100 or more workmen is required to define with sufficient precision the condition of employment and required to get it certified by the certifying authorities provided under Section 3 of this Act. Such certified conditions of service will prevail over the terms of contract of employment. In a significant judgment recently the Delhi High Court has held that a hospital even though employing more than 100 workmen is not covered under the provisions of this Act, as a hospital is not an Industrial Establishment as defined under this Act.

Distinctive Feature of Indian Labour and Employment Laws

A distinguishing feature of Indian Labour and Employment Laws are that in India there are three main categories of employees: government employees, employees in government controlled corporate bodies known as Public Sector Undertakings (PSUs) and private sector employees.

The rules and regulations governing the employment of government employees stem from the Constitution of India. Accordingly, government employees enjoy protection of tenure, statutory service contentions and automatic annually salary increases.

Public sector employees are governed by their own service regulations, which either have statutory force, in the case of statutory corporations, or are based on statutory orders.

In the private sector, employees can be classified into two broad categories namely management staff and workman. Managerial, administrative or supervisory employees drawing a salary of Rs.1600/-or more per month are considered management staff and there is no statutory provisions relating to their employment and accordingly in case of managerial and supervisory staff/employee the conditions of employment are governed by respective contracts of employment and their services can be discharged in terms of their contract of employment. Workmen category are covered under the provisions of the Industrial Disputes Act as already detailed above.

Voluntary Retirement Scheme and Golden Handshake

In the competitive time of globalization and liberalization the system of Voluntary retirement with golden handshake is widely prevalent both in public and private sectors in order to reduce the surplus manpower which for most of public sector undertakings is a major cause of losses.

The Unorganised Sector

Many of the labour and employment laws apply to the unorganised sector also. The unorganized sector can be defined as that part of the work force that have not been able to organize itself in pursuit of a common objective because of certain constraints such as casual nature of employment, ignorance or illiteracy, superior strength of the employer singly or in combination etc. viz. construction workers, labour employed in cottage industry, handloom/powerloom workers, sweepers and scavengers, beedi and cigar workers etc. Under this category are laws like the Building and Construction Workers Act 1996, the Bonded Labour System (Abolition) Act 1976, The Interstate Migrant Workers Act 1979, The Dock Workers Act 1986, The Plantation Labour Act 1951, The Transport Workers Act, The Beedi and Cigar Workers Act 1966, The Child Labour (Prohibition and Regulation) Act 1986, and The Mine Act 1952.

Women Labour and the Law

Women constitute a significant part of the workforce in India but they lag behind men in terms of work participation and quality of employment. According to Government sources, out of 407 million total workforce, 90 million are women workers, largely employed (about 87 percent) in the agricultural sector as labourers and cultivators. In urban areas, the employment of women in the organised sector in March 2000 constituted 17.6 percent of the total organised sector.

In addition to the Maternity Benefit Act, almost all the major central labour laws are applicable to women workers.

The Equal Remuneration Act was passed in 1976, providing for the payment of equal remuneration to men and women workers for same or similar nature of work. Under this law, no discrimination is permissible in recruitment and service conditions except where employment of women is prohibited or restricted by the law.

The situation regarding enforcement of the provisions of this law is regularly monitored by the Central Ministry of Labour and the Central Advisory Committee. In respect of occupational hazards concerning the safety of women at workplaces, in 1997 the Supreme Court of India in the case of Vishakha Vs. State of Rajasthan [(1997) 6 SCC 241] held that sexual harassment of working women amounts to violation of rights of gender equality. As a logical consequence it also amounts to violation of the right to practice any profession, occupation, and trade. The judgment also laid down the definition of sexual harassment, the preventive steps, the complaint mechanism, and the need for creating awareness of the rights of women workers. Implementation of these guidelines has already begun by employers by amending the rules under the Industrial Employment (Standing Orders) Act, 1946.

Focus on Elimination of Child Labour

Elimination of child labour continued to be one of the major focus areas of the Labour Ministry. It took an initiative for framing an omnibus legislation prescribing 14 years as the minimum age for employment and work in all occupations except agricultural activity in family and small holdings producing for own consumption. The proposed legislation would also fix a minimum age of not less than 18 years to any type of employment and work which by its nature or circumstances is likely to jeopardize the health, safety or morals of young persons. As of date, employment of children has been prohibited in 13 occupation and 51 processes in the country bringing the total to 64. It is proposed to raise their number to 73 by notifying additional nine hazardous occupations and processes.

In 2006, the Central Government has amended the Child Labour (Prohibition and Regulation) Act, 1986 prohibiting employment of children below 14 years of age even in non-hazardous industry like restaurants, motels and also as domestic servants.

To further augment resources for elimination of child labour, the Ministry of Labour signed a Memorandum of Understanding with the ILO extending International Programme on Elimination of Child Labour (IPEC) in India for another two years. India under the ILO's IPEC programme has taken up 154 action programmes on child labour covering more than ninety thousand children with direct funding by the ILO/Area Office to the NGOs.

The Reforms and Labour Law

Reforms in Labour laws is being much talked in recent years. It is being advocated that all talk of liberalization is futile without squarely facing up to the imperative of labour reforms. These are an integral part of the economic reforms process itself. Other efforts at raising the standard of performance on the economic front to world class are apt to stall if those managing enterprises find themselves hamstrung by outdated trade union laws and dilatory methods of adjudication of industrial disputes.

For instance, the unwieldy number of adjudicating authorities — conciliation officers, conciliation boards, courts of inquiry, labour courts, industrial tribunals and the national industrial tribunal — under the Industrial Disputes Act and the complex procedures are out of sync with the essential pre-requisites for the success and even the survival of companies in a globally integrated economy.

Productivity, customer service, cost-effectiveness, keeping to delivery schedules, technological up gradation and modernization have emerged as the criteria for judging the quality of management of companies, and labour reforms hold the key to increased competitiveness and investment flows in all these respects. The need for introducing labour market flexibility and simplifying labour laws has no doubt been emphasized by the President and Prime Minister of the country downwards from time to time.

The case for labour reforms could not have been argued better than in this extract from the Economic Survey of 2005-06: "... Indian Labour Laws are highly protective of labour, and labour markets are relatively inflexible. These laws apply only to the organised sector. Consequently, these laws have restricted labour mobility, have led to capital-intensive methods in the organised sector and adversely affected the sector's long-run demand for labour".

Violence Against Women

Violence against women is partly a result of gender relations that assumes men to be superior to women. Given the subordinate status of women, much of gender violence is considered normal and enjoys social sanction. Manifestations of violence include physical aggression, such as blows of varying intensity, burns, attempted hanging, sexual abuse and rape, psychological violence through insults, humiliation, coercion, blackmail, economic or emotional threats, and control over speech and actions. In extreme, but not unknown cases, death is the result. (Adriana, 1996) These expressions of violence take place in a man-woman relationship within the family, state and society. Usually, domestic aggression towards women and girls, due to various reasons remain hidden. Cultural and social factors are interlinked with the development and propagation of violent behaviour. With different processes of socialisation that men and women undergo, men take up stereotyped gender roles of domination and control, whereas women take up that of submission, dependence and respect for authority. A female child grows up with a constant sense of being weak and in need of protection, whether physical social or economic. This helplessness has led to her exploitation at almost every stage of life.

The family socialises its members to accept hierarchical relations expressed in unequal division of labour between the sexes and power over the allocation of resources. The family and its operational unit is where the child is exposed to gender differences since birth, and in recent times even before birth, in the form of sex-determination tests leading to foeticide and female infanticide. The home, which is supposed to be the most secure place, is where women are most exposed to violence.

Violence against women has been clearly defined as a form of discrimination in numerous documents. The World Human Rights Conference in Vienna, first recognised gender-based violence as a human rights violation in 1993. In the same year, *United Nations* declaration, 1993, defined *violence against women* as "any act of gender-based violence that results in, or is likely to result in, physical, sexual or psychological harm or suffering to a woman, including threats of such acts, coercion or arbitrary deprivations of liberty, whether occurring in public or private life". (Cited by Gomez, 1996)

Radhika Coomaraswamy identifies different kinds of violence against women, in the United Nation's special report, 1995, on *Violence Against Women*;

a) Physical, sexual and psychological violence occurring in the family, including battering, sexual abuse of female children in the household, dowry related violence, marital rape, female genital mutilation and other traditional practices harmful to women, non spousal violence and violence related to exploitation.

b) Physical sexual and psychological violence occurring within the general community, including rape, sexual abuse, sexual harassment and intimidation at work, in educational institutions and elsewhere, trafficking in women and forced prostitution.

c) Physical, sexual and psychological violence perpetrated or condoned by the state, wherever it occurs.

This definition added 'violence perpetrated or condoned by the State', to the definition by United Nations in 1993.

Coomaraswamy (1992) points out that women are vulnerable to various forms of violent treatment for several reasons, all based on gender.

1) Because of being female, a woman is subject to rape, female circumcision/genital mutilation, female infanticide and sex related crimes. This reason relates to society's construction of female sexuality and its role in social hierarchy.

2) Because of her relationship to a man, a woman is vulnerable to domestic violence, dowry murder, *sati*. This reason relates to society's concept of a woman as a property and dependent of the male protector, father, husband, son, etc.
3) Because of the social group to which she belongs, in times of war, riots. Or ethnic, caste, or class violence, a woman may be raped and brutalised as a means of humiliating the community to which she belongs. This also relates to male perception of female sexuality and women as the property of men.

Combining these types of abuse with the concept of hierarchical gender relations, a useful way to view gender violence is by identifying where the violence towards women occurs.

Essentially, violence happens in three contexts-the family, the community and the state and at each point key social institutions fulfil critical and interactive functions in defining legitimating and maintaining the violence.

1) The family socialises its members to accept hierarchical relations expressed in unequal division of labour between the sexes and power over the allocation of resources.
2) The community (i.e., social, economic, religious, and cultural institutions) provides the mechanisms for perpetuating male control over women's sexuality, mobility and labour.
3) The state legitimises the proprietary rights of men over women, providing a legal basis to the family and the community to perpetuate these relations. The state does this through the enactment of discriminatory application of the law.

Margaret Schuler has divided gender violence into four major categories;

1) Overt physical abuse (battering sexual assault, at home and in the work place)
2) Psychological abuse (confinement, forced marriage)

3) Deprivation of resources for physical and psychological well being (health/nutrition, education, means of livelihood)

4) Commodification of women (trafficking, prostitution)

Adriana Gomez has also talked about two basic forms of violence, that is; structural and direct. Structural violence arises from the dominant political, economic and social systems, in so far as they block access to the means of survival for large number of people; for example, economic models based on the super-exploitation of thousands for the benefit of a few, extreme poverty in opposition to ostentatious wealth, and repression and discrimination against those who diverge from given norms. Structural violence according to her is the basis of direct violence, because it influences the socialisation which causes individuals to accept or inflict suffering, according to the social function they fulfil. Open or direct violence is exercised through aggression, arms or physical force. (Larrain and Rodrigue, 1993)

The Fourth Conference of Women, 1995 has defined violence against women as a physical act of aggression of one individual or group against another or others. *Violence against women* is any act of gender-based violence which result in, physical, sexual or arbitrary deprivation of liberty in public or private life and violation of human rights of women in violation of human rights of women in situations of armed conflicts. (Conference on Women, Beijing, 1995 Country Report).

Violence is an act carried out with the intention or perceived intention of physically hurting another person (Gelles and Straus, 1979). *Gender Violence* is defined as "any act involving use of force or coercion with an intent of perpetuating promoting hierarchical gender relations". (APWLD, 1990, Schuler, 1992)

Adding gender dimension to that definition amplifies it to include violent acts perpetrated on women because they are women. With this addition, the definition is no longer simple or obvious. Understanding the phenomenon of gender violence requires an analysis of the patterns of violence directed towards women and the underlying mechanisms that permit the emergence and perpetuation of these patterns.

Liz Kelly (1998), Surviving Sexual Polity has defined violence as "any physical, visual, verbal or sexual act that is experienced by the woman or girl at the time or later as a threat, invasion or assault, that has the effect of hurting her or degrading her and/or takes away her ability to contest an intimate contact".

Dr Joanne Liddle modified this definition as "any physical, visual, verbal or sexual act that is experienced by the person at the time or later as a threat, invasion or assault, that has the effect of hurting or disregarding or removing the ability to control one's own behaviour or an interaction, whether this be within the workplace, the home, on the streets or in any other area of the community".

Human Trafficking

The Republic of India [map] is the second most populous country in the world, stretching from the Arabian Sea (W) to the Bay of Bengal (E), bordering Pakistan (W); China, Nepal, and Bhutan (N); Bangladesh (NE); and Myanmar (E). New Delhi is its capital and Bombay (Mumbai) its largest city. An estimated 400 million are children between 0 and 18 years of age. Although acceleration in economic growth has made India among the 10 fastest growing developing countries, the country's per capita income remains low and 26 per cent of the population live below the income poverty line.

India is a source, destination, and transit country for men, women, and children trafficked for the purposes of forced labour and commercial sexual exploitation. Internal forced labour may constitute India's largest trafficking problem; men, women, and children are held in debt bondage and face forced labour working in brick kilns, rice mills, agriculture, and embroidery factories. While no comprehensive study of forced and bonded labour has been completed, NGOs estimate this problem affects 20 to 65 million Indians. Women and girls are trafficked within the country for the purposes of commercial sexual exploitation and forced marriage. Children are subjected to forced labour as factory workers, domestic servants, beggars, and agriculture workers, and have been used as armed combatants by some terrorist and insurgent groups. India is also a destination for women and girls from Nepal and Bangladesh trafficked for the purpose of commercial sexual exploitation. Nepali children are also trafficked to India for forced labour in circus shows. Indian women are trafficked to the Middle East for commercial sexual exploitation. There are also victims of labour trafficking among the thousands of Indians who migrate willingly every year to the Middle East, Europe, and the United States for work as domestic servants and low-skilled laborers.

In some cases, such workers are the victims of fraudulent recruitment practices that lead them directly into situations of forced labour, including debt bondage; in other cases, high debts incurred to pay recruitment fees leave them vulnerable to exploitation by unscrupulous employers in the destination countries, where some are subjected to conditions of involuntary servitude, including non-payment of wages, restrictions on movement, unlawful withholding of passports, and physical or sexual abuse. Men and women from Bangladesh and Nepal are trafficked through India for forced labour and commercial sexual exploitation in the Middle East. Indian nationals travel to Nepal and within the country for child sex tourism.

India is a source, destination, and transit country for men, women, and children trafficked for the purposes of forced labour and commercial sexual exploitation. Internal forced labour may constitute India's largest trafficking problem; men, women, and children are held in debt bondage and face forced labour working in brick kilns, rice mills, agriculture, and embroidery factories. While no comprehensive study of forced and bonded labour has been completed, NGOs estimate this problem affects 20 to 65 million Indians. Women and girls are trafficked within the country for the purposes of commercial sexual exploitation and forced marriage. Children are subjected to forced labour as factory workers, domestic servants, beggars, and agriculture workers, and have been used as armed combatants by some terrorist and insurgent groups. India is also a destination for women and girls from Nepal and Bangladesh trafficked for the purpose of commercial sexual exploitation. Nepali children are also trafficked to India for forced labour in circus shows. Indian women are trafficked to the Middle East for commercial sexual exploitation. There are also victims of labour trafficking among the thousands of Indians who migrate willingly every year to the Middle East, Europe, and the United States for work as domestic servants and low-skilled laborers.

In some cases, such workers are the victims of fraudulent recruitment practices that lead them directly into situations of forced labour, including debt bondage; in other cases, high debts incurred to pay recruitment fees leave them vulnerable to exploitation by unscrupulous employers in the destination countries, where some are subjected to conditions of involuntary servitude, including non-payment of wages, restrictions on movement, unlawful withholding of passports, and physical or sexual abuse. Men and women from Bangladesh and Nepal are trafficked through India for forced labour and commercial sexual exploitation in the Middle East. Indian nationals travel to Nepal and within the country for child sex tourism.

The Government of India does not fully comply with the minimum standards for the elimination of trafficking; however, it is making significant efforts to do so. India is placed on Tier 2 Watch List for a fifth consecutive year for its failure to provide evidence of increasing efforts to combat trafficking in persons over the last year. Despite the reported extent of the trafficking crisis in India, government authorities made uneven efforts to prosecute traffickers and protect trafficking victims. During the reporting period, government authorities continued to rescue victims of trafficking for commercial sexual exploitation and forced child labour and child armed combatants, and began to show progress in law enforcement against these forms of trafficking.

Overall, the lack of significant federal government action to address bonded labour, the reported complicity of some law enforcement officials in trafficking and related criminal activity, and the critical need for an effective national-level law enforcement authority impeded India's ability to effectively combat its trafficking in persons problem. A critical challenge overall is the lack of punishment of traffickers, effectively resulting in impunity for acts of human trafficking.

Recommendations for India: Expand central and state government law enforcement capacity to conduct intrastate law enforcement activities against trafficking; consider expanding the central Ministry of Home Affairs "nodal cell" on trafficking to coordinate law enforcement efforts to investigate and arrest traffickers who cross state and national lines; significantly increase law enforcement efforts to punish labour trafficking offenders; significantly increase efforts to eliminate official complicity in trafficking, including prosecuting, convicting, and punishing complicit officials with imprisonment; continue to increase law enforcement efforts against sex traffickers, including prosecuting, convicting, and punishing traffickers with imprisonment; improve central and state government implementation of protection programmes and compensation schemes to ensure that certified trafficking victims actually receivc benefits, including compensation for victims of forced child labour and bonded labour, to which they are entitled under national and state law; increase the quantity and breadth of public awareness and related programmes to prevent both trafficking for labour and commercial sex.

Prosecution

Government authorities made no progress in addressing one of India's largest human trafficking problems – bonded labour – during the year, but made some improvements in law enforcement efforts against sex trafficking and forced child labour. The government prohibits some forms of trafficking for commercial sexual exploitation through the Immoral Trafficking Prevention Act (ITPA). Prescribed penalties under the ITPA—ranging from seven years' to life imprisonment—are sufficiently stringent and commensurate with those for other grave crimes. India also prohibits bonded and forced labour through the Bonded Labour Abolition Act, the Child Labour Act, and the Juvenile Justice Act. These laws are ineffectually enforced, however, and their prescribed penalties—a maximum of three years in prison—are not sufficiently stringent. Indian authorities also use Sections 366(A) and 372 of the Indian Penal Code, prohibiting kidnapping and selling minors into prostitution respectively, to arrest traffickers. Penalties under these provisions are a maximum of ten years' imprisonment and a fine. During the reporting period, the government did not make significant efforts to investigate, prosecute, convict, and sentence labour trafficking offenders. Despite the estimated millions of bonded laborers in India, only 19 suspects were arrested for trafficking for bonded labour during the reporting period. In the past several years, the State of Tamil Nadu reported convicting 803 employers, but those convicted did not receive significant punishments. In addition, despite widespread reports of fraudulent recruitment practices, the Indian government did not report any arrests, investigations, prosecutions, convictions, or punishments of labour recruiters who participate in or facilitate the trafficking of Indian workers into situations of forced labour abroad.

In addition, the government largely continued to ignore the pervasive problem of government complicity in trafficking. Corrupt officers reportedly continued to facilitate the movement of sex trafficking victims, protect brothels that exploit victims, and protect traffickers and brothel keepers from arrest and other threats of enforcement. There were no efforts to tackle the problem of government officials' complicity in trafficking workers for overseas employment. Despite the extent of the problem, authorities only made five arrests for complicity. India reported no prosecutions, convictions, or sentences of public officials for complicity in trafficking during the reporting period. State governments continued to make efforts to address forced child labour, but failed to punish traffickers. In January, the government sponsored 22 state and federal officials to attend an ILO training programme on child migration and trafficking. Since 2005, the Government of Maharashtra, through its task force against child labour, rescued 2,058 children and arrested 358 suspects.

The State of Andhra Pradesh also reported rescuing over 9,000 children in a door-to-door campaign and prosecuting 17 suspected traffickers in the same time period. During the reporting period, raids throughout the country yielded 333 children rescued and five individuals arrested. Nonetheless, government authorities did not report convicting or sentencing any individual for trafficking children for forced labour. In addition, although the government enacted a ban on children working as domestic servants and in hotels or tea stalls, the government did not demonstrate efforts to enforce this law. State governments sustained efforts in combating trafficking for commercial sexual exploitation, but convictions and punishments of traffickers were extremely infrequent, especially given the extent of the problem. During the reporting period, state governments arrested 1,289 suspects for sex trafficking. Nonetheless, only four traffickers were convicted and received prison sentences. In June, the State Government of West Bengal established a police Anti-Human Trafficking Unit, specializing in fighting sex trafficking, in Kolkata.

The State Government of Bihar established three similar units in November. India's Central Bureau of Investigation incorporated anti-trafficking training into its standard curriculum. In November, the State of Maharashtra developed an action plan to combat trafficking; it did not, however, allocate appropriate funding to accomplish the objectives of this plan. During the reporting period, the Ministry of Home Affairs developed a system to track ITPA arrests, prosecutions, and convictions at the national level in order to develop a baseline from which the government could measure progress. The government does not break down these statistics by sections of the law, meaning that law enforcement data regarding trafficking offenses may be conflated with data regarding arrests of women in prostitution pursuant to Section 8 of the ITPA.

Protection

India's efforts to protect victims of trafficking varied from state to state, but remained inadequate in many places during the year. Victims of bonded labour are entitled to 10,000 rupees ($225) from the central government for rehabilitation, but this programme is unevenly executed across the country. Government authorities do not proactively identify and rescue bonded laborers, so few victims receive this assistance. Although children trafficked for forced labour may be housed in government shelters and are entitled to 20,000 rupees ($450), the quality of many of these homes remains poor and the disbursement of rehabilitation funds is sporadic. Some states provide services to victims of bonded labour, but NGOs provide the majority of protection services to these victims. The central government does not provide protection services to Indian victims trafficked abroad for forced labour or commercial sexual exploitation. Indian diplomatic missions in destination countries may offer temporary shelter to nationals who have been trafficked; once repatriated, however, neither the central government nor most state governments offer any medical, psychological, legal, or reintegration assistance for these victims.

Section 8 of the ITPA permits the arrest of women in prostitution. Although statistics on arrests under Section 8 are not kept, the government and some NGOs report that, through sensitization and training, police officers no longer use this provision of the law; it is unclear whether arrests of women in prostitution under Section 8 have actually decreased. Because most law enforcement authorities lack formal procedures to identify trafficking victims among women arrested for prostitution; some victims may be arrested and punished for acts committed as a result of being trafficked. Despite instructions that law enforcement authorities should protect minors who are exploited in prostitution, in at least two instances during the reporting period, police officers released minors into the custody of their traffickers.

Some foreign victims trafficked to India are not subject to removal. Those who are subject to removal are not offered legal alternatives to removal to countries in which they may face hardship or retribution. NGOs report that some Bangladeshi victims of commercial sexual exploitation are pushed back across the border without protection services. The government also does not repatriate Nepali victims; NGOs primarily perform this function. Many victims decline to testify against their traffickers due to the length of proceedings and fear of retribution by traffickers. The government does not actively encourage victims to participate in investigations of their traffickers. The central government continued to give grants to NGOs for the provision of services to sex trafficking victims with funding available through its Swadhar Scheme and the recently developed Ujjawala Scheme. No such efforts were made to assist victims of labour trafficking. Government shelters for sex trafficking victims are found in all major cities, but the quality of care varies widely. In Maharashtra, state authorities operated a home exclusively for minor victims of sex trafficking this year. The Governments of West Bengal, Tamil Nadu, and Andhra Pradesh also operated similar homes. Though states have made some improvements to their shelter care, victims sheltered in these facilities still do not receive comprehensive protection services, such as psychological assistance from trained counselors.

Prevention

India made inadequate efforts this year aimed at the prevention of trafficking in persons. Several times during the year, the Ministry of Labour and Employment displayed full-page advertisements against child labour in national newspapers. The government also instituted pre-departure information sessions for domestic workers migrating abroad on the risks of exploitation. Nonetheless, the government did not report new or significant prevention efforts addressing the prominent domestic problems of trafficking of adults for purposes of forced labour and commercial sexual exploitation. The government also did not report any efforts to reduce the demand for commercial sex acts. Similarly, the government failed to take any steps to raise awareness of trafficking for nationals traveling to known child sex tourism destinations within the country. India has not ratified the 2000 UN TIP Protocol.

Legal Protection

The Constitution of India guarantees equality of sexes and in fact grants special favours to women. These can be found in three articles of the Constitution. Article 14 says that the government shall not deny to any person equality before law or the equal protection of the laws. Article 15 declares that government shall not discriminate against any citizen on the ground of sex. Article 15 (3) makes a special provision enabling the State to make affirmative discriminations in favour of women. Moreover, the government can pass special laws in favour of women. Article 16 guarantees that no citizen shall be discriminated against in matters of public employment on the grounds of sex. Article 42 directs the State to make provision for ensuring just and humane conditions of work and maternity relief. Above all, the Constitution imposes a fundamental duty on every citizen through Articles 15 (A) (e) to renounce the practices derogatory to the dignity of women.

All these are fundamental rights. Therefore, a woman can go to the court if one is subjected to any discrimination. When we talk about constitutional rights of women in India, we mainly pertain to those areas where discrimination is done against women and special laws formulated to fight those bigotries. The most important issues stand as those pertaining to marriage, children, abortion, crimes against women, and inheritance.

Before modern Hindu laws were passed, child marriages were the norms, inter-caste marriages were banned, the girl became a part of the husband's family, and polygamy was common. In the 19th century, the British rulers passed several laws to protect customs and traditions while abolishing detestable practices like Sati. Some such revolutionary laws were Hindu Widows Remarriage Act 1865 and the Brahmo Samaj Marriage Act 1872, the forerunner of the present Special Marriage Act. In the beginning, the Act sets four essential conditions for a valid Hindu marriage. They are:

1. Monogamy
2. Sound mind
3. Marriageable age
4. The parties should not be too closely related

Polygamy was permitted among Hindus before the Act was passed in 1955. However, after the act was passed, any man marrying again while his wife is living will be punished with fine and imprisonment up to seven years. Formerly, child marriages were common. The Child Marriage Act of 1929 was not very effective as such marriages were continued to be performed. Now, however, the bridegroom must be 21 years old and the bride 18 years. However, there is a separate Muslim

Code of Conduct, which allows polygamy of up to four wives as per Islamic laws.

A marriage may be invalid without the boy or the girl realizing it at the time of the wedding. A civil marriage would be void if four essential conditions are not complied with. These conditions are listed in the Special Marriage Act (Section 4), as enumerated below:

- If it is bigamy
- If either party was suffering from mental disorder
- If the boy has not completed 21 years and the girl 18 years
- The boy and the girl are too closely related, or in legal language, are "within degrees of prohibited relationship" unless custom governing at least one party permits the marriage between them. Prohibited relationships are listed in he Special Marriage Act.
- A fifth reason for invalidating a marriage is impotence of either party.

There are some grounds available to the wife only, both in Hindu and civil marriages. One such ground available exclusively to the wife is her husband's commission of rape, sodomy or bestiality. Under the Hindu Adoptions and Maintenance Act 1956, a Hindu wife is entitled to be maintained by her husband. Section 125 of the Criminal Procedure Code also deals with maintenance of wife and children. If there is a decree of maintenance against the husband and the couple have been living apart for over one year, it would be a ground for the wife to seek dissolution of marriage. Here again the Muslim Personal Law has a different set of conditions for the annulment of an Islamic marriage.

The Dowry Prohibition Act of 1961 says that any person who gives, takes, or abets the giving or taking of dowry shall be punished with imprisonment, which may extend to six months or with fine up to Rs. 5,000 or with both. Dowry that started off as a practice to give away presents to the departing daughter, usually some resources to begin her new married life, slowly assumed extraordinary proportions and turned into a social evil. Brides were expected to bring the "gifts" regardless of their personal willingness. The bride's family could no longer have an individual say; lists were prepared and sent to the girl's house before the final agreement between the two families. The condition being that the boy would marry the girl only if the demands were met. Such a custom is being practiced not only in India but also in other countries like Bangladesh and Nepal. The reason behind this custom is the poor economical condition of the people along with a lack of education; unawareness of legal rights among women and a general bias against the women.

Crimes like rape, kidnapping, eve teasing and indecent exposure can be grouped as crimes against women. Rape is the worst crime against women after murder and the maximum punishment under the Indian Penal Code (IPC) is life imprisonment. An abortion or miscarriage due to natural causes is not an offence. Therefore, the law does not deal with it. However, violent and forceful abortion is a crime. Sections 312 and 316 of the Indian Penal Code deal with abortion as crime. Section 313 deals with abortion without the consent of the woman. The punishment could even be life imprisonment.

The Hindu Succession Act gives male and female heirs almost equal right to inheritance. Section 14 says that any property possessed by a female Hindu shall be held by her as full owner and not as a limited owner.

Family Courts

A family court is a court convened to decide matters and make orders in relation to family law, such as custody of children. In common-law jurisdictions "family courts" are statutory creations primarily dealing with equitable matters devolved from a court of inherent jurisdiction, such as a superior court.

History of the Family Court

The family court is a branch of the Superior Court justice system and is created under s.21.1 of the Courts of Justice Act. Recently, some have questioned the validity of family court.

Case Types

Case types may include:

- Child support
- Child custody
- Visitation rights
- Restraining orders
- Emancipation of minors

Family Court in the United Kingdom

Cases involving children are primarily dealt with under The Children Act 1989, amongst other statutes. Two types of scenario are covered by The Children Act 1989: private law cases, where the applicant and respondent are usually the child's parents; and public law cases, where the applicant is the local authority and the parents are usually respondents. There is much debate at present over whether the manner in which the law is administered generally leads to outcomes that are beneficial to the families concerned. In this context, see fathers' rights. Cases involving divorce and the division of assets are primarily dealt with under the Matrimonial Causes Act 1973. Cases involving domestic violence are primarily dealt with under Part IV of the Family Law Act 1996.

Family Courts in India

Family Courts in India have been set up in several major cities and towns. Broadly, all matrimonial disputes like divorce, maintenance, alimony, custody of children, etc. are tried by the Family Courts. The concept of Family Courts in India imply an integrated broad based service to families in trouble. It stipulates that the Family Court structure should be such as to stabilize the marriage, to preserve the family, and where a marriage has been broken down irretrievably, to dissolve it with maximum fairness and minimum bitterness, distress and humiliation. The Family Court system also visualizes assistance of specialized agencies and persons.

Jurisdiction

Jurisdiction of the Family Courts: The following disputes fall within the jurisdiction of the Family Court:

a) Proceedings between a husband and wife for declaring a marriage as null and void;
b) Proceedings between a husband and wife for restitution of conjugal rights;
c) Proceedings between a husband and wife with respect to judicial separation and divorce;
d) Disputes with respect to the validity of a marriage or as to the matrimonial status of any person;
e) Property disputes between a husband and a wife;
f) Disputes pertaining to the legitimacy of any person;
g) Proceedings with respect to maintenance; and
h) Proceedings in relation to guardianship of the person or the custody of, or access to, any minor.

Confidentiality: It is now a part of the concept of Family Court that confidentiality of the Court record should be maintained and if the parties so desire or the Court so thinks proper, the proceedings should be in camera. The Family Courts Act makes it obligatory on the part of the Court to hold the proceedings in camera if any party so desires. They may also be held in camera if the Court so deems fit.

Procedure

The Family Courts are free to evolve their own rules of procedure, and once a Family Court does so, the rules so framed over ride the rules of procedure contemplated under the Code of Civil Procedure. The Act stipulates that a party is not entitled to be represented by a lawyer without the express permission of the Court (However, in reality, it is invariably a lawyer who represents a party. This is done by filing a formal application seeking the Courts permission to be represented by a lawyer, and such permission, more often than not, is always granted). The most unique aspect regarding the proceedings before the Family Court are that they are first referred to conciliation and only when conciliation proceedings fail, is the matter taken up for trial by the Court. The Conciliators are professionals who are appointed by the Court. Once a final order is passed, the aggrieved party has an option of filing an appeal before the High Court. Such appeal is to be heard by a bench consisting of two judges.

Enforcement Machinery—Police and Judiciary Human Rights as Women's Rights

The judiciary is a major means for the protection of rights. It has the power to receive complaints of the violation of rights, to hear evidence, and to provide redress for violations, including punishment for violators. The judiciary can only perform this function if the legal system is strong and well-organized. The members of the judiciary should be competent, experienced and have a commitment to human rights, dignity and justice. They should be independent of the legislature and the executive by vesting the power of their appointment in a judicial service commission and by constitutional safeguards of their tenure. Judicial institutions should fairly reflect the character of the different sections of the people by religion, region, gender and social class. This means that there must be a restructuring of the judiciary and the investigative machinery. More women, more under-privileged categories and more of the Pariahs of society must by deliberate State action be lifted out of the mire and instilled in judicial positions with necessary training. Only such a measure will command the confidence of the weaker sector whose human rights are ordinarily ignored in the traditional societies of Asia.

The legal profession should be independent. Legal aid should be provided for those who are unable to afford the services of lawyers or have access to courts, for the protection of their rights. Rules which unduly restrict access to courts should be reformed to provide a broad access. Social and welfare organizations should be authorised to bring legal action on behalf of individuals and groups who are unable to utilize the courts.

All states should establish Human Rights Commissions and specialized institutions for the protection of rights, particularly of vulnerable members of society. They can provide easy, friendly and inexpensive access to justice for victims of human rights violations. These bodies can supplement the role of the judiciary. They enjoy special advantages: they can help establish standards for the implementation of human rights norms; they can disseminate information about human rights; they can investigate allegations of violation of rights; they can promote conciliation and mediation; and they can seek to enforce human rights through administrative or judicial means. They can act on their own initiative as well on complaints from members of the public.

Civil society institutions can help to enforce rights through the organization of People's Tribunals, which can touch the conscience of the government and the public. The establishment of People's Tribunals emphasizes that the responsibility for the protection of rights is wide, and not a preserve of the state. They are not confined to legal rules in their adjudication and can consequently help to uncover the moral and spiritual foundations of human rights.

UNIT-IX

Women Issues

Portrayal of Women in Mass Media

We all know the stereotypes—the femme fatale, the supermom, the sex kitten, the nasty corporate climber. Whatever the role, television, film and popular magazines are full of images of women and girls who are typically white, desperately thin, and made up to the hilt—even after slaying a gang of vampires or dressing down a Greek legion.

Many would agree that some strides have been made in how the media portray women in film, television and magazines, and that the last 20 years has also seen a growth in the presence and influence of women in media behind the scenes. Nevertheless, female stereotypes continue to thrive in the media we consume every day.

This section of the site provides a snapshot of the issues around the media's portrayal of women and girls—from effects on body image and self-identity to ramifications in sports and politics. It looks at the economic interests behind the objectification and eroticization of females by the media as well as efforts to counter negative stereotyping. And it provides the latest articles and studies that explore the ways in which media both limit and empower women and girls in society.

Role of Women in Media

Hindi cinema has been a major point of reference for Indian culture in this century. It has shaped and expressed the changing scenarios of modern India to an extent that no preceding art form could ever achieve. Hindi cinema has influenced the way in which people perceive various aspects of their own lives. The three movies that we discuss here have three different points of view towards women. To some extent they identify areas where "modern feminism" comes into contact with "traditional values." The analysis which follows tries to decipher and articulate these points of view. It also attempts to determine the ways in which these films affect the discourse generated by the Women's Movement. But before the analysis we summarize the plots of these films.

A History of the Roles of Women in Newspapers: Media, Gender, and Journalism

In addition to providing the reader with an overview of the history of the media in general and newspapers in particular, this history of women and their role in newspapers, both as readers and journalists, also includes a consideration of women's history and the representation of women in the media. The literature review then tightens its focus to address specific ways in which businesswomen are represented in newspapers, with an emphasis on the portrayal of professional women in the media. Finally, this history of women in newspapers and as journalists and those depicted concludes with an integrative analysis that considers how all of these factors interact with one another in such a way that the newspaper shapes the way the public perceives businesswomen.

The purpose is to add to the body of existing knowledge about communications, which has implications not only for business, but also for media coverage and the portrayal of women in the media. While many existing studies have examined the portrayal of women in magazines (Signorelli, 1997), there are far fewer studies on the subject of how women are portrayed in newspapers, and how those portrayals shape public perceptions and, by extension, business policies and practices. Considering the paucity of studies in this area, it is important to create a system to review newspapers and audit the representation of women. While there is hope that the representation of women has increased proportionately as women continue to enter the field of business, and as women's rights have progressed, evidence to substantiate an increase is necessary.

In fact, almost 20 years after the transition from the era of women's pages, women remain underrepresented in news content. "Historically," writes Armstrong (2006), "the majority of news sources have been male" (p. 447). A recent study of international media revealed that "79 percent of experts quoted in the news media around the world are men while a mere 21 percent are women" ("Media mirror," 2006, p. 11). In addition, only 25% of newsmakers were women; at this rate, observed the author of the report, it will take at least 75 years to achieve gender parity in all aspects of representation in newspaper reporting ("Media mirror," 2006). While many newspapers are attempting to diversify their content in general, from the story idea to the subject, the source, and the reader, the fact of the matter is that in an attempt to be more inclusive of women, newspapers have often adopted the strategy of pushing article ideas that continue to reflect "women's issues" narrowly. In fact, the very term "women's issues" has become an ambiguous umbrella under which a category of stories and themes are clustered; the term itself has become so broad that it has begun to lose meaning (Armstrong, 2006, p. 448).

As Armstrong (2006) notes, "women's issues... ranges from topical issues like breast cancer and hormone replacement therapy to stories about weddings and parties...." (p. 448). Yet while more women take on positions in business and society that have traditionally been reserved for men, stories and sources in newspapers are not reflecting the shift (Armstrong, 2006). The problem, then, is that while more stories that are allegedly intended to *interest* women are being included in newspaper content, the number and quality of stories representing women in the general content of the newspaper remain scant. As Armstrong (2006) observes, the implications of such an approach to reporting is significant because it "may signal to readers that that women are unimportant for public events and activities and undeserving of leadership roles"; it may also push women away from newspapers as readers.

Despite newsroom editors' intentions to be inclusive in coverage, Rintala and Birrell (1984) argue that newspapers tend to preserve the status quo rather than act as agents of social change. Quite simply, although women have made increasing inroads in almost all areas of professional and social life, represented in politics, sports (Flatten, 1996), and corporate business, they remain inadequately and disproportionately underrepresented by all media, including newspapers.

Newspapers are not simply about text, photographs came to play an important role in newspapers across the country. One way in which the photograph was paired with text in the newspaper in such a way to appeal specifically to women readers was in those sections of the newspaper that came to be known as the women's pages, a tradition that can be traced at least as far back as the 1890s (Armstrong, 2006; Fahs, 2005). In women's pages, the "four Fs" were core content: "family, food, fashion, and furnishings" (Armstrong, 2006, p. 449). Special sections of the newspaper were developed for women, including society pages, which covered engagements and weddings; food sections, which included recipes and tips on being a good homemaker; and beauty sections, recently refashioned as women's health, in which women received advice—some clinical and most not—about how to look beautiful, if not stay healthy (Armstrong, 2006). Even when women were reporting the stories in the women's pages, the assumption of editors was that these types of stories were particularly appropriate for women—as opposed to "hard" news—because "women were assumed to have special abilities at the emotive storytelling, character sketches, and telling anecdotes that human interest stories demanded" (Fahs, 2005, p. 306). While many women journalists pushed their editors to assign them stories that were relevant to a general audience and which represented real news as opposed to filler, the majority of women were relegated to these special pages (Fahs, 2005).

The problem of the women's pages approach was that it marginalized women. By creating "special" sections that newspaper editors and—importantly—advertisers believed were geared expressly for women, the newspaper actually, if unconsciously, assumed that women were either uninterested in "real" news or that they were not qualified or capable of being a part of such news, either as subjects or as sources. Interestingly, although the women's pages may have had "content for women," such content was not always "content about women." In other words, even in articles themed around interests believed to be specifically feminine, men often remained more prominent than women as quoted sources, observers, and experts (Armstrong, 2006). The obvious shift away from women's pages began in the 1990s, as the traditionally female sections of the newspaper began to be renamed with less obviously gender-specific titles. Beauty sections were now called Health or Lifestyle, for instance. The intention and the effect, however, had not changed significantly.

One may argue that the bias against women in newspapers is merely a reflection of the bias that exists against women in society, both historical and contemporary. American women have long been in a position of not enjoying parity with men, whether the kind of parity being discussed is professional, political, social, or economic in nature (American Association of University Women Educational Foundation, 2005). In recent years, however, the gains made by the feminist/women's movement have made it possible for women to begin chipping away at the glass ceiling. More women than ever are participating in the workplace, more women than ever are occupying positions of professional authority and power, and more women than ever are beginning to approach salary earnings that are close—but not quite on par—to those of their male counterparts (American Association of University Women Educational Foundation, 2005). An examination, then, of how newspaper reporting has or has not evolved in its coverage of professional women and their workplace actions, challenges, and accomplishments cannot be possible without understanding some of the background and contextual factors that have brought women to this unprecedented point of professional participation.

An Alternative to Literacy Is it possible for community video and radio to play this role? a small experiment by the Deccan Development Society, Hyderabad, India.

Literacy has become a Holy Grail in the world of development. Development groups working in rural areas suffer from a feeling of inadequacy if they are not pursuing literacy programmes. They maybe doing excellent work through harnessing people's knowledge in the fields of forestry, fisheries, natural farming, land development, natural resource management whatever. But literacy programmes haunt them. The irony is that in most of these activities literacy has very little to offer. People's knowledge and peoples science in all these areas are so strong that they need very little external help in the form of technology. But still the feeling of inadequacy prevails very strong among non-literacy groups.

Time has come to question this exaggerated importance given to literacy in development. I would not like to be misunderstood as an anti-literacy person. I value literacy very much. What I am pointing to is in valuing literacy we should not devalue other capabilities and skills present in non-literate people. By doing so, we might kill all the self-confidence in these people. I am itching to tell a story which I had heard in my childhood. I still cherish it for the message it gives:

Three scholars decided to cross a river. They asked a boatman to help them cross the river. The boatman was glad to oblige them. As the boat sailed out, one scholar asked the boatman: Have you read Vedas. The boatman humbly replied "No Sir". He felt very ashamed. The scholar rubbed it in. "A quarter of your life is wasted". After they sailed a little further, the second scholar asked: "Have you read Upanishads?" The boatman felt further small. "No Sir". The scholar said contemptuously: "Half your life is wasted". They sailed halfway into the river.

The third scholar asked, "At least have you read Puranas?" The boatman felt totally humiliated. "No sir, not even that". "Then three quarter of your life is a waste". By then they hit a whirlpool. The boat started sinking. The boatman, for the first time, asked the scholars: "Sir, do you people know how to swim?" All the scholars said "No" in total panic. "All your lives are a waste now sir", said the boatman and leapt out of the boat.

What I am trying to say is that in our part of the world there is a generation of women and men, people who are in their thirties and above who are not literate. But they have deep reserves of knowledge in farming, forestry, ecology, natural resource management—areas where survival knowledge, which is paramount for the human race, eludes us the literates. Why should we discount this rich knowledge and skills with which they survive in the harshest of environments and push literacy towards them as THE SKILL? This has been one of the key questions that bothers my mind in my work with disadvantaged rural women in Medak District of Andhra Pradesh.

Historical Background of DDS

DDS started in this environment as the commitment of a group of professionals to the people in the Zaheerabad region to continue a rural development project abandoned by an industrial house due to its own compulsions. The earliest objectives of DDS was to combine ecological and employment parameters to regenerate the livelihoods of the people in the area through a string of activities:

- Ensure 100 days of employment per year per person
- Use these employment days to work on their lands to enhance the productivity of their soils through bunding, trenching, top soil addition etc.
- Galvanise communities of women to lease in lands from large farmers and work on it collectively.
- Green the area through planting in the village commons.

An associated objective was to transfer people-oriented technology. This included housing technologies, use of solar energy, permaculture way of organic farming etc. Gradually all these efforts have moved in a reverse direction. Today we recognise that people have more knowledge than us, more appropriate technologies than we can think of. Therefore our programmes have evolved into three principles:

- gender justice
- environmental-soundness and
- people's knowledge

Education at all levels was a very strong component in this string of efforts. Education, for DDS, encompasses a range of activities starting with balwadies to provide a creative learning environment for young children to Pachasaale, a unique school for working children which takes formal learning and life skills under one umbrella and redefines education into an area of relevance for rural children. Within this range are fitted intensive workshops for adult women, village night schools for out of school children etc.

Central to these attempts is the relocation of people's knowledge in the areas of health (through revitalising the traditional healthcare systems), agriculture (understanding, documenting and promoting people's knowledge of farming systems and practices) etc.

New Forms of Expression

When the commitment of an organisation is to value peoples knowledge and build its work on their confidence, the need to explore various tools of expression with which people can communicate with the outside world. Because the outside world is a reality and their necessity to communicate with it is also a reality.

In this effort, literacy was not the only choice. We felt literacy can actually become a constraint for non-literate people whose aural and visual narratives are so powerful. So what else can one think of? For me the possibility of providing video and audio technologies as a means of expression for the disadvantaged rural women was an exciting idea. So I have made efforts to equip a group of ten women with the skills to handle this media.

Communicating Through Video

I began a series of video workshops from January this year. Each workshop was for a duration of four days. Spread over eight months these workshops have trained a total of seven women of whom four are non-literate. Of these seven women, two are students and the four are farm labour and one is a DDS worker. All of them are dalits in an age group of 16-35 years.

The workshops started with a total of eleven persons, ten women and one man. But of them four dropped out during various phases of the workshops and seven have made it to all the workshops.

The women chose to learn video production for various reasons. Their own reasons

are as follows:

- We would like to let our issues known outside(Ippapally Mallamma)
- Our news must go outside (Zaheerabad Punyamma)
- We are working on the Gene Bank in our village. Several times you people come to shoot our work. But there are seasons when it is very important to shoot. At that time you people may not be available. Therefore when you people do not come, we can do our own recording and give it to you. (Humnapur Laxmi)
- So that we can communicate with people in other sanghams. Whenever some events take place in our sanghams, you people come to video it. When you don't come, we have to wait for you. Instead we can do the recording ourselves and take it out.(Pastapur Narsamma)
- To photograph; marriages etc.(Bopanpalli Nagamma)
- When big government people come to our village, we would like to record what they tell us. That becomes a document for us. (Eedulapalle Manjula)

Their expectations from the workshops were also varied.

- How can we tell about the work we are doing?
- To know whether it (the video) can record what we talk and say
- To understand what parts it (the video) has
- To know whether it records from a distance; how to make pictures big and small; how to make sound big and small;

The training objective was to familiarise the participants with the grammar of television, with the operation of video cameras and in editing their shoots and make their own stories. These workshops were conducted by three of us:

- P V Satheesh, a television Producer/Director (who incidentally is Director, Deccan Development Society and is an experienced producer and trainer and familiar with the rural ethos).
- Vijendra Patil, a Cameraman-producer who has a variety of experiences in training and production.
- Yesu, an 18-year old rural boy, who had recently apprenticed with a video production house and who was being simultaneously trained on video operations and editing.

The training was done with one DV Camera and two VHS video cameras and a makeshift editing set up.

Methodology

The trainings were conducted using the following methods:

- Group discussion on what the motivation of each person was to come for the training.
- Visual explanation with the use of drawings on the blackboard of the various concepts and terms.
- Creation of a new technical vocabulary in the local dialect using the women's words and their experiences. This became an exercise in participatory glossary formation in the local language.
- Creation of learning games to bring home the concepts. For eg. hopscotch was a game used to teach the principles of varying the image sizes, camera distances, heights and angles when shooting a given object for successive shots.
- Hands on training in using the camera and editing the pictures
- Group analysis of each other's work to facilitate a group learning process

Through these processes the women learnt the following:

- Parts of a video camcorder and how to operate each of them

- Use of a camera tripod
- Shots and image sizes
- Camera frame and simple principles of picture composition
- Camera distance, camera angle and camera movement
- Simple microphones and simple techniques of sound recording.
- Shot breakdown for a simple shoot
- Plotting camera positions for a simple shoot
- Logging the shoot and finding editing points
- Executing an edit on a VHS system

Outputs and Linkages

The training cum learning processes involved have been videoed and have been through a rough edit. After learning video skills for 30 days, the women have filmed one aspect of their sangham work namely pre-schools for their children and their significance to their lives. Together these two films highlight the capacities, experiences and communication skills of the village women.

In October there was unprecedented rain in our area and crops in the field were severely damaged. The women decided to tell their story on video. The group discussed their ideas and planned the story. Ms.Narasamma, a 25 year old non literate farm worker was selected as the reporter. The group also wanted to highlight in the story, that this video was being shot by the rural women themselves. Two cameras were taken to the field and the reporter stood in ankle deep water and gave her piece to the camera, briefly but passionately telling the facts regarding the destruction of bajra and jowar and the black future of the farmer and the women.

The quality of shooting with the play of light, close up of the blackened jowar was made more poignant as it was these women's fields that we were looking at. The story has gone on air on the regional Doordarshan network and on ETV, a commercial channel. This gave us confidence that the group can make short videos of broadcast quality. It was evident that the group had confidence in themselves and was beginning to handle their ideas, equipments and find space on air.

This gave us an idea and we have negotiated for a regular chunk on their channels both with the Doordarshan and with the ETV channel. Both have agreed to provide them space. Doordarshan has said that it is interested in giving them space on their Women's programme while ETV has in principle agreed provide a five minute slot per month for stories on organic farming.

Findings

- Video can be a very effective tool for use by non-literate rural people to express themselves to the outside world
- Being non literate is no barrier in learning video as a mode of expression. Therefore instead of literacy being pushed down the throats of adult rural women and men, new media of expressions can be found.
- Non literate women can turn into excellent videographers. Their traditional narrative and pictorial understanding of the world around them can find wonderful expression in the videos made by them.
- The trainers in these workshops who have long experiences in training professional television practitioners in the Afro Asian region, were struck with the ease and quickness with which non literate women were able to learn and use video. In many cases they started wondering whether literacy is after all a barrier in learning new media of expression.
- In their ability to understand and express through video the non literate women were not even a slight shade inferior to their urban counterparts who come to media education with formidable academic backgrounds.

Recommendations

- Video has a great potential for use in rural communities as a mode of exchange of ideas and thoughts. This must be recognised and the use of simple video by the rural communities in developmental communication must be supported and encoraged.

- Non literate communities can handle video extraordinarily well to express themselves and communicate with the outside world. Therefore as a tool for direct communication between communities and governments, policy makers, funders and international development organisations, video should be explored more widely. The burden of being non-literate gets lifted if video can substitute communication through literacy. With such and effort, non literate communities can regain their confidence for expression with outside world.
- Women in traditional communities are normally kept out of the realm of communicating with the external world. Interpersonal communication with outsiders, written communication and participation in large groups to express themselves normally becomes very difficult for thesse women. As a first stage of helping them find their own expression video can be used as a very effecive tool.
- Civil Society groups should be helped to establish and run Community Media Centres which include video and audio communication facilities. This prevents them from seeking literacy as the only tool of expression for their rural client groups. This also releases the latent energy among their communites whose confidences are normally shattered wit the existing heavy emphasis on literacy.
- This is not to suggest that efforts towards literacy must be stopped. On the contrary. What is being suggested is that we must recognise that to be effectively literate is a generational effort. In the meanwhile people of the middle generation who are past their teens should not be made to feel subhumans because they are not literate. If they are given other tools of expression their confidences can be rebuilt and literacy can follow as they start effectively communicating with the outside world with the new found tools. Video can be one such tool which they can easily master and handle.

The video training has tremendous value as it comes at a time when women are required to communicate more widely, their experiences and expertise in permaculture, empowerment and leadership training. Handling the camera also gives visibility in the community and empowers the women to document the stories of the community. Overall, the women have demonstrated the potential of becoming a rich independent, human resource for region in communicating indigenous development practises.

Community F M Radio

The other medium we are trying to explore with the non-literate rural women is Radio. Annexure A gives in detail their own expectations from a radio of their own. Their arguments are extraordinarily original and are unmatched for their logic. For the women who are equipped with extraordinary oral narrative skills radio is a natural medium. We feel very excited with the possibilities of using it. We have built a low cost radio station which is 90% complete and will be operationalised by January 1999. It is designed as an FM station capable of working on audio cassette technology. It has a 100 watts transmitter which can reach a radius of 30 kms. The station is part of the Women Speak to Women programme of UNESCO, which has supported us in this venture. Once the station is in operation dalit women from 75 villages will own and operate it. They will bring their form and content into it and make it a tool for their horizontal communication with their communities and to reach out to the outside world.

As the women get equipped with the capacities to express their thoughts, their knowledge and their vision for their future through pictures and sounds, we feel, we have made a major breakthrough in providing a technology for the education of deprived rural communities. And for the education of the outside world about what these communities are capable of.

Development of Communication Skills—Alternative Media—Folk Art

Folk art encompasses art produced from an indigenous culture or by peasants or other laboring tradespeople. In contrast to fine art, folk art is primarily utilitarian and decorative rather than purely aesthetic.

As a phenomenon that can chronicle a move towards civilization yet rapidly diminish with modernity, industrialization, or outside influence, the nature of folk art is specific to its particular culture. The varied geographical and temporal prevalence and diversity of folk art make it difficult to describe as a whole, though some patterns have been demonstrated.

Antique Folk Art

Antique folk art is distinguished from traditional art in that while it is collected today based mostly on its artistic merit; it was never intended as a category to be art for art's sake. Examples include: weathervanes, old store signs and carved figures, itinerant portraits, carousel horses, fire buckets, painted game boards, cast iron doorstops and many other similar lines of highly collectible "whimsical" antiques.

Characteristics

Characteristically folk art is not influenced by movements in academic or fine art circles, and, in many cases, folk art excludes works executed by professional artists and sold as "high art" or "fine art" to the society's art patrons. On the other hand, many 18th and 19th century American folk art painters made their living by their work, including itinerant portrait painters, some of whom produced large bodies of work.

Other terms that overlap with folk art are naïve art, Pop art, outsider art, traditional art, "self-taught" art and even "working class" art. As one might expect, all these terms have different connotations; but they are all at times used interchangeably with the term folk art, for which a satisfactory definition has proven hard to come by.

Theatre

After the Restoration in 1660, Charles II brought an innovative addition to the English theater: women were allowed to take the stage as actresses. The novelty of having women on stage created something of a stir, but for the most part the reaction of the public was positive, especially that of the young men who regularly chose their mistresses from the ranks of the new professionals. Many of the new actresses were women who intentionally used their position to achieve liaisons with titled gentlemen and thus increase their meager income. One of the most famous was of course Nell Gwyn, who became the mistress of Charles II.

Another, Elizabeth Barry, outlived her noble patron the Earl of Rochester by several decades, and later enjoyed the reputation of being one of the greatest actresses of the age. Not all actresses used the stage as a market, however: Mrs. Betterton helped manage the highly successful Duke's Company with her husband, training the younger actresses, and her pupil Anne Bracegirdle had the reputation of living a strict moral life.

Despite their popularity, women did not enjoy the same status as men in the theater. Their pay did not equal that of their male colleagues, and while many male actors became playwrights, very few women made the transition. One of the few who did, Charlotte Charke, wrote a total of three plays.

Aphra Behn, never an actress, may have possibly made her way into the world of Restoration theater through family connections. Her forte was comedy, often revolving around a plot of "forced marriage"—which was also the title of her first produced play in 1670. Even working within the constraints of the Restoration's male dominated society, Behn managed to create strong, independent female characters who made their own choices. Over the course of her nineteen year career, Behn probably wrote over twenty plays, as well as several novels and volumes of poetry.

The most well-known female dramatist to follow Behn, Susanna Centlivre, wrote nineteen plays during her career, beginning in 1700. Most of her plays were comedies of intrigue, although she did write two tragicomedies, *The Perjur'd Husband* (1700) and *The Cruel Gift* (1716). She was very popular in her time but has since been forgotten more effectively even than Aphra Behn.

In addition to actresses and playwrights, there were several women during this period who managed theaters, for example Charlotte Charke, who followed Henry Fielding as the manager of the Little Theatre in Haymarket. Lady Henrietta Maria Davenant succeeded her husband, the playwright Sir William Davenant, as manager of the Duke's Company, and with the assistance of the Bettertons lead the company until its merger with the King's Company.

Under her management, the Dorset Garden Theater, where Aphra Behn produced her plays, was the most successful theatrical company in London. She also acted as a mentor for actresses and actors, even putting young actresses up in her own house when they couldn't find affordable lodgings.

Women as Change Agents Indecent Representation of Women (Prohibition) Act, 1986

An Act to prohibit indecent representation of women through advertisements or in publications, writings, paintings, figures or in any other manner and for matters connected therewith or incidental thereto.

Be it enacted by Parliament in the Thirty-seven Year of the Republic of India as follows:-

1. Short title, extent and commencement.
   - (1) This Act may be called the Indecent Representation of Women (Prohibition) Act, 1986.
   - (2) It extends to the whole of India, except the State of Jammu and Kashmir.
   - (3) It shall come into force on such date as the Central Government may, by notification in the Official Gazette, appoint.
2. Definitions.-In this Act, unless the context otherwise requires,-

"advertisement" includes any notice, circular, label, wrapper or other document and also includes any visible representation made by means of any light, sound, smoke or gas;

"distribution" includes distribution by way of samples whether free or otherwise;

"indecent representation of women" means the depiction in any manner of the figure of a woman; her form or body or any part thereof in such way as to have the effect of being indecent, or derogatory to, or denigrating women, or is likely to deprave, corrupt or injure the public morality or morals;

"label" means any written, marked, stamped, printed or graphic matter, affixed to, or appearing upon, any package;

"package" includes a box, a carton, tin or other container;

"prescribed" means prescribed by rules made under this Act.

3 Prohibition of advertisements containing indecent representation of Women.-No person shall publish, or cause to be published, or arrange or take part in the publication or exhibition of, any advertisement which contains indecent representation of women in any form.

4 Prohibition of publication or sending by post of books, pamphlets, etc; containing indecent representation of women.-No person shall produce or cause to be produced, sell, let to hire, distribute, circulate or send by post any book, pamphlet, paper, slide, film, writing, drawing, painting, photograph, representation or figure which contains indecent representation of women in any form:

Provided that noting in this section shall apply to:

(a) any book, pamphlet, paper, slide, film, writing, drawing, painting, photograph, representation or figure:

(i) the publication of which is proved to be justified as justified as being for the public good on the ground that such book, pamphlet, paper, slide, film, writing, drawing, painting, photography, representation or figure is in the interest of science, literature, art, or learning, art, or learning or other objects of general concern; or

(ii) which is kept or used bona fide for religious purpose;

any representation sculptured, engraved, painted or otherwise represented on or in:

(i) any ancient monument within the meaning of the Ancient Monument and Archaeological Sites and Remains Act, 1958 (24 of 1958); or

(ii) any temple, or on any car used or the conveyance of idols, or kept or used for any religious purpose;

any film in respect of which the provisions of Part II of the Cinematograph Act, 1952 (37 of 1952), will be applicable.

5. Powers to enter and search.-(1) Subject to such rules as may be prescribed, any Gazetted Officer authorized by the State Government may, within the local limits of the area for which he is so authorized:-

enter and search at all reasonable times, with such assistance, if any, as he considers necessary, any place in which he has reason to believe that an offence under this Act has been or is being committed;

seize any advertisement or any book, pamphlet, paper, slide, film, writing, drawing, painting, photograph, representation or figure which he has reason to believe contravenes any of the provisions of this Act;

examine any record, register, document or any other material object found in any place mentioned in Cl.(a) and seize the same if he has reason to believe that it may furnish evidence of the commission of an offence punishable under this Act.

Provided that no entry under this sub-section shall be made into a private dwelling-house without a warrant:

(1) Provided further that the power of seizure under this sub-section may be exercised in respect of any document, article or thing which contains any such advertisement, including the contents, if any, of such document, article or thing if the advertisement cannot be separated by reason of its being embossed or otherwise from such document, article or thing without affecting the integrity, utility or saleable value thereof.

(2) The provisions of the Code of Criminal Procedure, 1973(2 of 1974), shall, so far as may be, apply to any search or seizure made under the authority of a warrant issued under Sec.94 of the said Code.

(3) where any person seizes anything under Cl.(b) or Cl.(c) of sub section (1), he shall, as soon as may be, inform the nearest Magistrate and take his orders as to the custody thereof.

6. *Penalty:* Any person who contravenes the provisions of Sec 3 or Sec 4 shall be punishable on first conviction with imprisonment of either description for a term which may extend to two years, and with fine which may extend to two thousand rupees, and in the event of a second or subsequent conviction with imprisonment for term of not less than six months but which may extend to five years and also with a fine not less than ten thousand rupees but which may extend to one lakh rupees.

7. *Offences by Companies:*

(1) Where an offence under this Act has been committed by a company, every person, who, at the time the offence was committed was in-charge of, and was responsible to, the company for the conduct of the business of the company, as well as the company, shall be deemed to be guilty of the offence and shall be liable to be proceeded against and punished accordingly:

Provided that nothing contained in this sub-section shall render any such person liable to any punishment, if he proves that the offence was committed without his knowledge or that he had exercised all due diligence to prevent the commission of such offence.

(2) Notwithstanding anything contained in sub-section (1), where any offence under this Act has been committed by a company and it is proved that the offence has been committed with the consent or

connivance of, or is attributable to any neglect on the part of, any director, manager, secretary or other officer of the company, such director, manager, secretary or other officer shall be proceeded against and punished accordingly.

Explanation – For the purpose of this section.-

"company" means any body corporate and includes a firm or other association of individuals; and

"director", in relation to a firm, means a partner in the firm.

8. Offences to be cognizable and bailable.

   (1) Notwithstanding anything contained in the Code of Criminal Procedure, 1973 (2of 1974), an offence punishable under this Act shall be bailable.

   (2) An offence punishable under this Act shall be cognizable.

9. Protection of action taken in good faith.-No suit, prosecution or other legal proceeding shall lie against the Central Government or any State Government or any officer of the Central Government or any State Government for anything which is in good faith done or intended to be done under this Act.

10. Power to make rules.

   (1) The Central Government may, by notification in the Official Gazette, make rules to carry out the provisions of this Act.

   (2) In particular and without prejudice to the generality of the foregoing power, such rules may provide for all or any of the following matters, namely:-

      (a) the manner in which the seizure of advertisement or other articles shall be made, and the manner in which the seizure list shall be prepared and delivered to the person from whose custody any advertisement or other article has been seized;

      any other matter which is required to be, or may be, prescribed.

(3) Every rule made under this Act, shall be laid, as soon as may be after it is made, before each House of Parliament, while it is in session for a total period of thirty days, which may be comprised in one session or in two or more successive sessions, and if, before the expiry of the session immediately following the session or the successive session aforesaid, both Houses agree in making any modification in the rule or both Houses agree that the rule should not be made, the rule shall thereafter have effect only in such modified form or be of no effect, as the case may be; so, however, that any such modification or annulment shall be without prejudice to the validity of anything previously done under that rule.

Indecent Representation of Women (Prohibition) Rules, 1987

G.S.R.822 (E), dated 25 September, 1987.-In exercise of the powers conferred by Sec.10 of the Indecent representation of Women (Prohibition) Act, 1986 (60 of 1986), the Central Government hereby makes the following rules, namely :

1. Short title and commencement.

(1) These rules may be called the Indecent Representation of Women (Prohibition) Rules, 1987.

(2) They shall come into force on the 2 October, 1987.

2. Definitions.

(1) In these rules, unless the context otherwise requires,-

(a) 'Act' means the Indecent Representation of women (Prohibition) Act, 1986 (60 of 1986);

(b) 'article' means any book, pamphlet, paper, slide, film, writing, drawing, painting, photograph, representation of figure;

(c) 'authorized officer' means any Gazetted Officer authorized by the State Government for the purpose of section 5 of the Act.

(d) 'section' means a section of the Act.

(2) Words and expressions used in these rules and not defined, shall have the meanings respectively, assigned to them in the Act.

3. Manner of seizure of articles.

(1) Every seizure made in pursuance of the provisions of sub-section (1) of section 5 shall be made in the manner hereinafter provided in these rules.

(2) The authorized officer seizing any advertisements or articles under sub-section (1) of section 5 shall prepare a list of such advertisements or articles containing such details relating to the description, quality, quantity, mark, number and other particulars thereof as he may consider relevant to the identity of such advertisements or articles in any proceeding under the Act, in the Form annexed to these rules.

(3) The authorized officer shall pack and seal such advertisements or articles in the manner provided in rule 4 and shall deliver a copy of the list so prepared to the person from whom such advertisements or articles are seized.

(4) The advertisements or articles so seized shall be marked with a distinguishing number and shall also be signed by the authorized officer, the person from whom such advertisements or articles have been seized and two respectable inhabitants of the locality. If it is not possible to mark any such advertisement or article, the marking may be done on the packaging or in any other manner which the authorised officer thinks proper.

4. Manner of packing and dealing with advertisements or articles seized.

(1) The advertisements or articles seized shall be packed in adequately strong paper, cloth or in any other packing material in such a way that the advertisements or articles may not be tampered with and the ends of the paper, cloth or other packing

material shall be neatly folded and affixed by means of gum or other adhesive or stitched in or tied.

(2) The package shall be further secured by means of strong twine or thread and the twine or thread shall be fastened on the package by means of sealing wax on which there shall be at least four distinct and clear impressions of the seal of the authorised officer of which one shall be on the top of the package, one at the bottom and the other two at the body of the package and knots of the twine or thread shall be covered by means of sealing wax bearing the impression of the seal of the authorized officer.

(3) Where necessary, the authorized officer shall put the advertisements or articles in a box, a container of a suitable material and size and seal it in the manner provided in sub-rule (2).

5. Manner of seizing and sealing advertisements or articles in certain cases.-Notwithstanding anything contained in rules 3 and 4, where the authorized officer is of the opinion that it is not possible to seize and seal any advertisement or article in the manner prescribed in rules 3 and 4 due to the size or the nature of such advertisement or article, he may take such steps as he thinks fit for the seizure and sealing of such advertisement or article without affecting the integrity, utility or saleable value thereof.

Impact of Media on Women

Women professionals and athletes continue to be under-represented in news coverage, and are often stereotypically portrayed when they are included.

Although there has been a steady increase in the number of women professionals over the past 20 years, most mainstream press coverage continues to rely on men as experts in the fields of business, politics and economics. Women in the news are more likely to be featured in stories about accidents, natural disasters, or domestic violence than in stories about their professional abilities or expertise.

Women in politics are similarly sidelined. Canadian journalist Jenn Goddu studied newspaper and magazine coverage of three women's lobby groups over a 15-year period. She discovered that journalists tend to focus on the domestic aspects of the politically active woman's life (such as "details about the high heels stashed in her bag, her habit of napping in the early evening, and her lack of concern about whether or not she is considered ladylike") rather than her position on the issues.

Quebec political analyst Denis Monière uncovered similar patterns. In 1998, Monière analysed 83 late evening newscasts on three national networks—the Canadian Broadcasting Corporation, Radio-Canada (the French-language public broadcaster) and TVA. He observed that women's views were solicited mainly in the framework of "average citizens" and rarely as experts, and that political or economic success stories were overwhelmingly masculine.

Monière also noted that the number of female politicians interviewed was disproportionate to their number in Parliament or in the Quebec National Assembly; nor, he noted, was this deficiency in any way compensated for by the depth and quality of coverage.

Inadequate women's coverage seems to be a worldwide phenomenon. In 2000 the Association of Women Journalists (Association des femmes journalistes–AFJ) studied news coverage of women and women's issues in 70 countries. It reported that only 18 per cent of stories quote women, and that the number of women-related stories came to barely 10 per cent of total news coverage.

News talk shows are equally problematic. The White House Project reports that only 9 per cent of the guests on Sunday morning news shows such as *Meet the Press* and *Face the Nation* are women, and even then they only speak 10 per cent of the time—leaving 90 per cent of the discussion to the male guests. Project president Marie Wilson warns that the lack of representation for women will have profound consequences on whether or not women are perceived as competent leaders, because "authority is not recognized by these shows. It is created by these shows."

Professor Caryl Rivers notes that politically active women are often disparaged and stereotyped by the media. When Hillary Clinton was still first lady, she was referred to as a "witch" or "witchlike" at least 50 times in the press. Rivers writes, "male political figures may be called mean and nasty names, but those words don't usually reflect superstition and dread. Did the press ever call Presidents Carter, Reagan, Bush, or Clinton warlocks?"

Women athletes are also given short shrift in the media. Margaret Carlisle Duncan and Michael Messner studied sports coverage on three network affiliates in Los Angeles. They report that only nine per cent of airtime was devoted to women's sports, in contrast to the 88 per cent devoted to male athletes. Female athletes fared even worse on ESPN's national sports show *Sports Center*, where they occupied just over two per cent of airtime. And, according to the Canadian Association for the Advancement of Women, Sports and Physical Activity, women athletes receive just three per cent of sports coverage in major Canadian dailies.

Margaret Carlisle Duncan notes that commentators (97 per cent of whom are men) use different language when they talk about female athletes. Where men are described as "big," "strong," "brilliant," "gutsy" and "aggressive," women are more often referred to as "weary," "fatigued," "frustrated," "panicked," "vulnerable" and "choking." Commentators are also twice as likely to call men by their last names only, and three times as likely to call women by their first names only. Duncan argues that this "reduces female athletes to the role of children, while giving adult status to white male athletes."

UNIT-X

Evaluation

Limitations of Methodology of Social Science

Evaluation is systematic determination of merit, worth, and significance of something or someone using criteria against a set of standards. Evaluation often is used to characterize and appraise subjects of interest in a wide range of human enterprises, including the arts, criminal justice, foundations and non-profit organizations, government, health care, and other human services.

Depending on the topic of interest, there are professional groups which look to the quality and rigor of the evaluation process.

The Joint Committee on Standards for Educational Evaluation has developed standards for educational programmes, personnel, and student evaluation. The Joint Committee standards are broken into four sections: *Utility, Feasibility, Propriety,* and *Accuracy*. Various European institutions have also prepared their own standards, more or less related to those produced by the Joint Committee. They provide guidelines about basing value judgments on systematic inquiry, evaluator competence and integrity, respect for people, and regard for the general and public welfare.

The American Evaluation Association has created a set of Guiding Principles for evaluators. The order of these principles does not imply priority among them; priority will vary by situation and evaluator role. The principles run as follows:

- *Systematic Inquiry:* Evaluators conduct systematic, data-based inquiries about whatever is being evaluated.
- *Competence:* Evaluators provide competent performance to stakeholders.
- *Integrity/Honesty:* Evaluators ensure the honesty and integrity of the entire evaluation process.
- *Respect for People:* Evaluators respect the security, dignity and self-worth of the respondents, programme participants, clients, and other stakeholders with whom they interact.
- *Responsibilities for General and Public Welfare:* Evaluators articulate and take into account the diversity of interests and values that may be related to the general and public welfare.

Furthermore, the international organizations such as the I.M.F. and the World Bank have independent evaluation functions. The various funds, programmes, and agencies of the United Nations has a mix of independent, semi-independent and self-evaluation functions, which have organized themselves as a system-wide UN Evaluation Group (UNEG), that works together to strengthen the function, and to establish UN norms and standards for evaluation. There is also an evaluation group within the OECD-DAC, which endeavors to improve development evaluation standards. Evaluation is an in depth analysis of an answer, using for instance diagrams. it basicly mean that evaluting anything that you are doing will have a result at the end.

Two classifications of evaluation approaches by House and Stufflebeam & Webster can be combined into a manageable number of approaches in terms of their unique and important underlying principles.

House considers all major evaluation approaches to be based on a common ideology, liberal democracy. Important principles of this ideology include freedom of choice, the uniqueness of the individual, and empirical inquiry grounded in objectivity. He also contends they are all based on subjectivist ethics, in which ethical conduct is based on the subjective or intuitive experience of an individual or group. One form of subjectivist ethics is utilitarian, in which "the good" is determined by what maximizes some single, explicit interpretation of happiness for society as a whole. Another form of subjectivist ethics is intuitionist/pluralist, in which no single interpretation of "the good" is assumed and these interpretations need not be explicitly stated nor justified.

These ethical positions have corresponding epistemologies—philosophies of obtaining knowledge. The objectivist epistemology is associated with the utilitarian ethic. In general, it is used to acquire knowledge capable of external verification (intersubjective agreement) through publicly inspectable methods and data. The subjectivist epistemology is associated with the intuitionist/pluralist ethic. It is used to acquire new knowledge based on existing personal knowledge and experiences that are (explicit) or are not (tacit) available for public inspection.

House further divides each epistemological approach by two main political perspectives. Approaches can take an elite perspective, focusing on the interests of managers and professionals. They also can take a mass perspective, focusing on consumers and participatory approaches.

Stufflebeam and Webster place approaches into one of three groups according to their orientation toward the role of values, an ethical consideration. The political orientation promotes a positive or negative view of an object regardless of what its value actually might be. They call this pseudo-evaluation. The questions orientation includes approaches that might or might not provide answers specifically related to the value of an object. They call this quasi-evaluation. The values orientation includes approaches primarily intended to determine the value of some object. They call this true evaluation.

When the above concepts are considered simultaneously, fifteen evaluation approaches can be identified in terms of epistemology, major perspective (from House), and orientation (from Stufflebeam & Webster). Two pseudo-evaluation approaches, politically controlled and public relations studies, are represented. They are based on an objectivist epistemology from an elite perspective. Six quasi-evaluation approaches use an objectivist epistemology. Five of them—experimental research, management information systems, testing programmes, objectives-based studies, and content analysis—take an elite perspective. Accountability takes a mass perspective. Seven true evaluation approaches are included. Two approaches, decision-oriented and policy studies, are based on an objectivist epistemology from an elite perspective. Consumer-oriented studies are based on an objectivist epistemology from a mass perspective. Two approaches—accreditation/certification and connoisseur studies—are based on a subjectivist epistemology from an elite perspective. Finally, adversary and client-centered studies are based on a subjectivist epistemology from a mass perspective.

Research for Women's Studies

Women's Studies is one of the most vibrant international fields of study, producing its own body of scholarship, at the same time challenging and altering traditional disciplines and having a profound effect on the wider world.One of feminism's success stories over the past four decades has been the establishment of Women's Studies programmes throughout every continent, and this expansion is continuing. As a discipline, Women's Studies addresses issues previously neglected by traditional disciplines, and adapts and refines theories and methods from those disciplines.Women's Studies is not simply the study of women and women's issues.

It is the study of women that places women's own experiences at the centre of enquiry and looks at how gender is a fundamental structure in all societies. Gender is the term used to describe the relationship between ideas about masculinity and femininity; gender describes the system of rules by which males and females are encouraged to relate to each other. What other disciplines use as assumptions about women and men, Women's Studies poses as questions. Feminist theory offers us the most sustained and nuanced understandings of how oppression works locally and globally and Women's Studies offers rich insight into the intersections among sexism, racism, homophobia, classism, ableism, religious sectarianism and other forms of oppression.Our classes are taught according to feminist teaching principles and so there is active student participation with a focus on empowering students to realise their competency. The classes are politically and socially relevant and students learn to think critically and develop a more open mind. Because issues relating to women's roles and needs are surfacing within government, service professions, science fields, industry and academic institutions, the Women's Studies degree is increasing in social, political and vocational relevance. Our programmes have practical applications for a variety of professional fields and after completion of their studies our graduates find themselves at the heart, or the vanguard, of a wide diversity of institutions and movements.

Over the past two decades greater numbers of courses and programmes in colleges and universities have emerged that explore the lives and roles of women who have been engaged in shaping and determining the cultural contexts in which we live, yet parity for women and girls within schools, the workplace, and the academy have changed only slightly. The differential treatment between males and females in classrooms from the nursery school to the postdoctoral experience impact females? academic and career opportunities, social treatment, and participation in power structures.

Throughtout the ages of Europe's history, society's views on the education of women has constantly changed. During the Renaissance age, noble women were encouraged to seek an education so they would be able to carry on intellectual conversations at social gatherings. The Reformation brought opinions which were completely opposed to the ideas of women getting an education and most people thought that women shouldn't learn and form their own opinions. The 17th and 18th centuries displayed a betterment in society's views on women's education because people believed that middle class women should also gain some knowledge so they'd be able to help their husbands in his trade. The Renaissance age's views on education were purely involved with noble women and no one else. Women who were below the noble class were not expectd or encouraged to gain an education at all. The women who were noble were encouraged to gain an education so they would make their husbands look good and they'd be useful at social gatherings because they would be able to socialize with other educated people. Society viewed women's potential to learn as equal to a man's, but the women were not completely expected to get involved or pursue the political or professional jobs that the educated men had.

The women of the Renaissance's education was almost entirely for entertainment purposes only. The Reformation brought opinions which were far more negative than the views brought on from the Renaissance age. Women were thought to only be useful for taking care of children and carrying out the duties of keeping the house clean. People believed that women were also physically built to do those jobs, so they believed that God wanted them to do only that. Men did not want women to gain any education because they believed that if women formed their own opinions, it would cause chaos.

The 17th and 19th centuries brought out more positive opinions toward the education of women compared to the opinions of the Renaissance and Reformation. Instead of just the noble women seeking an education, middle class women were now also encouraged to learn. The reasons why the middle class women should learn was a bit different from why the noble women were encouraged to learn though. While it was just for entertainment purposes with the noble women, middle class women were encouraged to learn so they would be able to help their husbands carry out the duties of his trade.

If the husband was to die, the woman had to know how to take over her husband's trade and continue it without him, so she needed to be educated. Women were not encouraged to seek knowledge about other things which did not involved the trade they were involved in though, but nevertheless, the 17th and 18th centuries broadened the scope of education for women and included more women into it. Society's views on the education of women changed throughout the times. There still is no clear distinction between the ages and their opinions because through all the ages, men still did not view women's education as being important. The evolution of women's education was also not a gradual step towards betterment. It was more like a roller coaster; going up and down, switching from positive to negative to positive again. In the end, everything eventually got better and led to the views and opinions on the capabilities of women that we have today.

Scope and Significance of Research in Women's Studies, Research Design and Methods-Survey

Survey research a research method involving the use of questionnaires and/or statistical surveys to gather data about people and their thoughts and behaviours. Sampling is that part of statistical practice concerned with the selection of individual observations intended to yield some knowledge about a population of concern, especially for the purposes of statistical inference. Each observation measures one or more properties (weight, location, etc.) of an observable entity enumerated to distinguish objects or individuals. Survey weights often need to be applied to the data to adjust for the sample design. Results from probability theory and statistical theory are employed to guide practice. In business, sampling is widely used for gathering information about a population.

Exploratory

Exploratory research is a type of research conducted because a problem has not been clearly defined. Exploratory research helps determine the best research design, data collection method and selection of subjects. Given its fundamental nature, exploratory research often concludes that a perceived problem does not actually exist.

Exploratory research often relies on secondary research such as reviewing available literature and/or data, or qualitative approaches such as informal discussions with consumers, employees, management or competitors, and more formal approaches through in-depth interviews, focus groups, projective methods, case studies or pilot studies. The Internet allows for research methods that are more interactive in nature: E.g., RSS feeds efficiently supply researchers with up-to-date information; major search engine search results may be sent by email to researchers by services such as Google Alerts; comprehensive search results are tracked over lengthy periods of time by services such as Google Trends; and Web sites may be created to attract worldwide feedback on any subject.The results of exploratory research are not usually useful for decision-making by themselves, but they can provide significant insight into a given situation. Although the results of qualitative research can give some indication as to the "why", "how" and "when" something occurs, it cannot tell us "how often" or "how many."Exploratory research is not typically generalizable to the population at large.

Diagnostic Experimental

Phases of Diagnostic Research

Phase 1: Do test results in patients with the target disorder differ from normal people? Phase 1 studies are conducted among groups of patients known to have the disease and in groups known not to have the disease. The diagnostic evaluation cannot be translated into diagnostic action at this stage, but adds to our biological insight into the processes behind the disease. It is quick and cheap. A negative result saves time in proceeding to further studies.

Phase 2: Are patients with certain test results more likely to have the target disorder than patients with other test results? If the phase 1 study produces a positive answer, it is logical to proceed to phase 2. This involves picking a cut-off point that distinguishes affected patients from normal controls. Specificity and sensitivity need to be compared with normal controls. Phase 2 also indicates whether or not a test shows diagnostic promise. The clinical utility of a test varies depending on the cut-off point chosen to define a negative result. Sensitivity rises and specificity falls as the cut-off point is lowered.

Phase 3: Is the test sufficiently sensitive to distinguish patients with and without the target disorder among patients in whom it is clinically reasonable to suspect that the disease is present? Phase 3 also questions the validity of the cut-off point. There are, however, limitations to phase 3 studies. Predictive values change as we move from the primary care setting to secondary and tertiary settings.

There is an assumption that sensitivity and specificity remain constant, but the spectrum of patients varies between settings primary care screening during asymptomatic early disease will produce different results from those obtained in patients with advanced disease in the tertiary care setting). Therefore, replicating a promising phase 3 study in another setting on a cohort of patients for which the test is designed to benefit avoids such problems.

Phase 4: Do patients who undergo this test fare better than those who are not tested? Phase 4 studies look at the health outcome that follows the therapeutic intervention indicated by test results. In essence, phase 4 questions can be answered by patient follow-up.

Analysis of Data: Each study design requires a different method of data analysis. The researcher should pay attention to how the data are collected. Confounders must be taken into consideration to improve the quality of the data.

Action Research

Action research is a reflective process of progressive problem solving led by individuals working with others in teams or as part of a "community of practice" to improve the way they address issues and solve problems. Action research can also be undertaken by larger organizations or institutions, assisted or guided by professional researchers, with the aim of improving their strategies, practices, and knowledge of the environments within which they practice. As designers and stakeholders, researchers work with others to propose a new course of action to help their community improve its work practices (Center for Collaborative Action Research). Kurt Lewin, then a professor at MIT, first coined the term "action research" in about 1944, and it appears in his 1946 paper "Action Research and Minority Problems". In that paper, he described action research as "a comparative research on the conditions and effects of various forms of social action and research leading to social action" that uses "a spiral of steps, each of which is composed of a circle of planning, action, and fact-finding about the result of the action".

Qualitative verses Quantative Research

Qualitative research is a field of inquiry that crosscuts disciplines and subject matters. Qualitative researchers aim to gather an in-depth understanding of human behavior and the reasons that govern such behavior. The discipline investigates the *why* and *how* of decision making, not just *what, where, when*. Hence, smaller but focused samples are more often needed rather than large random samples.

Qualitative researchers may use different approaches in collecting data, such as the grounded theory practice, narratology, storytelling, classical ethnography, or shadowing. Qualitative methods are also loosely present in other methodological approaches, such as action research or actor-network theory. Forms of the data collected can include interviews and group discussions, observation and reflection field notes, various texts, pictures, and other materials.

Qualitative research often categorizes data into patterns as the primary basis for organizing and reporting results. Qualitative researchers typically rely on the following methods for gathering information: *Participant Observation, Non-participant Observation, Field Notes, Reflexive Journals, Structured Interview, Unstructured Interview, Analysis of documents and materials* .

The ways of participating and observing can vary widely from setting to setting. Participant observation is a strategy of reflexive learning, not a single method of observing. In participant observation researchers typically become members of a culture, group, or setting, and adopt roles to conform to that setting. In doing so, the aim is for the researcher to gain a closer insight into the culture's practices, motivations and emotions. It is argued that the researchers' ability to understand the experiences of the culture may be inhibited if they observe without participating.

Some distinctive qualitative methods are the use of focus groups and key informant interviews. The focus group technique involves a moderator facilitating a small group discussion between selected individuals on a particular topic. This is a particularly popular method in market research and testing new initiatives with users/workers.

One traditional and specialized form of qualitative research is called cognitive testing or pilot testing which is used in the development of quantitative survey items. Survey items are piloted on study participants to test the reliability and validity of the items.

In the academic social sciences the most frequently used qualitative research approaches include:

1. Ethnographic Research, used for investigating cultures by collecting and describing data that is intended to help in the development of a theory. This method is also called "ethnomethodology" or "methodology of the people". An example of applied ethnographic research, is the study of a particular culture and their understanding of the role of a particular disease in their cultural framework.
2. Critical Social Research, used by a researcher to understand how people communicate and develop symbolic meanings.
3. Ethical Inquiry, an intellectual analysis of ethical problems. It includes the study of ethics as related to obligation, rights, duty, right and wrong, choice etc.
4. Foundational Research, examines the foundations for a science, analyses the beliefs and develops ways to specify how a knowledge base should change in light of new information.
5. Historical Research, allows one to discuss past and present events in the context of the present condition, and allows one to reflect and provide possible answers to current issues and problems. Historical research helps us in answering questions such as: Where have we come from, where are we, who are we now and where are we going?

6. Grounded Theory, is an inductive type of research, based or "grounded" in the observations or data from which it was developed; it uses a variety of data sources, including quantitative data, review of records, interviews, observation and surveys.
7. Phenomenological Research, describes the "subjective reality" of an event, as perceived by the study population; it is the study of a phenomenon.
8. Philosophical Research, is conducted by field experts within the boundaries of a specific field of study or profession, the best qualified individual in any field of study to use an intellectual analyses, in order to clarify definitions, identify ethics, or make a value judgment concerning an issue in their field of study.

Quantitative Research

Quantitative research is the systematic scientific investigation of quantitative properties and phenomena and their relationships. The objective of quantitative research is to develop and employ mathematical models, theories and/or hypotheses pertaining to natural phenomena. The process of measurement is central to quantitative research because it provides the fundamental connection between empirical observation and mathematical expression of quantitative relationships.

Quantitative research is widely used in both the natural sciences and social sciences, from physics and biology to sociology and journalism. It is also used as a way to research different aspects of education. The term quantitative research is most often used in the social sciences in contrast to qualitative research.

Quantitative research is generally made using scientific methods, which can include:

- The generation of models, theories and hypotheses
- The development of instruments and methods for measurement
- Experimental control and manipulation of variables

- Collection of empirical data
- Modeling and analysis of data
- Evaluation of results

Quantitative research is often an iterative process whereby evidence is evaluated, theories and hypothieses are refined, technical advances are made, and so on. Virtually all research in physics is quantitative whereas research in other scientific disciplines, such as taxonomy and anatomy, may involve a combination of quantitative and other analytic approaches and methods. D Pattni describes quantitative research as a very powerful tool for organisations.

In the social sciences particularly, quantitative research is often contrasted with qualitative research which is the examination, analysis and interpretation of observations for the purpose of discovering underlying meanings and patterns of relationships, including classifications of types of phenomena and entities, in a manner that does not involve mathematical models. Approaches to quantitative psychology were first modelled on quantitative approaches in the physical sciences by Gustav Fechner in his work on psychophysics, which built on the work of Ernst Heinrich Weber. Although a distinction is commonly drawn between qualitative and quantitative aspects of scientific investigation, it has been argued that the two go hand in hand. For example, based on analysis of the history of science, Kuhn (1961) concludes that "large amounts of qualitative work have usually been prerequisite to fruitful quantification in the physical sciences". Qualitative research is often used to gain a general sense of phenomena and to form theories that can be tested using further quantitative research. For instance, in the social sciences qualitative research methods are often used to gain better understanding of such things as intentionality (from the speech response of the researchee) and meaning (why did this person/group say something and what did it mean to them?).

Although quantitative investigation of the world has existed since people first began to record events or objects that had been counted, the modern idea of quantitative processes have their roots in Auguste Comte's positivist framework..

Case Studies

A case study is one of several ways of doing research whether it is social science related or even socially related. It is an intensive study of a single group, incident, or community.Other ways include experiments, surveys, multiple histories, and analysis of archival information .

Rather than using samples and following a rigid protocol to examine limited number of variables, case study methods involve an in-depth, longitudinal examination of a single instance or event: a case. They provide a systematic way of looking at events, collecting data, analyzing information, and reporting the results. As a result the researcher may gain a sharpened understanding of why the instance happened as it did, and what might become important to look at more extensively in future research. Case studies lend themselves to both generating and testing hypotheses .

Another suggestion is that case study should be defined as a research strategy, an empirical inquiry that investigates a phenomenon within its real-life context. Case study research means single and multiple case studies, can include quantitative evidence, relies on multiple sources of evidence and benefits from the prior development of theoretical propositions. Case studies should not be confused with qualitative research and they can be based on any mix of quantitative and qualitative evidence. Single-subject research provides the statistical framework for making inferences from quantitative case-study data. This is also supported and well-formulated in (Lamnek, 2005): "The case study is a research approach, situated between concrete data taking techniques and methodologic paradigms."

Bibliography

Ali, Aruna Asaf: *Resurgence of Indian Women,* Strosius Inc./Advent Books Division, 1991.

Bagilhole, Barbara *Sexual Harassment. Contemporary Feminist Perspective,* Open University Press, 1997.

Chakrapani, C.: *Changing Status and Role of Women in Indian Society,* South Asia Books, 1994.

Chilly Collective: *Breaking Anonymity: The Chilly Climate for Women Faculty,* Wilfrid Laurier University, 1995.

Cynthia Fuchs Epstein: *Women in Law,* University of Illinois Press, 1993.

Feldhaus, Anne: *Images of Women in Maharashtrian Literature and Religion,* SUNY Press, 1996.

Gandhi, Nandita and Nandita Shah: *The Issues at Stake: Theory and Practice in the Contemporary Women's Movement in India,* South Asia Books, 1992.

Jamison, Stephanie: *Sacrificed Wife / Sacrificer's Wife: Women, Ritual, and Hospitality in Ancient India,* Oxford. 1996.

Jayawardena, Kumari: *Feminism and Nationalism in the Third World,* London, Zed Books, 1986.

Jayawardena, Kumari: *The White Woman's Other Burden—Western Women and South Asia During British Rule,* New York: Routledge, 1995.

Liddle, Joanna and Rama Joshi: *Daughters of Independence: Gender, Caste and Class in India,* Rutgers Univ. Press, 1989.

Lois Benjamin: *Black Women in the Academy: Promises and Perils,* University Press of Florida, 1997.

Moore, Erin: *Gender, Law, and Resistance in India,* Univ. of Arizona Press, 1998.

Nadya Aisenberg: *Women of Academe: Outsiders in the Sacred Grove,* University of Massachusetts Press, 1988.

Ravitch, Diane: *Left Back: A Century of Failed School Reforms,* New York, Simon and Schuster, 2000.

Ray., Raka: *Fields of Protest: Women's Movements in India,* Univ. of Minnesota Press, 1999.

Roy, Manisha: *Bengali Women,* Univ. of Chicago Press, 1992.

Visram, Rozina: *Women in India and Pakistan: The Struggle for Independence from British Rule,* Cambridge Univ. Press, 1993.

Visweswaran, Kamala: *Fictions of Feminist Ethnography.* Univ. of Minnesota Press, 1994.

Index

□□□